ANDREW TAN &

KUMAR RAMAKRISHNA (eds.)

THE NEW TERRORISM

Anatomy,
Trends and
Counter-
Strategies

EASTERN UNIVERSITIES PRESS

© 2002 Times Media Private Limited

First published 2002 by Times Media Private Limited (Academic Publishing) under the
imprint **Eastern Universities Press.**
Times Centre, 1 New Industrial Road, Singapore 536196
Fax: (65) 6288 9254 E-mail: tap@tpl.com.sg
Online Book Store: http://www.timesacademic.com

Times Media Private Limited (Academic Publishing) is part of Times Publishing Limited
which has offices in:
London • New York • Shanghai • Bangkok • Kuala Lumpur • Singapore

Printed by B & Jo Enterprise Pte Ltd, Singapore

National Library Board (Singapore) Cataloguing in Publication Data
The New Terrorism : Anatomy, Trends and Counter-Strategies / Andrew Tan
and Kumar Ramakrishna (eds.). – Singapore : Eastern Universities Press, c2002.

p. cm.
ISBN : 981-210-210-8

1. Terrorism.
I. Tan, Andrew T. H. (Andrew Tian Huat)   II. Kumar Ramakrishna.

HV6431   363.32 — dc21   SLS2002044894

CONTENTS

Religion and Terrorism

Countering the New Terrorism

ACKNOWLEDGEMENTS

The authors would like to acknowledge the support and encouragement provided for the Workshop and this volume by Barry Desker, Director, Institute of Defence and Strategic Studies, Nanyang Technological University. The useful comments and advice of Professor Amitav Acharya, especially for the introduction, is also gratefully acknowledged. A special thanks also to Dr Bruce Hoffman for chairing the penultimate concluding session which generated a number of useful suggestions and perspectives, and also Dr Rohan Gunaratna, for his suggestions for the concluding chapter. The contributions of the authors, without which this volume would not have been possible, are much appreciated. The authors also wish to thank those who attended the Workshop and contributed so richly to enhancing our understanding of the new dimensions of terrorism and what to do about it. Regina Ariokasamy, Caroline Ng, Peter Ee and the administrative staff of IDSS have also rendered excellent administrative support for which the Workshop would not have been possible. Finally, the excellent copy-editing work of Eugene Tan is gratefully acknowledged, as has been the superb support given by Anthony Thomas of Times Media (Academic Publishing).

FOREWORD

The terrorist attacks on the World Trade Centre in New York, and the Pentagon in Washington, on 11 September 2001, shocked the entire world. The attacks are a watershed, with far-reaching implications for future security. They demonstrate that even the world's sole superpower is not safe from terrorism. The success of the attacks in causing a large number of casualties and the huge impact it engendered appear to validate the assertions of terrorist experts who have observed the emergence of a new form of terrorism that is global in orientation and much more lethal in its effects.

This new terrorism has been brought home to Southeast Asia with the discovery in December 2001 of an Al Qaeda-linked militant group that was planning terrorist attacks on Western and other targets in the region. This group, the Jemiah Islamiah (JI), operates in Singapore, Malaysia, Philippines and Indonesia, demonstrating a transnational mode of operation. The new terrorism is therefore not confined to the Middle East or the West, but has become a security problem for the region.

With this in mind, the Institute of Defence and Strategic Studies, Nanyang Technological University, Singapore, organized a Workshop on the New Dimensions of Terrorism in Singapore in May 2002, in order to better understand the nature of the new terrorism and explore possible strategies in dealing with it. The Workshop brought together Southeast Asian Muslims, several of the world's leading terrorism experts, and security analysts from throughout the region. It explored the characteristics of the new terrorism, its root causes, terrorism trends in Asia, the relationship between religion and terrorism in Southeast Asia, the threat of nuclear, biological and chemical (NBC) terrorism, information-age terrorism, and strategies in countering the new terrorism.

This edited volume is the result of this Workshop. We believe that the papers contained herein will prove to be both policy-relevant as well as a useful reference tool for those of us concerned with what is presently the major security threat to the region.

Barry Desker
Director
Institute of Defence and Strategic Studies
Nanyang Technological University
Singapore

CONTRIBUTORS

Bruce Hoffman is Vice-President for External Affairs and Director, The RAND Corporation, Washington D.C. office, and Editor-in-Chief of *Studies in Conflict and Terrorism*, considered the leading journal on terrorism today. He received his PhD from Oxford University and was the founding Director of the Centre for the Study of Terrorism and Political Violence at the University of St Andrew's, Scotland, where he was also Reader in International Relations and Chairman of the Department of International Relations. His latest book, *Inside Terrorism*, is published by Columbia University Press in the United States, and Orion Books in Britain, with foreign language editions in nine countries.

Gavin Cameron is Lecturer in Politics and Military History at the University of Salford, England. He received his PhD in International Relations from the University of St Andrew's, Scotland, has been a research fellow at the Centre for Nonproliferation Studies, Monterey, California, and at the Belfer Centre for Science and International Affairs, Harvard University. His research focuses on terrorism with non-conventional weapons, and on strategies to counter this threat. He is the author of *Nuclear Terrorism: A Threat Assessment for the 21ˢᵗ Century*, published by Palgrave in 1999.

Kevin O'Brien is Senior Policy Analyst at RAND Europe, Cambridge, where he works on the ICT program and on issues relating to counter-terrorism and intelligence policy in the global environment. He received his PhD in International Politics (Security Studies) from the University of Hull, and worked at the International Centre for Security Analysis (ICSA), King's College, London, where he was Deputy Director of the Canadian Institute of International Affairs, the Canadian Institute of Strategic Studies and the Institute for Security Studies, South Africa. He formed the Hussar International Research Group in 1995, and was appointed Chief Operations Officer for the International Assurance Advisory Council (IAAC) in 2000. His research interests include intelligence studies, asymmetric warfare (including terrorism, special forces, low-intensity conflict and insurgency), information operations, the privatization of security and African (especially southern and central) politics and security. He has published widely in academic journals and authored numerous articles for trade and industry magazines relating to information assurance and critical infrastructure protection.

Peter Chalk is Policy Analyst at the RAND Corporation, Washington D.C. Prior to joining RAND, Dr Chalk was Assistant Professor of Politics at the University of Queensland, Brisbane, and a Postdoctoral Fellow in the Strategic and Defence Studies Centre of the Australian National University, Canberra. At RAND, his projects include examining unconventional security threats in Southeast Asia, and evolving trends in national and international terrorism. In addition to numerous journal articles and other scholarly publications, Dr Chalk is a contributor to *Drugs and Democracy: In Search of New Directions* (2000) which examines Australia's unsuccessful attempts to control the illicit drug trade.

Rohan Gunaratna is British Chevening Scholar at the Department of International Relations, University of St Andrew's, Scotland. He was formerly Hesburg Scholar at the Institute for International Peace Studies, University of Notre Dame; Foreign Policy Fellow, Centre for International and Security Studies, University of Maryland; and Visiting Scholar, Office of Arms Control, Disarmament and International Security, University of Illinois. His research focuses on terrorist support networks, with particular emphasis on events in North America, Europe and the Far East, and terrorism in South Asia. He is the author of six books on armed conflict. His latest book, *Inside Al Qaeda: Global Network of Terror* (New York: Columbia University Press/London: Hurst, 2002), is the most definitive study of Al Qaeda to-date.

Farish A. Noor is a Malaysian political scientist. He is presently an Affiliated Fellow with the Institute for Malaysian and International Studies (IKMAS), National University of Malaysia (UKM) and Associate Fellow with the Bureau of Nation-Building and National Security at the Institute for Strategic and International Studies (ISIS), Malaysia. He has taught at the Centre for Inter-Civilizational Dialogue and the Department of Science and Philosophy at the University of Malaya (UM) and the Institute for Islamic Studies, Freie Universitat of Berlin. Dr Farish Noor has just completed his book on the historical development of the Pan-Malaysian Islamic Party (PAS) and is currently studying the socio-cultural and political impact of transnational religious movements in ASEAN. His book, *New Voices of Islam*, was published by the International Institute for the Study of Islam in the Modern World (ISIM), Leiden, Netherlands (2002).

Rizal Sukma was born in Aceh and is currently Director of Studies, Centre for Strategic and International Studies (CSIS), Jakarta, Indonesia. He is also a member of Indonesia's CSCAP National Committee and a visiting lecturer at the University of Indonesia. He received his PhD from the London School of Economics and Political Science (LSE). His research interests include Southeast Asian security issues, ASEAN cooperation, Indonesian foreign policy and domestic political changes in Indonesia. He has published extensively; his latest publication, *Values, Governance and Indonesia's Foreign Policy*, is forthcoming with JCIE, Tokyo.

Ely Karmon is Senior Research Fellow at the Interdisciplinary Centre in Herzliya, lectures on international terrorism at Bar-Ilan University, Israel, and is an advisor to the Israeli Ministry of Defence. He received his MA and PhD from Haifa University and has served as advisor to the Anti-Semitism Monitoring Forum of the Israeli Government Secretariat. His research focuses on international terrorism, political violence and extremism, and the strategic influence of terrorism and subversion in the Middle East. His book, *Coalitions Between Terrorist Organisations (1968–1990): European Revolutionaries and Palestinian Nationalists—Painful Partnership*, is forthcoming by Kluwer Law International (The Hague, London and Boston).

Kumar Ramakrishna is Assistant Professor at the Institute of Defence and Strategic Studies, Nanyang Technological University. He received his MA from the University of New South Wales, Australia, and PhD from Royal Holloway, University of London, and has taught at the National University of Singapore and the Department of Strategic Studies, Singapore Command and Staff College. He has published in journals such as *The Washington Quarterly, Intelligence and National Security, The Journal of Southeast Asian Studies, The Journal of the Malaysian Branch of the Royal Asiatic Society*, and *The Journal of Imperial and Commonwealth History*. His book, *Emergency Propaganda: The Winning of Malayan Hearts and Minds, 1948–1958*, has been published by Routledge Curzon.

Andrew Tan is Assistant Professor at the Institute of Defence and Strategic Studies, Nanyang Technological University, Singapore. He received his M Phil from Cambridge and PhD from the University of Sydney, and has worked in both private and public sectors, including being desk officer for Russia/Eastern Europe, and Malaysia, at Singapore's Foreign Ministry. He also worked and taught at an institute of the University of Technology, Sydney. His research interests are conflicts (inter-state tensions, insurgencies, terrorism and force modernization) in Southeast Asia and security issues in Asia. He has published numerous articles and book reviews in various academic journals. His recent books and monographs include *Intra-ASEAN Tensions* (Royal Institute of International Affairs), *Armed Rebellion in the ASEAN States: Persistence and Implications* (Australian National University) and *Malaysia–Singapore Relations: A Troubled Past and Uncertain Future?* (University of Hull) as well as two co-edited volumes, *Non-Traditional Security Issue in Southeast Asia* (Select Books, Singapore) and *Seeking Alternative Perspectives on Southeast Asia* (ASEAN Academic, London).

THE NEW
TERRORISM

CHAPTER 1

THE NEW TERRORISM: DIAGNOSIS AND PRESCRIPTIONS

Kumar Ramakrishna and Andrew Tan

That the terrorist attacks of September 11, 2001 on the World Trade Centre in New York and the Pentagon in Washington represented a true watershed in world history is no longer a matter for serious debate. The impact of the strikes was instantaneously transmitted throughout the globalized electronic web that binds far-flung world communities in an ever-tighter embrace, in the process amplifying not just the psychic, but also the economic and financial aftershocks. More than that, however, the attacks had deeper resonance for global security. First and foremost, they proved beyond a shadow of a doubt that even unipolar hegemons are no longer completely invulnerable in a world in which globalization has helped diffuse power to some extent.

In this sense, it is worth recalling that box-cutters—in all their low-tech glory—were the weapons with which the September 11 hijackers commandeered the passenger jets that were transformed into the manned missiles that rained war-scale death and destruction on America that fateful day. In the process, the suicide terrorists made America's conventional and nuclear military muscle—and planned missile defence schemes—look, if not outright irrelevant, then at the very least, worryingly inadequate. Worryingly inadequate because surely the key lesson that the September 11 strikes reinforce is that, despite *prima facie* appearances, the central conflict in the world today is not between states competing for global hegemony. It is between secularizing, homogenizing and avaricious global capitalism on the one hand, and ethnic and religious fundamentalism on the other.[1]

It is worth arguing, therefore, that perhaps the central security requirement facing the international community is to devise ideological, political, social and economic structures capable of peacefully and equitably accommodating these dialectical forces of globalization and fragmentation. Tanks, aircraft, and ballistic missile shields have at best a subsidiary, rather than a central, role in this most pressing challenge of the new millennium. Seen in this light, therefore, the September 11 attacks may be interpreted as a powerful indictment of the abject failure of governments to contain and mesh the forces of secular globalization and ethnic-religious fragmentation. More specifically, the failure of the international community to construct durable and equitable structures of accommodation has manifested itself in the rise of the so-called "new terrorism" which among other things, has demonstrated how, left unmediated, secular modernity and religious fundamentalism may well fuse in virulent and destructive ways. It would be wise not to overestimate, as some have, the degree to which the rampantly puritanical Al Qaeda terrorist organization is at the same time "modern" and comfortable with "modern methods."[2] Rather than a comfortable accommodation, an unmediated collision between the retrogressive and the modern often creates "a soul that feels corrupted by the modern world," thereby generating psychic tensions that demand a "purge through a spasm of violence." David Ignatius, in this connection, commented on the strange ambivalence of the terrorists the night before they immolated themselves and their victims: While some visited a strip club, others "draped a towel over an offending picture of a woman on the wall of their motel room."[3]

Coping with the wider problem of meshing secular modernity with religious tradition, as well as its lethal corollary, the new terrorism, concerns not just Americans and Westerners but Southeast Asians as well. It has been widely suggested that following the U.S.-led ouster of the radical Taliban regime in Afghanistan that provided Al Qaeda sanctuary, the Southeast Asian archipelago, with its huge Muslim population and difficult-to-police borders, has become the "second front in the war on terror." Certainly, the disruption of allegedly Al Qaeda-linked radical Islamic groups in Singapore and Malaysia especially has confirmed the region's importance in Washington's eyes. However, while there has been general agreement within Southeast Asia and elsewhere that the United States was justified in dismantling the Taliban regime, there has been increasing concern about what America has done since: After Afghanistan, Washington has appeared, in Yemen, Georgia and in the

Philippines especially, to evince a preference for military and enforcement measures. In July and August 2002, for instance, U.S. Secretary of State Colin Powell, on a visit to Southeast Asia, signed agreements with the 10 countries of the Association of Southeast Asian Nations (ASEAN) that called for enhanced cooperation in sharing intelligence, cutting terrorist funding, and tightening border and immigration controls.[4] Powell also pledged US$50 million in aid to Indonesia's police and military.[5]

Will this evident American focus on military and operational matters, however, suffice in the war on terror? This is one central question this volume seeks to grapple with. In this respect, early in 2002, the feeling amongst some Southeast Asian analysts was that such approaches, while certainly necessary in the short term, would not be sufficient to deal with the terror threat in a comprehensive fashion over the longer term.[6] Hence, it was felt that there was a need for officials and analysts to not only come to grips with the peculiar characteristics of the new terrorism—in itself a pressing necessity—but to also ponder the appropriate counter-measures to neutralize it. Consequently, a conference was organized in Singapore in late March 2002 that brought together a number of leading experts from a wide range of backgrounds from America, Europe and Asia, and the key findings have now made their way into this present volume. It is no real surprise that in general, the contributors to this volume, reflecting their diverse backgrounds, have, to varying degrees, differing views on the root causes of, and appropriate responses to, the September 11 strikes. Nevertheless, the editors believe that there is more than sufficient reason to commend the positioning of this study within the wider body of literature that interprets the September 11 attacks as a particularly horrific manifestation of the tussle between the forces of secular globalization and ethnic-religious fragmentation. Specifically, then, the volume attempts three things: First, it addresses the precise characteristics of the bastard child of the unconsummated union between secular modernity and religious tradition, the new terrorism. Second, it sheds light on how the modernity-religion dialectic, in the particular manifestation of domestic and transnational terrorist trends and linkages, has objectively overlaid Asian politics and societies—and how it has also been subjectively constructed, especially from Southeast Asian religious perspectives. Finally, the volume seeks to suggest appropriate anti-terror counter-strategies—with perhaps a distinctly Southeast Asian flavour—that take into account the wider context of the contest between globalization and fragmentation.

Anatomy of the New Terrorism

Fittingly, Bruce Hoffman, one of the leading experts on the new terrorism phenomenon, leads the contributors by examining how the September 11 strikes confirmed both the characteristics as well as the terrifying destructive potential of the new terrorism. He shows that the new terrorism is "new" most of all because of its sheer lethality. To be sure, other analysts had noted that "the 1993 World Trade Centre bombings in New York, and related conspiracies; the 1996 Oklahoma City bombing; the 1998 East Africa bombings; and the Tokyo sarin gas attack in 1995," were all "unmistakable harbingers of a new and vastly more threatening terrorism, one that aims to produce casualties on a mass scale."[7] This increasingly obvious trend toward greater lethality appears to have culminated in the September 11 attacks, which as Hoffman rightly notes, "were unparalleled in their severity and lethal ambitions." Another important feature of the new terrorism—and related to the first characteristic—is its unmistakably religious dimension. Hoffman writes that despite the best efforts of America and its Coalition partners not to portray the war as a "clash of civilizations" as first postulated by Samuel Huntington, bin Laden has deliberately and effectively painted it as such. More than just manipulating Islam as a tool of mass mobilization, moreover, bin Laden appears to believe in the intrinsic incompatibility of Islam with other, especially Western, creeds, and genuinely sees the conflict with America and the West in apocalyptic terms. The nexus between religious motivation and violence is reflected in the fact that while previous secular, nationalist terrorist organizations understood that "wanton violence" could be politically counter-productive,[8] religiously motivated terrorists' nebulous, apocalyptic world-views hamper their articulation of a "plausible political agenda," and this contributes to an "absence of constraints on violence."[9] In this vein, Hoffman writes of the stunning willingness of the new terrorists to kill not just their targets but themselves in the process. He notes that the radical Islamic martyr is convinced that at his death, he would proceed to heaven—a realm of lakes of honey as well as rivers of milk and wine—where "he will see the face of Allah," enjoy the company of 72 virgins and "be joined by 70 chosen relatives." He argues for a more nuanced understanding of "terrorism motivated by a religious imperative in particular and the concept of martyrdom."

A third key feature of the new terrorism is its peculiar *networked* organizational structure. As Kevin O'Brien—building upon the work of his distinguished RAND colleagues John Arquilla and David Ronfeldt—

points out in his comprehensively-researched contribution to this volume, the new terrorists are organized not in large centralized hierarchies like conventional armies but rather "are likely to consist of dispersed small groups who communicate, coordinate, and conduct their campaigns in a networked manner, without a precise central command." O'Brien attributes the networked nature of Al Qaeda to "the revolution in computing, telecommunications, and data-transference capacities—commonly referred to as the Information Revolution." This has enabled terrorist organizations like Al Qaeda to engage in "coordinating and planning activities from around the world," by enabling them to "leave messages of future or planned activities on websites or by e-mail." Moreover, the implications of the Information Revolution for leadership have not been lost on bin Laden, who after all, has a background in "business administration and modern management techniques." As Hoffman argues, bin Laden functions like a "terrorist CEO," defining a "flexible strategy" for Al Qaeda that enables the organization to function at "multiple levels, using both top-down and bottom-up approaches." On the one hand, like a CEO of a multinational organization, bin Laden has defined specific goals, issued directives and monitored their implementation, as he has done with respect to "high-visibility, usually high-value and high-casualty operations like September 11." On the other hand, Hoffman notes that bin Laden is also enabled by the networked structure of Al Qaeda to operate like a "venture capitalist": hence, he is also engaged in "soliciting ideas from below, encouraging creative approaches and 'out of the box' thinking and providing funding to those proposals he thinks promising." O'Brien also sheds light on how the new terrorists have leveraged on the Information Revolution to support their activities. He notes how, in this regard, terrorist organizations are well-capable of exploiting the Internet "to gather detailed targeting information; gathering and moving money to support activities—or even manipulating stocks to benefit the terrorist organizations."

If globalization in the sense of what has been called the "democratizations of finance, technology and information"[10] has expedited the creation of flexible, diffuse and more robust organizational structures of the new terrorists, it has also helped define their fourth characteristic: their greatly enhanced striking power. In this regard, O'Brien warns that "the populations and governments of Western countries rely almost entirely on national critical information infrastructures (NCII) consisting of government and corporate computer servers, telecommunications facilities and Internet service providers."

Thus many states have become extremely vulnerable to cyber-attacks from "insiders, rogue hackers and foreign military jammers." O'Brien cites in this respect the damage done to Western economies by the Distributed-Denial-of-Service (DDoS) attacks on the Internet-based companies Yahoo, Amazon and E-Bay in 1999–2000, as well as the ILOVEYOU e-mail virus in 2000. He is therefore correct in asserting the irony that "the more the world digitizes, the more vulnerable it becomes." Cyberspace not only expedites organizational control over widely dispersed units and acts as an actual medium of conflict; by accessing the voluminous information available online, terrorists can also develop fresh ideas for planning operations involving "kidnapping, bomb-making and assassination."[11]

Furthermore, given that technical information for assembling weapons of mass destruction (WMD) is now virtually accessible online, and, as Gavin Cameron emphasizes in this volume, the September 11 attacks have "undoubtedly raised the bar for future terrorism," the threat of terrorism involving WMD must inevitably be addressed. However, it is important to keep the WMD threat in proper perspective. This is because, as Cameron notes, there are very real practical difficulties of "weaponization and delivery" of "either chemical or biological weapons." Cameron observes moreover that a "nuclear-yield weapon is likely to be the hardest type of CBRN [Chemical, Biological, Radiological, Nuclear] device for terrorists to acquire." He argues that while the collapse of the Soviet Union has given rise to concerns over "loose nukes" and the potential for "nuclear materials and nuclear expertise to leave the country and be exploited by rogue states or terrorists," the technical obstacles to terrorist organizations actually building a workable nuclear weapon are formidable. Either considerable affluence or state support would be required, and even then, "many state programs spend millions and take years trying to enrich enough material for a viable nuclear weapons" project—and success is "far from assured." He opines that a "radiological device" would be the "easiest type of CBRN weapon for terrorists to acquire," because "radioactive sources remain widespread and poorly protected," relative to other types of nuclear materials. This observation is particularly telling in light of the capture in June 2002 of Jose Padilla following his alleged involvement in a plot to detonate a "dirty bomb" in Washington.

The upshot is that governments should not be over-focused in planning to counter the threat of WMD use in potential future attacks. Cameron is of the view that "conventional weapons remain more likely instruments for terrorists intent on causing mass destruction, at least in the short term." For his part, Ely Karmon also opines in this volume that "the known terrorist organizations do not have the capability to produce or acquire real non-conventional weapons." He suggests that governments should be alert to the possibilities of "the more deadly use of conventional weapons." Similarly, Hoffman observes that the new terrorists "retain an enormous capability to inflict pain and suffering" without necessarily resorting to CBRN weapons. He notes that American authorities prior to the terrorist strikes in New York and Washington had tended to focus on terrorist scenarios involving, *inter alia*, "germ or chemical agents," presuming in the process that "any conventional or less extensive incident could be addressed simply by planning for the most catastrophic threat." September 11 revealed how tragically flawed this supposition had been. Thomas Homer-Dixon has in this connection also pointed out that:[12]

> ...modern societies are filled with supercharged devices packed with energy, combustibles, and poisons, giving terrorists ample opportunities to destructive ends. To cause horrendous damage, all terrorists must do is figure out how to release this power and let it run wild or, as they did on September 11, take control of this power and retarget it.

Homer-Dixon identifies, for instance, large gas pipelines running through urban areas, the radioactive waste pools of nuclear reactors, and chemical plants as providing "countless opportunities for turning supposedly benign technology to destructive ends."[13] There is thus a need, as Hoffman attests, to think of a wider range of unconventional terrorism scenarios involving the use of conventional weapons.

The final characteristic of the new terrorism suggests a degree of continuity with previous secular, nationalistic forms: It is fundamentally an asymmetric method by which a weaker actor seeks to obtain its ends by breaking the will of a stronger power. Hence as Ramakrishna writes, "Like Vo Nguyen Giap before him, Osama bin Laden knows that he cannot engage American forces directly as he does not have the military strength to do so. Hence, like Giap, he intends to defeat America by targeting not its military might but rather what he perceives to be its critical vulnerability or soft underbelly: the American public." In this way therefore, bin Laden's "tactical concept follows a classical insurgent approach."[14] In other to strike the "soft underbelly" of the U.S. public, Al Qaeda basically seeks not so much its annihilation but rather, as Hoffman points out, "to create unbridled fear, dark insecurity and reverberating panic." Thus Cameron notes that while Al Qaeda certainly seeks to acquire CBRN weapons, and would almost certainly use them if they had them, securing such a capability is not meant to be an end in itself but merely as another means of attaining its operational objective of undermining American public morale. For his part, Karmon notes that perhaps the greatest value of the use of CBRN weapons—no matter how limited—would be the "political and psychological consequences" of such attacks, which would be "enormous"— as the anthrax scare in the U.S. in late 2001 and the more recent "dirty bomb" case in mid-2002 suggest. As Hoffman puts it, "Terrorists do not have to kill 3,000 people to create panic and foment fear and insecurity: five persons dying in mysterious circumstances is quite effective at unnerving an entire nation." It is in this sense, therefore, that Hoffman is surely right when he asserts that in the final assessment, the new terrorism remains a form of "psychological warfare" aimed at helping the materially-inferior actor impose its will on a stronger power.

Terrorist Trends and Patterns in the Asia-Pacific

As Rohan Gunaratna, perhaps the foremost Asian expert on Al Qaeda, asserts in these pages, in the past decade "the centre of gravity of terrorism" shifted from the Middle East to the Asia-Pacific region—an area that occupies almost 30 percent of the world's surface and holds 61 percent of the total global population. The shift essentially occurred when Lebanon was replaced by Afghanistan as the "major centre of international terrorist training" in the early 1990s.[15] Gunaratna asserts that the Asia-Pacific region today hosts several foreign and indigenous groups, ranging from Islamist Sunni organizations such as Al Qaeda, and Shiite, like Hezbollah, as well as other "ideological and ethno-nationalist groups." Especially important, ever-improving global communications have ensured that Asia-Pacific terrorist organizations have not been insulated but rather empowered to cooperate with like-minded "transnational constituencies" with "compatible aims and objectives." Consequently, Asia-Pacific groups, by penetrating "diaspora and migrant communities" in Africa, the Middle East, the Balkans, the Caucuses, Western Europe and North America, have set up advanced international support structures beyond the Asia-Pacific region for "disseminating propaganda, raising funds, training, procuring weapons, and shipping." These interconnections have expedited the penetration of radical Arab Islamist ideas into the region. Gunaratna is of the view that of all the varieties of terrorist groups extant in the Asia-Pacific today, "the Islamist category"—as exemplified by Al Qaeda—poses the "biggest challenge today and in the foreseeable future."

Specifically, Gunaratna identifies a "free-floating" terrorist "core" comprising battle-hardened and dedicated Asian, Middle Eastern, Caucasian, Balkan, African, American and European Muslims who participated in the anti-Soviet Afghan *jihad* in the 1980s as a key security concern. In addition, he reminds us that while Al Qaeda "is a small group of only 3,000 members dedicated to fighting the West, the organization, together with the Afghan-based Taliban regime" trained and indoctrinated "over 110,000" Muslims from numerous countries to "provide support to disparate groups active from the Philippines to Algeria, all aiming to establish Islamic states." Gunaratna first shows how Pakistan, thanks to American disengagement following the Soviet pullout, became both "a safe haven for many Afghan veterans" as well as a "centre for ideological training." In addition, Peter Chalk shows how the initially home-grown Muslim insurgency in Indian-controlled Kashmir was transformed by the decision of Pakistan's Inter-Services Intelligence (ISI) to "replicate the success of the anti-Soviet *mujahideen* campaign it coordinated in Afghanistan by exhorting foreign Islamists to participate in a *jihad* that is being fought on behalf and in the name of oppressed co-religionists." Both Gunaratna and Chalk then outline how "the inflow of Afghan Arabs"—including Al Qaeda elements—not only ratcheted up the scale of violence but also resulted in the injection into the Kashmiri theatre of the Al Qaeda *modus operandi* that included, *inter alia*, "kidnapping and murdering Western nationals," as well as "suicide attacks." Gunaratna also avers that the dissolution of the Soviet Union in the early 1990s provided opportunities for India, Pakistan, Saudi Arabia, Iran and Turkey to build ties with the former Soviet Central Asian Republics, namely, Kazakhstan, Tajikistan, Turkmenistan, Uzbekistan and Kyrgyzstan. Particularly pertinent is the fact that from Afghanistan, "the gateway to Soviet Central Asia," radical Islamist ideas have found fertile soil in the Ferghana valley, linking Uzbekistan, Kyrgyzstan and Tajikistan: Afghan and Pakistani radical Islamist propaganda, for instance, has been found outside mosques in the former Soviet Central Asian countries. Hence, the Ferghana is becoming yet another "centre for Islamist ideological training," and in fact Islamist parties from Uzbekistan in particular have received military instruction in Afghanistan.

Nevertheless, it is the Southeast Asian sub-region of the Asia-Pacific that has received the most attention from Western officials and analysts, following the ouster of the Taliban regime by the U.S.-led Coalition at the end of 2001. There are good reasons for this: About 20 percent of the world's 1.2 billion Muslims live in the area, and Indonesia is, in fact, the world's largest Muslim country. In addition, the majority of the populations of Malaysia and Brunei are Muslim, and significant Muslim minorities reside in the Philippines, Singapore, and Thailand. This large Muslim population aside, Indonesia and the Philippines in particular are large archipelagoes with difficult-to-police maritime boundaries. Thus in January 2002, U.S. Deputy Defence Secretary Paul Wolfowitz expressed concern that parts of the southern Philippines, such as Basilan, as well as Sulawesi and Maluku in Indonesia, are relatively "ungoverned" and may prove to be potential "lawless regions where it's easy for terrorist cells and terrorist groups to breed, in effect."[16] Subsequently, in late April, General Richard Myers, the Chairman of the U.S. Joint Chiefs of Staff, asserted while on an official visit to Manila that "links" had been discerned between Al Qaeda and radical Islamic terrorist organizations in the region.[17] In fact, Gunaratna argues that even before September 11 "Afghanistan and Middle Eastern-trained Islamists and philanthropists" had been active in Southeast Asia, "establishing links with domestic political and violent groups," and recruiting Asian Muslims. To be sure, Southeast Asian governments have long had to contend with home-grown radical Islamist groups espousing their own violent national agendas, and in this volume, Gunaratna identifies and discusses, for instance, indigenous Islamist separatist groups in southern Thailand that re-emerged in the late 1990s, such as Bersatu and the New Patani United Liberation Organization (PULO). And yet it is also increasingly clear that the danger of transnationalization of Southeast Asian radical Islam through its incorporation into a wider, global *jihad* waged by the likes of Al Qaeda is very real. Gunaratna has argued elsewhere that:[18]

> Whenever Al Qaeda interacted with a terrorist group or a government, its potent Islamist ideology and the irresistible financial rewards it offered saw them either become fully absorbed into the wider Al Qaeda network or fall within its sphere of influence.

In like vein, Gunaratna claims in the present study that in the past decade, Thailand has served as a "safe haven for a number of terrorist and criminal groups" such as the Lebanese Hezbollah, which has, he claims, used the country as a base from which to conduct terrorist support operations in the region.

As far as Al Qaeda is concerned, Gunaratna has argued in his own work that it commenced its infiltration into Southeast Asia in the early 1990s when Osama bin Laden forged a personal relationship with Abdurajak Janjalani, the founder of the Philippines-based Abu Sayyaf Group (ASG).[19] In this volume moreover, Gunaratna—as does Peter Chalk—not only reiterates the relatively clear links between Al Qaeda and the ASG, they also discuss bin Laden's connections with the Moro Islamic Liberation Front (MILF). Chalk for his part argues that the evident "internationalist orientation" of the ASG gives it special relevance and "a threat quotient far beyond" the relatively small number of "hardcore activists that the group is currently able to mobilize in the southern Philippine theatre." Chalk also opines that as far as Indonesia is concerned, the most important radical Islamist group is Laskar Jihad (LJ). Led by Jafar Umar Thalib, a veteran of the anti-Soviet Afghan *jihad*, the group adheres to the view that there is a worldwide Jewish/Christian conspiracy to undermine Islam. LJ thus seeks to impose *shariah* law across Indonesia, as well as launch a *jihad* aimed at liberating the country from the influence of the U.S. and its "infidel" cohorts. LJ is particularly worrying because of its regional and even global pretensions. Chalk cites Indonesian intelligence sources in claiming that Al Qaeda agents, including affiliated terrorists from Malaysian groups Kumpulan Militan Malaysia (KMM) and Jemiah Islamiah (JI), have participated in LJ attacks in Maluku and Sulawesi as well as bombings in Jakarta.

With respect to Malaysia, both Chalk and Gunaratna appear to suggest the country's importance lies in the fact that it is known to contain radical Islamist elements that have formed the basis for "a loose logistical network" that has supported the activities of Muslim militants, both within Southeast Asia and beyond. Of particular interest, it has been confirmed that in January 2000, Al Qaeda operatives met in Kajang in the Malaysian state of Selangor to discuss plans for several attacks on U.S. targets. Khalid al-Midhar and Nawaf Al Hazmi, two of the September 11 hijackers attended this meeting, while Zacarias Moussaoui, the so-called "14th hijacker" currently standing trial in the United States, also visited Malaysia later in 2000. As Gunaratna notes, the Islamist terrorist support network in Malaysia "spilled over to Singapore in the early 1990s." Hence, Chalk shows how even Singapore, with its highly professional internal security apparatus, was not spared from radical Islamist infiltration. Indeed, as is now well-known, in December 2001, Singaporean JI extremists with links to Malaysia were implicated in a wider Al Qaeda plan to attack several high-profile Western targets in Singapore, including the island-nation's deep-water naval base at Changi, the Ministry of Defence, a shuttle bus used by U.S. military personnel to travel on the Yishun subway, the U.S. and Israeli embassies, the British and Australian High Commissions and commercial complexes housing American firms. JI—a group formed by Indonesian radical Islamists and infiltrated by Al Qaeda in the early 1990s[20]— has since been identified in at least four Southeast Asian countries, including Malaysia, the Philippines, Indonesia and Singapore. As Chalk observes, JI appears to be closely affiliated with the KMM, a group first formed by the Malaysian Afghan veteran Zainon Ismail in October 1995,[21] and that appears to have been heavily influenced by the radical Al Qaeda world-view.

Islam and Terrorism: Southeast Asian Perspectives

Bernard Lewis, whom the *New York Times* has described as the "doyen of Middle Eastern studies," asserted in a 1990 article entitled "The Roots of Muslim Rage:"[22]

> It should now be clear that we are facing a mood and a movement far transcending the level of issues and policies and governments that pursue them. This is no less than a clash of civilizations—that perhaps irrational but surely historic reaction of an ancient rival against our Judeo-Christian heritage, our secular present, and the worldwide expansion of both.

Lewis appeared to have influenced the well-known American political scientist, Samuel P. Huntington, who, in 1996, published *The Clash of Civilizations and the Remaking of World Order*, in which he followed Lewis' lead in constructing an image of a monolithic, hostile Islamic world:[23]

> The underlying problem for the West is not Islamic fundamentalism. It is Islam, a different civilization whose people are convinced of the superiority of their culture and are obsessed with the inferiority of their power.

As the erudite scholar of Islam, John Esposito observes, both scholars were "seminal in defining the parameters of a debate that has gripped diplomats,

policymakers, journalists, and academic analysts."[24] Certainly, in the wake of
September 11, the prevailing orthodoxy in American and Western circles of a
retrogressive, violent, and monolithic Islamic world appears to have been
reinforced. For instance, the well-respected American military analyst, Ralph
Peters, recently averred with barely-concealed venom:[25]

> Bigoted, hopelessly corrupt, close-minded, uneducated, psychologically
> infantile, self-important, and incapable of dealing not only with the
> twenty-first century, but even with the demands and developments of
> the twentieth, Muslim states and societies are rotting while their ancient
> competitors flourish…the Islamic world will continue to be a source
> of trouble for every other civilization…A civilization that is anti-
> meritocratic, that oppresses and torments women, that mocks the rule
> of law, that neglects education and lacks a work ethic simply cannot
> prosper under modern conditions.

Is Islam as guilty as charged by Peters? Edward Said, for one, demurs. He has
long argued that there is more to Islam than both Lewis, Huntington and now
Peters suggest. In a recent article, for example, Said deconstructs the prevailing
Lewis–Huntington schema with characteristic vigour, arguing forcefully that
"the many Islams cannot be simplified:"[26]

> For anyone with any clarity of thought and common-sense ideas about
> the complexity and variety of concrete human experience, it is much
> more sensible to try to talk about different kinds of Islam, at different
> moments, for different people, in different fields…Once one gets a
> tiny step beyond core beliefs (since even those are very hard to reduce
> to a simple set of rules) and the centrality of the Koran, one has entered
> an astoundingly complicated world whose enormous—one might even
> say unthinkable—collective history alone has yet to be written.

It is in this spirit that the Southeast Asian Muslim intellectuals Rizal Sukma
and Farish Noor argue in this volume for a more nuanced understanding of
Islam, especially as it applies to the Southeast Asian context. Significantly
both contributors paint a picture of a far-from-monolithic Southeast Asian
Islam; Sukma himself, in analyzing the Indonesian response to September
11 delineates three groups: "the radical Islamic," "mainstream Islamic," and
an essentially secularist faction. In speaking of "differences within a pluralistic

ummah," Sukma is not breaking new ground. Observers have long noted that in Southeast Asia, Islam has fused with other civilizational and indigenous influences and is "basically, tolerant, peaceful, and smiling."[27] No surprise then that Noor laments the fact that "Islam and the culture of Muslims have been equated with terrorism and violence." He warns against the error of "cultural essentialism" in equating terror with Islam simply because the terrorists justify their heinous behaviour in the syntax of Islamic discourse. He advocates penetrating the surface of "religio-political discourse" to examine how the "socio-political terrain of societies" serve as the *real* "backdrop where such discourses and counter-discourses" emerge in the first instance. Thus, Noor points out that the "Islamic threat" must not be taken seriously as an "epistemic category," but rather as a "discursive tool crafted for specific political and ideological reasons." Noor argues in this respect that while Southeast Asian political opposition movements in the 1960s and 1970s tended to adopt secular, nationalist platforms, from the 1980s onwards, "religious militant movements" arose that employed the "discourse of religion rather than secular politics." These movements were by and large driven by radical Islamist ideologies.

What explains the rise of radical Islamism in Southeast Asia? As Singapore's far-sighted geopolitical analyst and elder statesman Lee Kuan Yew observed in May 2002, three factors were particularly pertinent. First, after the quadrupling of oil prices in 1973, Saudi Arabia was able to finance the *Dakwa* (missionary) movement by building mosques and *madrasahs* around the world and paying for religious teachers or *ulamas*. This meant that the severe Saudi form of Wahhabi Islam was disseminated to Southeast Asia. Second, the Iranian Revolution led by Islamist clerics played a major role in restoring Muslim belief in the power of the faith. Third, the participation of large numbers of Southeast Asian Muslims in the ultimately successful Afghan *jihad* against the Soviet Union inevitably had a radicalizing effect. Noor himself adds a fourth, crucial reason for the radicalization of some Southeast Asian Muslims: their disillusionment with ruling elites, conventional modes of political dialogue and the failure of democratic structures to provide effective governance. Noor therefore argues that radical Islam provides a "framework for a moral/ethical critique of power and that it foregrounds a religiocentric viewpoint from which society can be reconstructed." Hence, what links radical Islamist groups such as Laskar Jihad and Jemiah Islamiah together is "the use of religious discourse as a means of gaining leverage over their co-religionist competitors and adversaries." In other words, Southeast Asian radical Islamists, by "upping the ante in the 'holier than thou' race" against their more mainstream, moderate competitors, seek to win the battle for Muslim hearts and minds and hence establish the "religio-political hegemony" required to underpin the Islamic order they see as the solution to their real-world woes.

While Noor proceeds to analyze the post-911 struggle for the Muslim and wider Malaysian ground between Mahathir Mohamad's secular, moderate United Malays National Organization (UMNO) and the Islamist PAS in Malaysia, Sukma shows how a similar struggle has ensued for Indonesian Muslim hearts and minds, between moderate Islamist organizations like Nadhlatul Ulama and Muhammadiyah and radical Islamist groups like Laskar Jihad. However, as Sukma cogently argues, the potential for Indonesia, the world's largest Muslim country, to represent "a moderate face of Islam in the years to come," is not something to be taken for granted. The essential need, Sukma argues, is to eradicate "the grounds for grievances and prevent them from turning into support for radicalism." In other words, a Southeast Asian prescription for countering the radical Islamism that largely fuels the new terrorism would involve much more than a preoccupation with military-operational measures.

Formulating Counter-Strategies: The Need for Two Tracks

It would appear that the general consensus of the contributors to this volume is that effectively dealing with the radical Islamist threat exemplified by Al Qaeda requires the co-ordinated application of what may be termed "dual-track" counter-strategies. Track One must involve the crucial, immediate military-operational measures of physically detecting and eliminating armed terrorist groups and clandestine cells, organization, funding and planning. Simultaneously, on a second parallel Track Two, as it were, non-military measures aimed at "draining the swamp" that nurtures terrorists must also be pursued. As Hoffman puts it, "counter-measures" are needed that are "at once designed to blunt that threat," but that at the same time also "utilize the full range of means we can bring to bear in countering terrorism: psychological as well as physical; diplomatic as well as military; economic as well as moral." In terms of Track One counter-strategies, Ely Karmon argues that effectively mitigating the existential threat of NBC terrorism in particular must involve several parallel measures: securing sound intelligence; the denial of chemical, biological, radiological and nuclear agents, specific hardware and know-how to terrorist and rogue elements; the preparation of specialized teams to deal with NBC attacks in the field; investment in the research and development of detection, protection, decontamination and treatment equipment and supplies; and importantly, global coordination in police intelligence and law enforcement in the monitoring and tracking of suspected NBC terrorists. Nevertheless, it is worth iterating that the thread that links the Hoffman, Cameron, and Karmon contributions is that while one should not be complacent about the threat of terrorists deploying WMD weapons, there is an equally pressing requirement to visualize and guard against a wider range of unconventional terrorism scenarios involving the use of conventional weapons.

To guard against the worst terrorist outrages requires the imagination to foresee what they are capable of perpetrating in today's networked world—and this is in turn utterly reliant on first-class intelligence. As Andrew Tan rightly points out, in the short term, information-sharing at the inter-agency level both domestically and internationally is absolutely essential in confronting the new terrorism, given its global reach and transnational mode of operations. Tan argues that while huge Western investment in technical surveillance has been helpful, what has been sorely lacking is quality human intelligence and in particular the in-house expertise to evaluate the collected data. There is thus "a clear need to develop specialists who can build up the necessary expertise on specific terrorist or militant groups, and to share their expertise and information with other agencies and countries." The key task of such in-house experts would be to construct "a shared profile of radical terrorist groups." This, Tan says, would "enable deeper analysis of their organizational capability, political intent, links to other organizations and political forces, willingness to act, the motivation for their actions, and the domestic context in which they operate." Only detailed, long-term, on-going monitoring of targeted terrorist organizations will provide governments with opportunities for "early warning and preventive actions." But even this in itself would not be sufficient. It is worth reiterating that all the information in the world will be useless if it were not subjected to imaginative, critical thinking of the highest order: Only by constantly challenging assumptions, exchanging ideas and experimentation can analysts provide the policy-relevant inputs that will help governments keep a step ahead of the new terrorists.

If Track One counter-strategies would help governments stay ahead of the new terrorists in the short term, Track Two approaches may in the longer haul help, in U.S. Deputy Defence Secretary Paul Wolfowitz's words, "drain the swamp" from which the new terrorists emerge. It is apparent, at least to the editors, that a substantive discussion of Track Two counter-strategies is long overdue: It is not entirely clear to what extent non-military measures in the war on terror are even seriously considered by the Bush administration in particular. In this respect, Nicholas Kristof has noted that one strain of thought that has been increasingly evident in Washington circles is aptly summarized by Cicero's dictum: *Oderint, dum metuant*—let them hate, as long as they fear.[28] Certainly, Ralph Peters appears to be one of the more hawkish voices promoting the Cicero approach. He argues in his recent book that America must "not waste an inordinate amount of effort trying to win unwinnable hearts and minds. Convince hostile populations through victory."[29] He adds that America must not shrink from using its "raw power" and that its "responses to terrorist acts should make the world gasp."[30] He urges American forces to focus "on the basic mission—the destruction of the terrorists," and asserts that "all other issues, from future nation-building, to alliance consensus, to humanitarian concerns, are secondary."[31] He urges the adoption of one overriding consideration:[32]

> This is a fight to protect the American people, and we must proceed, whatever the cost, or the price in American lives will be devastating. In a choice between "them" and "us," the choice is always "us."

Peters essentially argues, therefore, America, the "new Rome," can only ensure its security against terror by being feared.[33]

While the sheer horror of the September 11 terror attacks have provoked a not unnatural impulse on the part of many Americans to retaliate against Al Qaeda in kind, this study suggests that America, in seeking to destroy the radical Islamist threat, would do well to heed the essential advice of the ancient Chinese sage Sun Tzu to use *wisdom* in fighting one's enemies.[34] In the specific context of the war on terror, this would imply developing an appreciation that over-reliance on the mailed fist would not be sufficient to defeat Al Qaeda; in fact, it may well *energize* Al Qaeda and exacerbate the terror threat. As Ramakrishna argues, even if the U.S.-led Coalition succeeds in eliminating most of the Al Qaeda cells round the globe, denies access to WMD technologies and freezes terrorist funds, "the threat would not necessarily be eradicated." Because of the reality of a globalized, networked world, "a fanatically-determined radical Islamic core that is scattered throughout the world—but leveraging on communications technology to coordinate activities and manpower movement—can, over time, generate new cells, reconstruct disrupted logistics and funding networks while clandestinely restoring access to WMD capabilities." Ramakrishna argues that the basic problem is that as long as "sizable pockets of disgruntled, anti-American young Muslims remain in countries from Nigeria to the Philippines, there will always be a radical Islamic movement posing an existential threat to Western and especially U.S. interests." Al Qaeda should be seen not merely as a dispersed guerilla army but more as a self-regenerating hydra. Hence, to truly defeat Al Qaeda, America really needs "to *kill the radical Islamic hydra*, not interminably snip at its many heads."

To kill the terrorist hydra requires, as Hoffman argues, pinpointing the "inner logic" that "motivates terrorists and animates terrorism." Any attempt to dissect this "inner logic" brings us back to our over-arching theme: the fact that the new terrorism is the product of a failed accommodation between secular modernity and religious tradition. One central aspect of this failure is surely the inability of secular political, economic and social structures, so well-configured for participation in global capitalism, to absorb and in so doing make their peace with traditional elements in societies worldwide. Fareed Zakaria puts it well:[35]

> Radical Islam has risen on the backs of failed states that have not improved the lots of their people. It festers in societies where contact with the West has produced more chaos than growth and more uncertainty than wealth. It is, in a sense, the result of failed and incomplete modernization.

Similarly, Andrew Tan argues cogently in these pages that "the roots of Muslim rage and alienation lie fundamentally in local political, economic and social issues and conflicts, whether in Kashmir, Chechnya, Aceh, Patani or Mindanao, or indeed, even in Western Europe." Tan then shows how in Southeast Asia, all three separatist rebellions in Aceh, Patani and Mindanao, "predated September 11 and Al Qaeda, and have been driven by the presence of local grievances," such as continuing poverty, unemployment and military abuses in Aceh, and Muslim Moro landlessness in Mindanao. Tan, therefore, asserts that while countering the new terrorism "must include military and defensive measures," these must be complemented by "attention to winning hearts and minds, for which development and the addressing of fundamental political, economic and social grievances which lie at the root cause of rebellion and terrorism, are essential."

To be sure, there have been analysts like Daniel Pipes who have eloquently disagreed that radical Islamists are the children of economic despair. Pipes marshals evidence to show that, in fact, radical Islamists tend to be young, of middle-class origin, achievement-oriented, upwardly mobile, with science or engineering backgrounds and from stable families.[36] Tan asserts that while it is undeniable that the new terrorism is animated by a middle-class militant core, this in no way invalidates the importance of promoting political and economic development as a key instrument of Track Two counter-strategies. There are two reasons for this. First, if foreign aid can at the very least help prevent state failure, then it may well deprive terrorist organizations like Al Qaeda of safe havens. It has been observed that after all, Osama bin Laden "based himself in Sudan and then Afghanistan because dysfunctional countries afforded him maximum freedom."[37] Second, the middle-class "counter-elites" that reside at the core of the new terrorism after all need manpower to carry out their schemes, and they thus need to "recruit a following among the poor, who make valuable foot-soldiers."[38] This suggests that the true centre of gravity of the new terrorism—in Clausewitz's classic formulation, "the hub on which everything else depends"—resides in the hearts and minds of the middle-class militant core. Hence, what is it that drives them? Martin Kramer suggests that despite their wealth, they are frustrated as they "cannot translate their socio-economic assets into political clout."[39] Hence, as Shibley Telhami adds, they deeply resent "their inferior position in society because they 'know better,' and because they are also more aware of their capacity to affect change."[40] If this is the case, then Sebastian Mallaby is surely right in arguing that foreign aid can do much to mute the "political passions" of the disaffected middle-class militants by reducing poverty, improving social welfare and promoting "honest and representative governance."[41]

Targeted foreign aid, it should be pointed out, must also be complemented by profound adjustments in U.S. foreign policy. It is particularly instructive, as Rizal Sukma shows in these pages, that most Indonesian Muslims, who are far from radical, nevertheless attributed the September 11 attacks to Muslim disillusionment with American policy towards the Middle East. There is, in particular, much latent bitterness over the status of Palestine. In this regard, Surin Pitsuwan, the respected former foreign minister of Thailand and an Arabic-speaking Southeast Asian

Muslim, has explained that a strong sense of "primordial" resentment exists among "all Muslims around the world, particularly here in Southeast Asia," that their sentiments about Jerusalem, which after Mecca and Medina is the third holiest site in Islam, have been ignored by the international community.[42] According to Pitsuwan, the failure to seek a just solution to the Palestine question has resulted in Southeast Asian Muslim "frustration, inadequacy, the sense of being left out, the sense of being done injustice;" sentiments that have been "overwhelming to the point of desperation."[43] For his part, Sukma asserts that Indonesian Muslims have long felt that the U.S. pursues a double standard in three policy areas. First, although preaching the norms of democracy in other parts of the world, the U.S. is regarded as guilty of backing many non-democratic regimes in the Middle East. Second, although portraying itself as the chief exemplar of human rights, Washington is perceived to be consistently oblivious to human rights violations by Israel against Palestinians. Third, and more generally, America is considered to be largely indifferent whenever the victims of oppression happen to be Muslims—and in this connection, American backing for the authoritarian Suharto regime during the Cold War has not been forgotten. In fact, in the wake of September 11, Indonesian intellectuals are increasingly concerned "that while some of their more authoritarian neighbours, like Malaysia or Pakistan, have suddenly become the new darlings of Washington," Indonesia "is being orphaned because it is a messy, but real, democracy."[44]

Given the long-held perception—predating September 11—that America has never been a friend of Islam, it is no surprise that in many parts of the Islamic realm, including Muslim Southeast Asia, Washington has, in fact, precious little credibility. Sukma notes in this respect that even amongst moderate Indonesians, there was disbelief that Muslims could have carried out the September 11 terror attacks. Instead, as elsewhere in the Muslim world, the CIA and Israel were fingered. As Ramakrishna argues, therefore, there certainly needs to be more resources pumped into augmenting American public diplomacy in the Muslim world. However, Philip Taylor has correctly argued that "to be effective, propaganda requires image and reality to go hand in hand."[45] Thus, America must not only seek to *tell* the Muslim world that it is a friend of Islam—it is equally important to *prove* it through concrete action. There is a wide range of ways in which America can, over the long term, seek to persuade Muslims of the veracity of its pronouncements, not least of which is through a concerted effort to seek a just solution of the Palestinian problem. Another important—but apparently woefully neglected—way in which Washington can ensure that the message sent out by its words is not flatly contradicted by that emanating from its deeds is by taking care to ensure that all military action is carefully calibrated and controlled. As Ramakrishna suggests, all the extra funding pumped into enhancing public diplomacy will be well nigh worthless if, through collateral Muslim civilian deaths arising from American air strikes and countless other ways, America inadvertently suggests that despite its apparently conciliatory rhetoric, it is *indeed* at war with the *ummah*. It is of the utmost necessity, therefore, that American officials and commanders, like their British counterparts of a previous era, develop the art of being "propaganda-minded."[46]

Apart from socio-economic and political elements, there is a further strand that must be woven into the complex picture that constitutes new terrorist motivations: ideology. As noted, Farish Noor argues that in Southeast Asia, radical Islam is appealing because it offers a "framework for a moral/ethical critique of power." In a similar vein, the Islamic scholar John Esposito has pointed out that an "Islamic ideology" provides counter-elites "with a critique of society and an agenda for radical social change."[47] In the final analysis, therefore, a comprehensive effort to mesh secular modernity with religious tradition must not only involve the construction of political, economic and social structures of accommodation, but also *ideological* ones as well. Significantly, the leaders of the two key Muslim countries in Southeast Asia hold this view. Malaysian Prime Minister Mahathir Mohamad, for instance, has argued that the main problem facing Islam is an inherent conservatism that militates against acquisition of new knowledge. He opines that too many Muslims equate the fundamentalist return to traditional dress codes as evidence of a "Muslim Renaissance" when in fact a genuine Islamic revival can only occur with a "change in attitude, a change in the mindset and values which always hold us back whenever we seek to empower ourselves."[48] Mahathir laments that, for too long, Muslims have been "taught to uphold the forms rather than the substance of the religion we believe in," and to emphasize religious knowledge while regarding "other kinds of knowledge" as "either sinful or lacking in merit, as not contributing to the afterlife." Mahathir insists:[49]

> It is not Islam which obstructs our progress. It is the wrong and rigid interpretations which we are taught which hinder progress.

Former Indonesian President and leading moderate intellectual, Abdurrahman Wahid (Gus Dur), agrees that it is not Islam *per se*, but rather the interpretation of Islam that is the key. Gus Dur in fact takes the argument further. He suggests that young Muslim students not only need to acquire an "understanding of modern science and technology," as Mahathir says, but also to mesh this with a similarly modern conception of their faith. However:

> Because they have not been trained in the rich disciplines of Islamic scholarship, they tend to bring to their reflection on their faith the same sort of simple modelling and formulistic thinking that they have learnt as students of engineering or other applied sciences.

As a result, these students take a

> more or less literalistic approach to the textual sources of Islam…[and] use these texts in a reductionistic fashion without being able to undertake, or even appreciate, the subtly-nuanced task of interpretation required of them if they are to understand how documents from the 7th to 8th centuries, from the tribal Arab society among the desert sands, are to be applied correctly to the very different world that we live in today.

If young Muslims are not taught how, Gus Dur argues, "to approach their faith with the intellectual sophistication that the demands of the modern world require of them," then when "alienation, loneliness and the search for identity" encroach upon them, they will be vulnerable to the "formalistic understanding of Islamic law" that breeds "violent radicalism." He therefore asserts that a real problem is that "precious few young Muslims from developing nations have the privilege of undertaking liberal arts courses in Western universities."[50] On the other hand, as Ramakrishna observes in this volume, if young Muslims cannot go abroad to get a liberal arts education, then perhaps a liberal arts education can come and get them. He cites Roy Mottahedeh, who has argued that more vernacular-based liberal arts undergraduate courses would help expedite much-needed economic growth. Foreign aid programmes that help governments expand the number of secular schools would therefore help obviate the need for desperate parents to send their children to certain "religious ones that are little more than terror training colleges."[51]

Taking Stock

The upshot of all this is that to effectively neutralize the radical Islamist new terrorism best exemplified by Al Qaeda, the West in general and America in particular cannot afford to make do with a primarily military-operational strategy. While these measures do have an immediate, important place as part of what we have termed Track One counter-strategies, these simply have to be complemented by Track Two approaches that essentially address the more fundamental longer-term problem of creating structures of political, economic, social and ideological accommodation between global, secular, homogenizing capitalism and religious tradition. In a very real sense, the central struggle is ideological. The radical Islamist hydra will be disembowelled only when what Graham Fuller calls a "Muslim Reformation" has given rise to "a politics at once authentically Islamist yet also authentically liberal and democratic."[52] To attain this genuine Islamic Renaissance would require that young Muslims worldwide be not only encouraged but properly taught the principles of *ijtihad*, or independent reasoning. This would enable them to adopt lifestyles according to conscientious individual interpretations of Islam and free them from the medieval *fatwas* of radical Islamic clerics.

In light of the above, and to fight, as Sun Tzu always counselled, with wisdom, America must take a leaf out of the strategy manual of the great French strategist Andre Beaufre, and adopt an *indirect strategy* for countering Al Qaeda. While a "direct" strategy involves the application of military force as the primary means of imposing one's will on an enemy, with diplomatic, economic and propaganda instruments orchestrated in support of the main military thrust, in an "indirect" strategy, military force is carefully calibrated to support and not scupper the primarily non-military means to impose one's will on the enemy.[53] More specifically, to comprehensively neutralize the Al Qaeda threat by draining the swamp from which bin Laden draws his recruits, an indirect strategy must be adopted involving the circumspect application of Track One counter-measures in ways that promote and not scupper, the simultaneous implementation of Track Two approaches. Unfortunately, at the time of writing, the preference in official Washington circles seems to be for the *reverse*: an emphasis on Track One military-operational measures, potentially against Iraq, and an under-emphasis on Track Two approaches such as a concerted effort to justly resolve the Palestinian conflict. In other words, a *direct* strategy is being adopted, in which Washington's multilateral machinations are designed to erect a multinational, multidimensional framework integrating political, diplomatic, and economic measures with one overriding purpose in mind: to more effectively and efficiently expedite the unilateral exercise of American military power against Al Qaeda. This explains why Tony Judt has observed that several months into the war on terror, it became clear that "the 'coalition' was an inch deep," and that in essence, "most of its members were not being asked to do anything much beyond lining up behind American military action."[54]

American hawks who believe that homeland security can only be assured by being feared underestimate the depth of the anger, humiliation and disaffection of many in the Islamic world. In fact, the ongoing Palestinian "martyrdom operations" despite stepped-up Israeli security offer a microcosmic hint of what America might have to endure in future if it persists with a short-sighted, primarily military-operational, policy. As Ramakrishna warns, "an American invasion of Iraq without concomitant progress in ending Israeli-Palestinian violence would generate additional political oxygen which—in a supreme irony—would not only create the civilizational enmity America seeks to avoid, but also ensure a steady supply of fresh recruits into Al Qaeda's ranks." And in a globalized, networked world, is it wise to believe that the new terrorists of Al Qaeda and perhaps even other disaffected millennial groups will not be able to find creative ways to penetrate American defences again? Lasting security for America will be assured only when Osama bin Laden can no longer find willing recruits for his skewed schemes. As the contributions in this volume will hopefully show, to grasp the essence of the new terrorism would be to understand that a great deal more than raw military force would be required to permanently neutralize it.

Notes

1   For two exemplary expositions of this view, see Thomas L. Friedman, *The Lexus and the Olive Tree* (New York: Anchor Books, 2000); and Benjamin R. Barber, *Jihad vs McWorld: How Globalism and Tribalism Are Reshaping the World* (New York: Ballantine Books, 1996).
2   Simon Reeve, *The New Jackals: Ramzi Yousef, Osama bin Laden and the Future of Terrorism* (London: Andre Deutsch, 1999), p. 4.
3   David Ignatius, "See the bin Ladenites as Excrescence of a Painful Transition," *International Herald Tribune* (*IHT*), 29 October 2001.
4   Todd S. Pergum, "Powell Treading a Thin Line in Rallying Antiterror Support," *The New York Times*, 31 July 2002, Late edn., Final, Section A, p. 7.
5   Phil Zabriskie, "The Never-Ending Battle," *Time*, 12 August 2002, p. 21.

6 Barry Desker and Kumar Ramakrishna, "Forging an Indirect Strategy in Southeast Asia," *The Washington Quarterly*, Vol. 25, No. 2 (Spring 2002), pp. 161–176.

7 Steven Simon and Daniel Benjamin, "America and the New Terrorism," *Survival*, Vol. 42, No. 1 (Spring 2000), p. 59.

8 Peter L. Bergen, "Picking Up the Pieces: What We Can Learn From—and About—9/11," *Foreign Affairs*, Vol. 81, No. 2 (March/April 2002), p. 172.

9 Steven Simon and Daniel Benjamin, "The Terror," *Survival*, Vol. 43, No. 4 (Winter 2002), pp. 5–6.

10 Friedman, *The Lexus and the Olive Tree*, Chapter Four.

11 Thomas Homer-Dixon, "The Rise of Complex Terrorism," *Foreign Policy* (January/February 2002), pp. 54–55.

12 Homer-Dixon, "Rise of Complex Terrorism," p. 55.

13 Homer-Dixon, "Rise of Complex Terrorism," p. 60.

14 John Mackinlay, "NATO and Bin Laden," *RUSI Journal*, Vol. 146, No. 6 (December 2001), p. 37.

15 Rohan Gunaratna, *Inside Al Qaeda: Global Network of Terror* (New York: Columbia University Press, 2002), p. 5.

16 Transcript of Paul Wolfowitz interview with James Dao and Eric Schmitt, 7 January 2002, Royal Institute of Lingustics and Anthropology (KITLV) website, available at http://iiasnt.leidenuniv.nl:8080/DR/2002/01/DR_2002_01_15/2.

17 Luz Baguiro, "Al-Qaeda 'may set up base in South-east Asia'," *The Straits Times Interactive* (Singapore), available at http://straitstimes.asia1.com.sg, 28 April 2002.

18 Gunaratna, *Inside Al Qaeda*, p. 5.

19 Gunaratna, *Inside Al Qaeda*, p. 174.

20 Gunaratna, *Inside Al Qaeda*, p. 186.

21 Gunaratna, *Inside Al Qaeda*, p. 196.

22 Cited in Samuel P. Huntington, *The Clash of Civilizations and the Remaking of World Order* (London: Simon and Schuster, 1996), p. 213.

23 Huntington, *The Clash of Civilizations*, p. 217.

24 John L. Esposito, *The Islamic Threat: Myth or Reality?* 3rd edn. (New York and Oxford: Oxford University Press, 1999), p. 219.

25 Ralph Peters, *Beyond Terror: Strategy in a Changing World* (Mechanicsburg, PA: Stackpole, 2002), pp. 6–7.

26 Edward W. Said, "Impossible Histories: Why the Many Islams Cannot Be Simplified," *Harper's* (July 2002), pp. 69–70.

27 Azyumardi Azra, "The Megawati Presidency: Challenge of Political Islam," paper delivered at the "Joint Public Forum on Indonesia: The First 100 Days of President Megawati," organized by the Institute of Southeast Asian Studies (Singapore) and the Centre for Strategic and International Studies (Jakarta), 1 November 2001, Singapore.

28 Nicholas D. Kristof, "Cicero was Wrong," *The New York Times on the Web*, available at http://www.nytimes.com/2002/03/12/opinion/12KRIS.html, 12 March 2002.

29 Peters, *Beyond Terror*, p. 59.

30 Peters, *Beyond Terror*, p. 59.

31 Peters, *Beyond Terror*, p. 60.

32 Peters, *Beyond Terror*, pp. 61–62.

33 Peters, *Beyond Terror*, pp. 18–19.

34 See Sun Tzu, *The Art of War*, ed. by Tao Hanzhang (Hertfordshire: Wordsworth Reference, 1993), p. 19.

35 Fareed Zakaria, "The Return of History: What September 11 Hath Wrought," in James F. Hoge, Jr. and Gideon Rose (eds.), *How Did This Happen? Terrorism and the New War* (New York: Public Affairs/Council on Foreign Relations, 2001), p. 316.

36 Daniel Pipes, "God and Mammon: Does Poverty Cause Militant Islam?" *The National Interest* (Winter 2001/2002), p. 16.

37 Sebastian Mallaby, "Poverty Causes Terror? Either Way, Aid Works," *The IHT Online*, available at http://www.iht.com/articles/58280.html, 21 May 2002.

38 Martin Kramer, cited in Pipes, "God and Mammon," p. 17.

39 Cited in Pipes, "God and Mammon," p. 17.

40 Shibley Telhami, "It's Not About Faith: A Battle for the Soul of the Middle East," *Current History*, Vol. 100, No. 650 (December 2001), p. 415.

41 Mallaby, "Poverty Causes Terror?"

42 Surin Pitsuwan, "Strategic Challenges Facing Islam in Southeast Asia," lecture delivered at a forum organized by the Institute of Defence and Strategic Studies and the Centre for Contemporary Islamic Studies, Singapore, 5 November 2001.

43 Pitsuwan lecture.

44 Thomas L. Friedman, "The War on What?", *The New York Times on the Web*, available at http://www.nytimes.com/2002/05/08/opinion/08FRIE.html, 8 May 2002.

45 Philip Taylor, "Spin Laden," *The World Today*, December 2001, p. 7.

46 For an explanation of the concept as it came to be applied in Malaya during the Emergency (1948–60), see Kumar Ramakrishna, *Emergency Propaganda: The Winning of Malayan Hearts and Minds 1948–58* (Richmond, Surrey: Curzon, 2002).

47 Esposito, *The Islamic Threat*, p. 147.

48 Mahathir Mohamad, "Breaking the Muslim Mindset," *The Sunday Times* (Singapore), 28 July 2002.

49 Mahathir, "Breaking the Muslim Mindset."

50 Abdurrahman Wahid, "Best Way to Fight Islamic Extremism," *The Sunday Times* (Singapore), 14 April 2002.

51 Mallaby, "Poverty Causes Terror?"

52 Graham E. Fuller, "The Future of Political Islam," *Foreign Affairs*, Vol. 81, No. 2 (March/April 2002), p. 59.

53 Andre Beaufre, *Strategy of Action* (London: Faber and Faber, 1967).

54 Tony Judt, "The War on Terror," *The New York Review of Books*, Vol. XLVIII, No. 20 (20 December 2001), pp. 102–103.

CHAPTER 2

THE EMERGENCE OF THE NEW TERRORISM

Bruce Hoffman

A few hours after the first American air strikes against Afghanistan began on October 7, 2001, a pre-recorded videotape was broadcast around the world. A tall, skinny man with a long, scraggily beard, wearing a camouflage fatigue jacket and the headdress of a desert tribesman, with an AK-47 assault rifle at his side, stood before a rocky backdrop. In measured, yet defiant, language, Osama bin Laden again declared war on the United States. Only a few weeks before, his statement would likely have been dismissed as the inflated rhetoric of a sabre-rattling braggart. But with the World Trade Centre now laid to waste, the Pentagon heavily damaged and the wreckage of a fourth hijacked passenger aircraft strewn across a field in rural Pennsylvania, bin Laden's declaration was regarded with a preternatural seriousness that would previously have been unimaginable. How bin Laden achieved this feat, and the light his accomplishment sheds on understanding the extent to which terrorism has changed and, in turn, how our responses must change as well, is the subject of this essay.

The September 11 Attacks by the Numbers

The enormity and sheer scale of the simultaneous suicide attacks on September 11 eclipsed anything we have previously seen in terrorism. Among the most significant characteristics of the operation were its ambitious scope and dimensions, impressive coordination and synchronization, and the unswerving dedication and determination of the 19 aircraft hijackers who willingly and wantonly killed themselves, the passengers and crews of the four aircraft they commandeered and the approximately three thousand persons working in or visiting both the World Trade Centre and the Pentagon.

Indeed, in lethality terms alone the September 11 attacks are without precedent. For example, since 1968, the year credited with marking the advent of modern, international terrorism, one feature of international terrorism has remained constant despite variations in the number of attacks from year to year. Almost without exception,[1] the United States has annually led the list of countries whose citizens and property were most frequently attacked by terrorists.[2] But until September 11, over the preceding 33 years, a total of no more than perhaps 1,000 Americans had been killed by terrorists either overseas or even within the U.S. itself. In less than 90 minutes that day, nearly three times that number were killed.[3] To put those uniquely tragic events in context, during the entirety of the twentieth century, no more than 14 terrorist operations killed more than 100 persons at any one time.[4] Or, viewed from still another perspective, until the attacks on the World Trade Centre and Pentagon, no single terrorist operation had ever killed more than 500 persons at one time.[5] Whatever the metric, therefore, the attacks that day were unparalleled in their severity and lethal ambitions.

Significantly, too, from a purely terrorist operational perspective, *spectacular* simultaneous attacks—using far more prosaic and arguably conventional means of attack (such as car bombs, for example)—are relatively uncommon. For reasons not well understood, terrorists typically have not undertaken coordinated operations. This was doubtless less of a choice than a reflection of the logistical and other organizational hurdles and constraints that all but the most sophisticated terrorist groups are unable to overcome. Indeed, this was one reason why we were so galvanized by the synchronized attacks on the American embassies in Nairobi and Dar-es-Salaam three years ago. The orchestration of that operation, coupled with its unusually high death and casualty tolls, stood out in a way that, until September 11, few other terrorist operations had. During the 1990s, perhaps only one other terrorist operation evidenced those same characteristics of coordination and high lethality: the series of attacks that occurred in Bombay in March 1993, when ten coordinated car bombings rocked the city, killing nearly 300 persons and wounding more than 700 others.[6] Apart from the attacks on the same morning in October 1983 of the U.S. Marine barracks in Beirut (241 persons were killed) and a nearby French paratroop headquarters (where 60 soldiers perished), the 1981 hijacking of three Venezuelan passenger jets by a mixed commando of Salvadoran leftists and Puerto Rican *independistas*, and the dramatic 1970 hijacking of four commercial aircraft by the PFLP (Popular Front for the Liberation of Palestine), two of which were brought to and then dramatically blown up at Dawson's Field in Jordan, there have been few successfully executed, simultaneous terrorist spectaculars.[7]

Finally, the September 11 attacks not only showed a level of patience and detailed planning rarely seen among terrorist movements today, but the hijackers stunned the world with their determination to kill themselves as well as their victims. Suicide attacks differ from other terrorist operations precisely because the perpetrator's own death is a requirement for the attack's success.[8] This dimension of terrorist operations, however, arguably remains poorly understood. In no aspect of the September 11 attacks is this clearer than in the debate over whether all 19 of the hijackers knew they were on a suicide mission or whether only the four persons actually flying the aircraft into their targets did. It is a debate that underscores the poverty of our understanding of bin Laden, terrorism motivated by a religious imperative in particular, and the concept of martyrdom.

The so-called *Jihad Manual*, discovered by British police in March 2000 on the hard drive of an Al Qaeda member's computer is explicit about operational security (OPSEC) in the section that discusses tradecraft. For reasons of operational security, it states, only the leaders of an attack should know all the details of the operation and these should only be revealed to the rest of unit at the last possible moment.[9] Schooled in this tradecraft, the 19 hijackers doubtless understood that they were on a one-way mission from the time they were despatched to the U.S. on their mission of martyrdom. Indeed, the videotape of bin Laden and his chief lieutenant, Dr Ayman Zawahiri, recently broadcast by the Arabic television news station Al-Jazeera contains footage of one of the hijackers acknowledging his impending martyrdom in an illusion to the forthcoming September 11 attacks.

The phenomenon of martyrdom terrorism in Islam has, of course, long been discussed and examined. The act itself can be traced back to the Assassins, an off-shoot of the Shia Ismaili movement, who some 700 years ago waged a protracted struggle against the European Crusaders' attempted conquest of the Holy Land. The Assassins embraced an ethos of self-sacrifice, where martyrdom was regarded as a sacramental act—a highly desirable aspiration and divine duty commanded by religious text and communicated by clerical authorities—that is evident today. An important additional motivation then as now was the promise that the martyr would feel no pain in the commission of his sacred act and would then ascend immediately to a glorious heaven, described as a place replete with "rivers of milk and wine . . . lakes of honey, and the services of 72 virgins," where the martyr will see the face of Allah and later be joined by 70 chosen relatives.[10] The last will and testament of Muhammad Atta, the ringleader of the September 11 hijackers, along with a "primer" for martyrs that he wrote, entitled *The Sky Smiles, My Young Son* clearly evidences such beliefs.[11]

Equally as misunderstood is the attention focused on the hijackers' relatively high levels of education, socio-economic status and stable family ties.[12] In point of fact, contrary to popular belief and misconception, suicide terrorists are not exclusively derived from the ranks of the mentally unstable, economically bereft, or abject, isolated loners. In the more sophisticated and competent terrorist groups, such as the LTTE (Liberation Tigers of Tamil Eelam, or Tamil Tigers), it is precisely the most battle-hardened, skilled and dedicated cadre who enthusiastically volunteer to commit suicide attacks.[13] Observations of the patterns of recent suicide attacks in Israel and on the West Bank and Gaza similarly reveal that the bombers are not exclusively drawn from the maw of poverty, but have included two sons of millionaires. Finally, in the context of the ongoing Palestinian-Israeli conflict, suicide attacks—once one of the more infrequent (albeit dramatic, and attention-riveting) tactics—are clearly increasing in frequency, if not severity, assuming new and more lethal forms.

Where We Went Wrong in Failing to Predict the 9/11 Attacks

But most importantly, we were perhaps lulled into believing that mass, simultaneous attacks in general and those of such devastating potential as we saw in New York and Washington on September 11 were likely beyond the capabilities of most terrorists—including those directly connected to, or associated with, Osama bin Laden. The tragic events of that September day demonstrate how profoundly misplaced such assumptions were. In this respect, we perhaps overestimated the significance of our past successes (e.g., in largely foiling a series of planned terrorist operations against American targets between the August 1998 embassy bombings to the November 2000 attack on the USS *Cole*, including more than 60 instances when credible evidence of impending attack forced the temporary closure of American embassies and consulates around the world) and the terrorists' own incompetence and propensity for mistakes (e.g., Ahmed Ressam's bungled attempt to enter the United States from Canada in December 1999). Both impressive and disturbing is the likelihood that there was considerable overlap in the planning for these attacks with the one in November 2000 against the USS *Cole* in Aden, thus suggesting Al Qaeda's operational and organizational capability to coordinate major, multiple attacks at one time.[14]

Attention was also arguably focused too exclusively either on the low-end threat posed by car and truck bombs against buildings or the more exotic high-end threats, against entire societies, involving biological or chemical weapons or cyber-attacks. The implicit assumptions of much of American planning scenarios on mass-casualty attacks were that they would involve germ or chemical agents or result from widespread electronic attacks on critical infrastructure. It was therefore presumed that any conventional or less extensive incident could be addressed simply by planning for the most catastrophic threat. This left a painfully vulnerable gap in our anti-terrorism defences where a traditional and long-proven tactic—like airline hijacking—was neglected in favour of other, less conventional threats and where the consequences of using an aircraft as a suicide weapon seem to have been ignored. In retrospect, it was not the 1995 sarin nerve gas attack on the Tokyo subway and the nine attempts to use bio-weapons by Aum that should have been the dominant influence on our counter-terrorist thinking, but a 1986 hijacking of a TWA flight in Karachi, where the terrorists' intention was reported to have been to crash it into the centre of Tel Aviv and the 1994 hijacking in Algiers of an Air France passenger plane by terrorists belonging to the Armed Islamic Group (GIA), who similarly planned to crash the fuel-laden aircraft with its passengers into the heart of Paris. The lesson, accordingly, is not that we need to be unrealistically omniscient, but rather that we need to be able to respond across a broad technological spectrum of potential adversarial attacks.

We also had long consoled ourselves—and had only recently begun to question and debate the notion—that terrorists were more interested in publicity than killing and therefore had neither the need nor the interest in annihilating large numbers of people.[15] For decades, there was widespread acceptance of the observation made famous by Brian Jenkins in 1975 that, "terrorists want a lot of people watching and a lot of people listening and not a lot of people dead."[16] While entirely germane to the forms of terrorism that existed in prior decades, for too long we adhered to this antiquated notion. On September 11, bin Laden wiped the slate clean of the conventional wisdom on terrorists and terrorism and, by doing so, ushered in a new era of conflict.

Finally, before September 11, the United States arguably lacked the political will to sustain a long and determined counter-terrorism campaign. The record of inchoate, unsustained previous efforts effectively retarded significant progress against this menace. The carnage and shock of the September 11 attacks laid bare America's vulnerability and too belatedly resulted in a sea change in national attitudes and accompanying political will to combat terrorism systematically, globally and, most importantly, without respite. [17]

Terrorism's CEO

We also violated the cardinal rule of warfare: "Know your enemy." We failed to understand and comprehend Osama bin Laden: his vision, his capabilities, his financial resources and acumen as well as his organizational skills. The broad outline of bin Laden's curriculum vitae is by now well-known; remarkably, it attracted minimal interest and understanding in most quarters prior to September 11. [18] The scion of a porter-turned-construction magnate whose prowess at making money was perhaps matched only by his countless progeny and devout religious piety, the young Osama pursued studies not in theology (despite his issuance of *fatwas*, or Islamic religious edicts), but in business and management sciences. Osama bin Laden is a graduate of Saudi Arabia's prestigious King Abdul-Aziz University, where in 1981 he obtained a degree in economics and public administration. He subsequently cut his teeth in the family business, later applying the corporate management techniques learned both in the classroom and on the job to transform the terrorist movement he founded, Al Qaeda, into the world's pre-eminent terrorist organization. [19]

Osama bin Laden achieved this by cleverly combining the technological munificence of modernity with a rigidly puritanical explication of age-old tradition and religious practice. He is also the quintessential product of the 1990s and globalism. Osama bin Laden, the terrorism CEO, could not have existed—and thrived—in any other era. He was able to overcome the relative geographical isolation caused by his expulsion from the Sudan to Afghanistan, that the U.S. engineered in 1996, by virtue of the invention of the satellite telephone. With this most emblematic technological artifice of 1990s globalism technology, bin Laden was therefore able to communicate with his minions in real time around the world.[20] Al Qaeda operatives, moreover, routinely made use of the latest technology themselves: encrypting messages on Apple PowerMacs or Toshiba laptop computers, communicating via e-mail or on Internet bulletin boards,[21] using satellite telephones and cell phones themselves and, when travelling by air, often flying first-class. This "grafting of entirely modern sensibilities and techniques to the most radical interpretation of holy war," Peter Bergen compellingly explains in *Holy War, Inc.*, "is the hallmark of bin Laden's network."[22]

For bin Laden, the weapons of modern terrorism critically are not only the guns and bombs that they have long been, but the mini-cam, videotape, television and the Internet. The professionally produced and edited two-hour Al Qaeda recruitment videotape that bin Laden circulated throughout the Middle East during the summer of 2001—which according to Bergen also subtly presaged the September 11 attacks—is exactly such an example of bin Laden's nimble exploitation of "twenty-first century communications and weapons technology in the service of the most extreme, retrograde reading of holy war."[23] The tape, with its graphic footage of infidels attacking Muslims in Chechnya, Kashmir, Iraq, Israel, Lebanon, Indonesia and Egypt, children starving under the yoke of United Nations economic sanctions in Iraq, and most vexatiously, the accursed presence of "Crusader" military forces in the holy land of Arabia, was subsequently converted to CD-ROM and DVD formats for ease in copying onto computers and loading onto the World Wide Web for still wider, global dissemination. An even more stunning illustration of his communications acumen and clever manipulation of media was the pre-recorded, pre-produced, B-roll, or videoclip, that bin Laden had queued and readied for broadcast within hours of the commencement of the American air strikes on Afghanistan on Sunday, October 7.

In addition to his adroit marrying of technology to religion and of harnessing the munificence of modernity and the West as a weapon to be wielded against his very enemies, bin Laden has demonstrated uncommon patience, planning and attention to detail. According to testimony presented at the trial of three of the 1998 East Africa embassy bombers in Federal District Court in New York last year by a former bin Laden lieutenant, Ali Muhammad,[24] planning for the attack on the Nairobi facility commenced nearly five years before the operation was executed. Muhammad also testified that bin Laden himself studied a surveillance photograph of the embassy compound, pointing the spot in front of the building where he said the truck bomb should be positioned. Attention has already been drawn to Al Qaeda's ability to commence planning of another operation before the latest one has been executed in the case of the embassy bombings and the attack 27 months later on the USS *Cole*. Clearly, when necessary, bin Laden devotes specific attention—perhaps even to the extent of micro-managing—to various key aspects of Al Qaeda "spectaculars." In the famous "home movie"/videotape discovered in an Al Qaeda safe-house in Afghanistan that was released by the U.S. government in December 2001, bin Laden is seen discussing various, intimate details of the September 11 attack. At one point, bin Laden explains how "we calculated in advance the number of casualties from the enemy, who would be killed based on the position of the tower. We calculated that the floors that would be hit would be three or four floors. I was the most optimistic of them all. . . due to my experience in this field . . ." alluding to his knowledge of construction techniques gleaned from his time with the family business.[25] Osama bin Laden also knew that Muhammad Atta was the operation's leader[26] and states that he and his closest lieutenants "had notification [of the attack] since the previous Thursday that the event would take place that day [September 11]."[27]

The portrait of bin Laden that thus emerges is richer, more complex, and more accurate than the simple caricature of a hate-filled, mindless fanatic. "All men dream: but not equally," T. E. Lawrence, the legendary Lawrence of Arabia, wrote. "Those who dream by night in the dusty recesses of their minds wake in the day to find that it was vanity: but the dreamers of the day are dangerous men, for they may act their dream with open eyes, to make it possible."[28] Osama bin Laden is indeed one of the dangerous men that Lawrence described. At a time when the forces of globalization, coupled with economic determinism, seemed to have submerged the role of the individual charismatic leader of men beneath far more powerful, impersonal forces, bin Laden has cleverly cast himself as a David against the American Goliath; one man standing up to the world's sole remaining superpower and able to challenge its might and directly threaten its citizens.

Indeed, in an age arguably devoid of ideological leadership, when these impersonal forces are thought to have erased the ability of a single man to affect the course of history, bin Laden—despite all our efforts—managed to taunt us and strike at us for years even before September 11. His effective melding of the strands of religious fervour, Muslim piety and a profound sense of grievance into a powerful ideological force stands—however invidious and repugnant—as a towering accomplishment. In his own inimitable way, bin Laden cast this struggle as precisely the "clash of civilizations" that America and its Coalition partners have laboured so hard to negate. "This is a matter of religion and creed; it is not what Bush and Blair maintain, that it is a war against terrorism," he declared in a videotaped speech broadcast over Al-Jazeera television on November 3, 2001. "There is no way to forget the hostility between us and the infidels. It is ideological, so Muslims have to ally themselves with Muslims." [29]

Osama bin Laden, though, is perhaps best viewed as a "terrorist CEO," essentially having applied business administration and modern management techniques to the running of a transnational terrorist organization. Indeed, what bin Laden apparently has done is to implement for Al Qaeda the same type of effective organizational framework or management approach adapted by corporate executives throughout much of the industrialized world. Just as large, multinational business conglomerates moved during the 1990s to flatter, more linear, and networked structures, bin Laden did the same with Al Qaeda.

Additionally, he defined a flexible strategy for the group that functions at multiple levels, using both top-down and bottom-up approaches. On the one hand, bin Laden has functioned like the president or CEO of a large multinational corporation, defining specific goals and aims, issuing orders, and ensuring their implementation. This mostly applies to the Al Qaeda "spectaculars": those high-visibility, usually high-value and high-casualty operations like September 11, the attack on the *Cole*, and the East Africa embassy bombings. On the other hand, he has operated as a venture capitalist, soliciting ideas from below, encouraging creative approaches and "out of the box" thinking and providing funding to those proposals he thinks promising. Al Qaeda, unlike many other terrorist organizations, therefore, deliberately has no one set *modus operandi*, making it all the more formidable. Instead, bin Laden encourages his followers to mix and match approaches, employing different tactics and different means of attack and operational styles as needed. At least four different levels of Al Qaeda operational styles can be identified:

1. *The professional cadre*. This is the most dedicated, committed and professional element of Al Qaeda: the persons entrusted with only the most important and high-value attacks—in other words, the "spectaculars." These are the terrorist teams that are pre-determined

and carefully selected, are provided with very specific targeting instructions and who are generously funded (e.g., to the extent that during the days preceding the September 11 attacks, Atta and his confederates were sending money back to their paymasters in the United Arab Emirates and elsewhere).

2. *The trained amateurs.* At the next level down are the trained amateurs. These are individuals much like Ahmed Ressam, who was arrested in December 1999 at Port Angeles, Washington State, shortly after he had entered the U.S. from Canada. Ressam, for example, had some prior background in terrorism, having belonged to Algeria's Armed Islamic Group (GIA). After being recruited into Al Qaeda, he was provided with a modicum of basic terrorist training in Afghanistan. In contrast to the professional cadre above, however, Ressam was given open-ended targeting instructions before being despatched to North America. All he was told was to attack some target in the U.S. that involved commercial aviation. Ressam confessed that he chose Los Angeles International Airport because at one time he had passed through there and was at least vaguely familiar with it. Also, unlike the well-funded professionals, Ressam was given only US$12,000 in "seed money" and instructed to raise the rest of his operational funds from petty thievery—e.g., swiping cell phones and laptops around his adopted home of Montreal. He was also told to recruit members for his terrorist cell from among the expatriate Muslim communities in Canada and the U.S. In sum, a distinctly more amateurish level of Al Qaeda operations than the professional cadre deployed on September 11; and which also relied on someone far less steeled, determined and dedicated than the hijackers proved themselves to be. Ressam, of course, panicked when he was confronted by a Border Patrol agent immediately upon entering the U.S. By comparison, nine of the 19 hijackers were stopped and subjected to greater scrutiny and screening by airport personnel on September 11. Unlike Ressam, they stuck to their cover stories, did not lose their nerve and, despite having aroused suspicion, were still allowed to board. Richard Reid, the individual who attempted to blow up an American Airlines passenger plane en route from Paris to Miami with an explosive device concealed in his shoe, is another example of the trained amateur. It should be emphasized, however, that as inept or even

moronic as these individuals might appear, their ability to be lucky even once and then to inflict incalculable pain and destruction should not be lightly dismissed. As distinctly second-tier Al Qaeda operatives, they are likely seen by their masters as expendable, having neither the investment in training nor the requisite personal skills that the less numerous, but more professional, first-team Al Qaeda cadre have.

3. *The local walk-ins.* These are local groups of Islamic radicals who come up with a terrorist attack idea on their own and then attempt to obtain funding from Al Qaeda for it. This operational level plays to bin Laden's self-conception as a venture capitalist. An example of the local walk-in is the group of Islamic radicals in Jordan who, observing that American and Israeli tourists often stay at the Raddison Hotel in Amman, proposed to, and were funded by, Al Qaeda to attack the tourists on the eve of the millennium. Similarly, the cell of Islamic militants who were arrested in Milan in October 2001 after wiretaps placed by Italian authorities revealed discussions of attacks on American interests being planned in the expectation that Al Qaeda would fund them, is another example.

4. *Like-minded insurgent guerillas and terrorists.* This level embraces existing insurgent or terrorist groups who over the years have benefited from bin Laden's largesse and/or spiritual guidance, received training in Afghanistan from Al Qaeda, or have been provided with arms, materiel and other assistance by organization. These activities reflect bin Laden's "revolutionary philanthropy," that is, the aid he provides to Islamic groups as part of furthering the cause of global *jihad*. Among the recipients of this assistance have been insurgent forces in Uzbekistan and Indonesia, Chechnya and the Philippines, Bosnia and Kashmir, etc. This philanthropy is meant not only to hopefully create a *jihad* "critical mass" out of these geographically scattered, disparate movements, but also to facilitate a *quid pro quo* situation, where Al Qaeda operatives can call on the logistical services and manpower resources provided locally by these groups.

Underpinning these operational levels is bin Laden's vision, self-perpetuating mythology and skilled acumen at effective communications.

His message is simple. According to bin Laden's propaganda, the U.S. is a hegemonic, status quo power, opposing change and propping up corrupt and reprobate regimes that would not exist but for American backing. Osama bin Laden also believes that the U.S. is risk- and casualty-averse and therefore cannot bear the pain or suffer the losses inflicted by terrorist attacks. Americans and the American military, moreover, are regarded by bin Laden and his minions as cowards, "sissies" who only fight with high-tech, airborne-delivered munitions. The Red Army, he has observed, at least fought the *mujahideen* in Afghanistan on the ground; America, bin Laden has maintained, only fights from the air with cruise missiles and bombs. In this respect, bin Laden has often argued that terrorism works—especially against America. He cites the withdrawal of the U.S. Marines, following the 1983 barracks bombing, from the multinational force deployed to Beirut and how the deaths of 18 U.S. Army Rangers (an account of which is described in the best-selling book by Mark Bowden, *Black Hawk Down*, and current film of the same title)—a far smaller number—prompted the precipitous U.S. withdrawal from Somalia a decade later.

Finally, it should never be forgotten that some 20 years ago, bin Laden consciously sought to make his own mark in life as a patron of *jihad*—holy war. In the early 1980s, he was drawn to Afghanistan, where he helped to rally—and even more critically, fund—the Muslim guerilla forces resisting that country's Soviet invaders. Their success in repelling one of the world's two superpowers had a lasting impact on bin Laden. To his mind, Russia's defeat in Afghanistan set in motion the chain of events that resulted in the collapse of the U.S.S.R. and the demise of communism. It is this same self-confidence coupled with an abiding sense of divinely ordained historical inevitability that has convinced bin Laden that he and his fighters cannot but triumph in the struggle against America. Indeed, he has often described the U.S. as a "paper tiger" on the verge of financial ruin and total collapse, with the force of Islam poised to push America over the precipice.

Remarkably, given his mindset, bin Laden would likely cling to the same presumptions despite the destruction of the Taliban and liberation of Afghanistan during this first phase of the war against terrorism. To him and his followers, the U.S. is doing even more now than before to promote global stability (in their view, to preserve the status quo) and ensure the longevity of precisely those morally bankrupt regimes in places like Egypt, Saudi Arabia, the Gulf, Pakistan, Uzbekistan and elsewhere which bin Laden and his followers despise. In bin Laden's perception of the war in Afghanistan, most of the fighting has been done by the Northern Alliance—the equivalent of the native levies of imperial times, though instead of being led by British officers as in the past, are now guided by U.S. military special operations personnel. Moreover, for bin Laden—like guerillas and terrorists everywhere—not losing is winning. To his mind, even if terrorism did not work on September 11 in dealing the knock-out blow to American resolve that bin Laden hoped to achieve, he can still persuasively claim to have been responsible for having a seismic effect on the U.S., if not the entire world. Whatever else, bin Laden is one of few persons who can argue that they have changed the course of history. The U.S. itself, in his view, remains fundamentally corrupt and weak, on the verge of collapse, as bin Laden crowed in the videotape released last year about the "trillions of dollars" of economic losses caused by the September 11 attacks. More recently, Ahmed Omar Sheikh, the chief suspect in the killing of the American journalist, Daniel Pearl, echoed this same point. While being led out of a Pakistani court in March, he exhorted anyone listening to "sell your dollars, because America will be finished soon."[30]

Today, added to this fundamental enmity is now the even more potent and powerful motivation of revenge for the destruction of the Taliban and America's "war on Islam." To bin Laden and his followers, despite overwhelming evidence to the contrary, the U.S. is probably still regarded as a "paper tiger," a favourite phrase of bin Laden's, whose collapse can be attained provided Al Qaeda survives the current onslaught in Afghanistan in some form or another. Indeed, although weakened, Al Qaeda has not been destroyed and at least some of its capability to inflict pain, albeit at a greatly diminished level from September 11, likely still remains intact. In this respect, the multi-year time lag of all prior Al Qaeda spectaculars is fundamentally disquieting since it suggests that some monumental operation might have already been set in motion just prior to September 11.

Future Threats and Potentialities

Rather than asking what could or could not happen, we might more profitably focus on understanding what has not happened in the light this inquiry can shed on possible future Al Qaeda attacks. This approach actually remains among the most understudied and, in turn, conspicuous lacunae of terrorism studies. Many academic terrorism analyses when they venture into the realm of future possibilities, if at all, do so only tepidly. In the main, they are self-limited to mostly lurid hypotheses of worst-case scenarios, almost exclusively involving CBRN (chemical, biological, radiological or nuclear) weapons, as opposed to trying to understand why—with the exception of September 11— terrorists have only rarely realized their true killing potential.

Among the key unanswered questions are:

- Why haven't terrorists regularly used man-portable surface-to-air missiles (SAMs/MANPADS) to attack civil aviation?
- Why haven't terrorists employed such simpler and more easily obtainable weapons like rocket-propelled grenades (RPGs) to attack civil aviation by targeting planes while taking off or landing?
- Why haven't terrorists used unmanned drones or one-person ultra-light or micro-light aircraft to attack heavily-defended targets from the air that are too difficult to gain access to on the ground?
- Why haven't terrorists engaged in mass simultaneous attacks with very basic conventional weapons, such as car bombs, more often?
- Why haven't terrorists used tactics of massive disruption—both mass transit and electronic (cyber)—more often?
- Why haven't terrorists perpetrated more maritime attacks, especially against cruise ships loaded with holidaymakers or cargo vessels carrying hazardous materials (such as liquefied natural gas or LNG)?
- Why haven't terrorists engaged in agricultural or livestock terrorism (which is far easier and more effective than against humans) using biological agents?
- Why haven't terrorists exploited the immense psychological potential of limited, discrete use of CBRN weapons and cyber-attacks more often?
- Why haven't terrorists targeted industrial or chemical plants with conventional explosives in hopes of replicating a Bhopal with thousands dead or permanently injured?
- And, finally, why—again with the exception of September 11—do terrorists generally seem to lack the rich imaginations of Hollywood movie producers, thriller writers, and others?

Alarmingly, many of the above tactics and weapons have in fact already been used by terrorists—and often with considerable success. The 1998 downing of a civilian Lion Air flight from Jaffna to Colombo by Tamil Tigers using a Russian-manufactured SA-14 is a case in point. The aforementioned series of car bombings that convulsed Bombay in 1993 is another. The IRA's effective paralyzing of road- and rail-commuting traffic around London in 1997 and 1998 is one more as were the similar tactics used by the Japanese Middle Core to shut down commuting in Tokyo a decade earlier. And in 1997, the Tamil Tigers launched one of the few documented cyber-terrorist attacks when they shut down the servers and e-mail capabilities of the Sri Lanka embassies in Seoul, Washington, D.C., and Ottawa. As these examples illustrate, terrorists retain an enormous capability to inflict pain and suffering without resorting to mass destruction or mass casualties of the order of the September 11 attacks. This middle range, between worst-case scenario and more likely means of attack is where the U.S. remains dangerously vulnerable. Terrorists seek constantly to identify vulnerabilities and exploit gaps in our defences. It was precisely the identification of this vulnerability in the middle range of our pain threshold that led to the events of that tragic day.

Conclusion

Terrorism is perhaps best viewed as the archetypal shark in the water. It must constantly move forward to survive and indeed to succeed. While survival entails obviating the governmental counter-measures designed to unearth and destroy the terrorists and their organization, success is dependent on overcoming the defences and physical security barriers designed to thwart attack. In these respects, the necessity for change in order to stay one step ahead of the counter-terrorism curve compels terrorists to change, adjusting and adapting their tactics, *modus operandi*, and sometimes even their weapons systems as needed. [31] The better, more determined and more sophisticated terrorists will therefore always find a way to carry on their struggle.

The loss of physical sanctuaries—the most long-standing effect that the U.S.-led war on terrorism is likely to achieve—will signal only the death knell of terrorism as we have known it. In a new era of terrorism, "virtual" attacks from "virtual sanctuaries," involving anonymous cyber-assaults may become more appealing for a new generation of terrorists unable to absorb the means and methods of conventional assault techniques as they once did in capacious training camps. Indeed, the attraction for such attacks will likely grow as American society itself becomes ever more dependent on electronic means of commerce and communication. One lesson from last October's anthrax cases and the immense disruption it caused the U.S. Postal

Service may be to impel more rapidly than might otherwise have been the case for the use of electronic banking and other online commercial activities. The attraction therefore for a terrorist group to bring down a system that is likely to become increasingly dependent on electronic means of communication and commerce cannot be dismissed. Indeed, Zawahiri once scolded his followers for not paying greater attention to the fears and phobias of their enemy, in that instance, Americans' intense preoccupation with the threat of bio-terrorism. The next great challenge from terrorism may therefore be in cyberspace.

Similarly, the attraction to employ more exotic, but crude, weapons like low-level biological and chemical agents may also increase. Although these materials might be far removed from the heinous capabilities of true WMD (weapons of mass destruction) another lesson from last October's anthrax exposure incidents was that terrorists do not have to kill 3,000 people to create panic and foment fear and insecurity: five persons dying in mysterious circumstances is quite effective at unnerving an entire nation.

This essay has hitherto discussed and hypothesized about terrorism. What, in conclusion, should we do about it? How should we view it? First, we should recognize that terrorism is, always has been, and always will be instrumental: planned, purposeful and premeditated. The challenge that analysts face is in identifying and understanding the rationale and "inner logic"[32] that motivates terrorists and animates terrorism. It is easier to dismiss terrorists as irrational homicidal maniacs than to comprehend the depth of their frustration, the core of their aims and motivations, and to appreciate how these considerations affect their choice of tactics and targets. To effectively fight terrorism, we must gain a better understanding of terrorists and terrorism than has been the case in the past.

Second, we need to recognize that terrorism is fundamentally a form of psychological warfare. This is to say that people do not tragically die or that assets and property are not wantonly destroyed. It is, however, to note that terrorism is designed, as it has always been, to have profound psychological repercussions on a target audience. Fear and intimidation are precisely the terrorists' timeless stock-in-trade. Significantly, terrorism is also designed to undermine confidence in government and leadership and to rent the fabric of trust that bonds society. It is used to create unbridled fear, dark insecurity, and reverberating panic. Terrorists seek to elicit an irrational, emotional response. Our counter-measures, therefore, must be at once designed to blunt that threat but also to utilize the full range of means we can bring to bear in countering terrorism: psychological as well as physical; diplomatic as well as military; economic as well as moral.

Third, the U.S. and all democratic countries that value personal freedom and fundamental civil liberties will remain vulnerable to terrorism. The fundamental asymmetry of our inability to protect all targets all the time against all possible attacks ensures that terrorism will continue to remain attractive to our enemies. In this respect, both political leaders and the American public must have realistic expectations of what can and cannot be achieved in the war on terrorism and, indeed, the vulnerabilities that exist inherently in any open and democratic society.

Fourth, the enmity felt in many places throughout the world towards the U.S. will likely not diminish. America is invariably targeted as a hegemonic, status quo power and more so as the world's lone superpower. Diplomatic efforts, particularly involving renewed public diplomacy activities, are therefore needed at least to affect and influence successor generations of would-be terrorists, even if we have already missed the current generation.

Finally, terrorism is a perennial, ceaseless struggle. While a war against terrorism may be needed to sustain the political and popular will that has often been missing in the past, war by definition implies finality. The struggle against terrorism, however, is never-ending. Terrorism has existed for 2,000 years and owes its survival to an ability to adapt and adjust to challenges and counter-measures, and to continue to identify and exploit its opponent's vulnerabilities. For us to succeed against terrorism, our efforts must be as tireless, innovative and dynamic as our opponents'.

Notes

1 The lone exception was 1995, when a major increase in non-lethal terrorist attacks against property in Germany and Turkey by the PKK (Kurdistan Workers' Party) not only moved the U.S. to the number two position but is also credited with accounting for that year's dramatic rise in the total number of incidents from 322 to 440. See Office of the Coordinator for Counterterrorism, *Patterns of Global Terrorism 1999*, Washington, D.C., U.S. Department of State Publication 10321, April 1996, p. 1.

2 Several factors can account for this phenomenon, in addition to America's position as the sole remaining superpower and leader of the free world. These include the geographical scope and diversity of America's overseas business interests, the number of Americans travelling or working abroad, and the many U.S. military bases around the world.

3 See "Timetables of the Hijacked Flights," in Reporters, Writers, and Editors of *Der Spiegel* Magazine, *Inside 9-11: What Really Happened* (New York: St. Martin's, 2002), pp. 261–262.

4 Brian M. Jenkins, "The Organization Men: Anatomy of a Terrorist Attack," in James F. Hoge, Jr. and Gideon Rose (eds.), *How Did This Happen? Terrorism and the New War* (New York: Public Affairs/Council on Foreign Relations, 2001), p. 5.

5 Some 440 persons perished in a 1978 fire deliberately set by terrorists at a movie theatre in Abadan, Iran.

6 Celia W. Dugger, "Victims of '93 Bombay Terror Wary of U.S. Motives," *The New York Times*, 24 September 2001.

7 Several other potential high-lethality simultaneous attacks during the 1980s were averted. These include a 1985 plot by Sikh separatists in India and Canada to simultaneously bomb three aircraft while inflight (one succeeded—the downing of an Air India flight while en route from Montréal, Québec, to London, England, in which 329 persons were killed), a Palestinian plot to bomb two separate Pan Am flights in 1982 and perhaps the most infamous and ambitious of all pre-September 11 incidents: Ramzi Ahmed Yousef's *Bojinka* plan to bring down 12 American airliners over the Pacific. See Jenkins, "The Organization Men," p. 6.

8 See Yoram Schweitzer, "Suicide Terrorism: Development and Main Characteristics," in The International Policy Institute for Counter-Terrorism at the Interdisciplinary Centre Herzliya, *Countering Suicide Terrorism: An International Conference* (Jerusalem and Hewlett, New York: Gefen, 2001), p. 76.

9 See bin Laden's comments about this on the videotape released by the U.S. Government in November 2001, a verbatim transcript of which is reproduced in *ibid.*, pp. 313–321.

10 "Wedded to death in a blaze of glory——Profile: The suicide bomber," *The Sunday Times* (London), 10 March 1996; and Christopher Walker, "Palestinian 'Was Duped into Being Suicide Bomber'," *The Times* (London), 27 March 1997.

11 See Reporters, Writers, and Editors, *Inside 9-11*, on pp. 304–313.

12 See, for example, Jenkins, "The Organization Men," p. 8.

13 See, in particular, the work of Dr Rohan Gunaratna of St Andrew's University in this area and specifically his "Suicide Terrorism in Sri Lanka and India," in International Policy, *Countering Suicide Terrorism*, pp. 97–104.

14 It is now believed that planning for the attack on an American warship in Aden harbour commenced some two to three weeks before the August 1998 attacks on the East Africa embassies. Discussion with U.S. Naval Intelligence Service agent investigating the *Cole* attack, December 2001.

15 See Steven Simon and Daniel Benjamin, "America and the New Terrorism," *Survival*, Vol. 42, No. 1 (Spring 2000), pp. 59–75 and Olivier Roy, Bruce Hoffman, Reuven Paz, Steven Simon and Daniel Benjamin, "America and the New

Terrorism: An Exchange," *Survival*, Vol. 42, No. 2 (Summer 2000), pp. 156–172. In it, Simon and Benjamin aver that I had become "too closely bound to the academic fashion of the moment…" (p. 171). As I told both Simon and Benjamin after September 11, their observation was indeed correct.

16 Brian Michael Jenkins, "International Terrorism: A New Mode of Conflict," in David Carlton and Carlo Schaerf (eds.), *International Terrorism and World Security* (London: Croom Helm, 1975), p. 15.

17 See, for example, the discussion of two former members of the U.S. National Security Staff, Daniel Benjamin and Steven Simon, on the effects of the al-Shifa on the Clinton administration and its counter-terrorism policy after the August 1998 embassy bombings. Daniel Benjamin and Steven Simon, "A Failure of Intelligence?" in Robert B. Silvers and Barbara Epstein (eds.), *Striking Terror: America's New War* (New York: New York Review of Books, 2002), pp. 279–299.

18 It should be noted that on many occasions, the Director of Central Intelligence, George Tenet, warned in Congressional testimony and elsewhere of the profound and growing threat posed by bin Laden and Al Qaeda to U.S. national security.

19 See Peter L. Bergen, *Holy War, Inc.: Inside the Secret World of Osama bin Laden* (New York: Free Press, 2001), pp. 14–15.

20 Bruce Hoffman, "Terrorism's CEO: An On-Line Interview with Peter Bergen, Author of *Holy War, Inc.*," available at http://www.theatlantic.com, January 2002.

21 Bergen, *Holy War, Inc.*, p. 28.

22 *Ibid.*, p. 28.

23 *Ibid.*, p. 27.

24 Ali Muhammad, a former major in the Egyptian Army, enlisted in the U.S. Army, where he served as a non-commissioned officer at Fort Bragg, North Carolina, teaching U.S. Special Forces about Middle Eastern culture and politics. Mohammed, among other Al Qaeda operatives, like Wadi el-Hoge, demonstrates how Al Qaeda found the U.S. a comfortable and unthreatening operational environment. See Hoffman, "Terrorism's CEO," available at http://www.theatlantic.com/unbound/interviews/int2002-01-09.html.

25 Reporters, Writers, and Editors, *Inside 9-11*, p. 317.

26 *Ibid.*, p. 319.

27 *Ibid.*, p. 317.

28 T. E. Lawrence, *Seven Pillars of Wisdom* (Harmondsworth: Penguin Books, 1977), p. 23.

29 Neil MacFarquhar with Jim Rutenberg, "Bin Laden, in a Taped Speech, Says Attacks in Afghanistan Are a War Against Islam," *The New York Times*, 4 November, 2001, p. B2.

30 Raymond Bonner, "Suspect in Killing of Reporter Is Brash and Threatening in a Pakistani Court," *The New York Times*, 13 March 2002.

31 Bruce Hoffman, *Inside Terrorism* (London: Orion, and New York: Columbia University Press, 1998), pp. 180–183.

32 My colleague at St Andrew's University, Dr Magnus Ranstorp's, formulation.

CHAPTER 3

TERRORISM AND WEAPONS OF MASS DESTRUCTION: PROSPECTS AND PROBLEMS

Gavin Cameron

Introduction

The acts of terrorism on September 11, 2001, appear to herald a new era of high-casualty and high-consequence terrorism, unmatched even by previous incidents such as Aum Shinrikyo's release of sarin in the Tokyo subway in March 1995. Although relying on a familiar tactic—airline hijacking—the attacks on the World Trade Centre and Pentagon were unlike their predecessors in the 1970s. Moreover, the hijacking was not the principal aspect of the terrorists' action, but was merely a means to the greater act of violence: crashing the planes and the passengers aboard into the World Trade Centre and Pentagon.

Until relatively recently, Aum Shinrikyo's attack was regarded as being a watershed, itself supposed to be the start of a wave of high-consequence terrorist attacks with CBRN (Chemical, Biological, Radiological, Nuclear) weapons. Such pessimism was not borne out of events in the subsequent years. The central question of this paper is whether the events of September 11 are really indicative of a greater likelihood of terrorists resorting to CBRN weapons.

Terrorism and WMD

Falkenrath *et al.* list a dozen cases of mass-casualty terrorism within the twentieth century, all of which resulted in over 100 fatalities.[1] The majority of cases on the list are examples of attacks using a single weapon, usually a bomb containing conventional explosives, rather than being the results of assaults with multiple weapons. An example of the latter, not on the list, is the November 1997 massacre, predominantly using guns, in Luxor, Egypt, of 62 people by members of the Al-Gama'at al-Islamiyya (IG). Of Falkenrath's examples, five were of planes that were destroyed in mid-air, the most destructive of which was the Air India bombing in 1985, in which 328 people were killed. All twelve examples involved conventional weapons, as did the attacks on September 11. The September 11 terrorists used two traditional tactics, hijacking and crashing a vehicle into a building. Their innovation was to combine these tactics and to use planes rather than trucks as the vehicle of destruction. In doing so, the September 11 terrorists killed almost 3,000 people. By comparison, the most notable terrorist use of CBRN weapons, Aum Shinrikyo's March 1995 attack on the Tokyo subway, killed 12 people and injured thousands. This may suggest that September 11 is indicative of further acts of high-casualty terrorism rather than of terrorism with CBRN weapons. The two are not synonymous.

Moreover, despite the attempts to acquire CBRN weapons by groups such as Aum Shinrikyo and Al Qaeda, and the use of such weapons by several groups, including Aum Shinrikyo, no terrorist organization has perpetrated a high-casualty incident using CBRN weapons. The one possible exception is DIN ("Avenging Israel's Blood") who, in 1946, contemplated killing nearly two million Germans by poisoning the water supplies of four major cities in revenge for the Holocaust. DIN did not carry out this attack, but rather a much smaller one against Stalag 13 near Nuremberg. DIN used an arsenic-based agent to poison the bread of thousands of German prisoners of war in April 1946, and may have killed hundreds.[2] If fatalities are the key factor in defining a terrorist incident as mass-destructive, then we have yet to see a clearcut example involving non-conventional weapons.

When terrorist groups had sought to cause high levels of casualties, they did so using conventional weapons, such as explosives. The overwhelming majority of incidents involving CBRN materials were hoaxes or threats, particularly in the United States since 1998, and the instances of use of an agent tended to be examples of "low-end" or household products. It was questionable whether such uses had anything significant to do with terrorist use of CBRN weapons for high-casualty events, except maintaining the issue of CBRN terrorism in the forefront of public, media, academic and governmental awareness. The threat from high-end CBRN terrorism arose because groups, such as Al Qaeda, continued to seek those weapons that remained, at the very least, theoretically available to a well-financed and connected organization, one that would likely be willing to use such weapons to cause high levels of casualties. In the past, there has been a disconnection between those sub-state actors who have used CBRN weapons and those which one most feared would use such weapons. This paper argues that this disconnection has continued analytical validity in the wake of September 11, the subsequent anthrax attacks in the United States and elsewhere, and the continued evidence of Al Qaeda, among others, seeking CBRN weapons.

In addition, the attacks certainly revealed Al Qaeda's organizational ability and the willingness of the group to commit attacks that resulted in thousands of casualties. In that respect, the attacks of September 11 were unprecedented, causing numbers of casualties that exceeded any previous terrorist attack by several orders of magnitude. However, Al Qaeda committed these attacks using conventional weapons, albeit in an unusual and highly innovative way, and the political and social effect of the attacks could scarcely have been greater if the group had used a CBRN weapon. On the other hand, though, the group's attack raises the issue of whether other like-minded organizations could create the same effect without resorting to CBRN weapons. Assuming that an exact replication of Al Qaeda's attacks is not possible, are there other ways a group could inflict similar levels of casualties or destruction? The answer is almost certainly that the destruction of a highly-populated skyscraper, by whatever means, could have a similar effect in terms of casualties, but it is difficult to imagine many targets that would be suitable for such a visible and overt strike against a country's prestige. The attacks had a variety of motivations but one of those was certainly symbolic: to strike the United States at its military and economic centres, in full view of the world's media. The attacks of September 11, against the Pentagon but more particularly against the World Trade Centre towers, have undoubtedly raised the bar for future terrorism. It is now more difficult for other groups to match Al Qaeda's impact, and groups that regard themselves as rivals to Al Qaeda for attention, leverage or resources may believe themselves compelled to consider alternative strategies for their campaigns, including possibly new types of weapon.

This dynamic occurs when the September 11 attacks have created an unprecedented backlash against terrorism of all varieties. It is likely to be increasingly difficult, at least in the short term, for groups to find overtly sympathetic sponsors. In such circumstances, groups may find themselves resorting to one of two opposed strategies: a "quietist" approach where violence is temporarily minimized, or a campaign of more extreme coercion where new types of weapon or new levels of violence are used.

However, terrorism cannot be viewed as a linear process. The most obvious example of this is the aftermath of Aum Shinrikyo's sarin attack in Tokyo in 1995. Although not the first use of a chemical or biological weapon by a terrorist group, Aum's attack seemed different, using a high-end agent to cause indiscriminate casualties. Most analysts and those charged with countering terrorism assumed that Aum's attack represented a harbinger of the future, that other, increasingly lethal, attacks with CBRN weapons would follow and that terrorism was on an escalatory spiral. Such assessments were not supported by the experience of the following years: There was not a wave of similar attempts. This was in spite of the increasing knowledge of CBRN weapons and availability of weapons-usable technologies from a range of sources.[3] Moreover, due to increased fear of attacks in many countries, using these weapons increased the coercive power available for any terrorist group willing and able to make a convincing threat to use CBRN weapons. Al Qaeda's attacks of September 11, far from relying on CBRN weapons, used a technologically conservative weapon, depending on variants of familiar tactics—hijacking and vehicle bombing—to cause carnage. Although Al Qaeda was and remains undoubtedly interested in a range of CBRN weapons, and clearly investigated each for their potential value in committing an attack, ultimately the organization chose a different route from the one implied by Aum's 1995 attack. The precise reason for this tactical choice is not currently certain, but it seems likely that Al Qaeda decided to use methods that its leaders believed had the best chances of success. Although CBRN weapons have supposedly grown increasingly accessible in the past ten years, there remain major challenges in successfully acquiring, weaponizing and delivering an effective CBRN weapon. Although the wealth, resources and contacts of an organization such as Al Qaeda would undoubtedly have helped to reduce this risk, the example of Aum Shinrikyo, also wealthy and well-connected, but unable to deliver a successful attack with chemical or biological weapons, shows that such problems still exist. Al Qaeda therefore, appears to have chosen a method that, as well as being cheaper and technologically less sophisticated, also had a better probability of causing mass casualties than an attack using CBRN weapons.[4]

The central question is this: What, if anything, changed on September 11, with respect to the likelihood of CBRN terrorism? The answer may be that, in spite of the clear indication of Al Qaeda's willingness to cause mass casualties and the subsequent confirmation of continuing interest by the organization in CBRN materials, the attack has limited effect on the future likelihood of terrorism with such weapons. In order to answer the key question, this article will assess whether September 11 taught us anything new, and will analyze the likely impact of the attacks on future terrorism, looking not only at Al Qaeda, but also other terrorist groups. This article will note also that the majority of attacks involving CBRN materials are small-scale attacks, rather than terrorist incidents as traditionally perceived.

There are two lessons to be learned from the attacks of September 11 and its aftermath, both of which should have been clear before then, but which have a clear bearing on Al Qaeda's willingness to use CBRN weapons. First, Al Qaeda is willing to inflict high levels of casualties, and second, the organization has a long-standing interest in CBRN weapons. Although the attacks of September 11 were unprecedented as terrorist incidents, the number of fatalities exceeding any previous attack by several orders of magnitude, the willingness of Al Qaeda to use high levels of violence has been clear for years. In addition to numerous statements by bin Laden and others, justifying attacks against the United States, the West, Israel, and corrupted Islamic regimes, there have also been a history of attacks against such targets. Many of the perpetrators of these attacks have connections to Al Qaeda or to its associated groups. Several such attacks were intended to result in heavy casualties, or actually did so. Ramzi Yousef's attack on the World Trade Centre in 1993 is one such example; others include the destruction of U.S. military facilities in Saudia Arabia in the mid-1990s and the 1998 East African embassy bombings. Ahmed Ressam's plot to attack Los Angeles International Airport around the millennium is an example of a similarly destructive plot that was intercepted. Such a long history of high-casualty incidents or attempts to cause high-casualty events supports the supposition that Al Qaeda or its associated groups would be willing to use any means, including CBRN weapons, to create mass destruction or casualties. Such a supposition is credible because the organization has a long-standing interest in CBRN weapons. There is no doubt that Al Qaeda sought and continues to seek CBRN weapons. In late May 2002, U.S. Secretary of State Powell, speaking more generally about terrorist groups, said that he believed groups are trying every way they can to get their hands on weapons of mass destruction, whether radiological, chemical, biological or nuclear.[5] Secretary of Defence Rumsfeld said he believed it "inevitable" terrorists would acquire weapons of mass destruction and "they would not hesitate one minute to use them."[6]

Al Qaeda

Al Qaeda appears to have actively pursued an all-options strategy for its attempts to acquire CBRN, simultaneously seeking chemical, biological, radiological, and nuclear weapons. Osama bin Laden purportedly went to contacts in the former Soviet Union to attempt to acquire an intact nuclear weapon, although his contacts were in the Ukraine[7] and the Central Asian Republics. Israeli military intelligence claims that he paid around £2 million to an intermediary in Kazakhstan, believing that, because of its substantial Muslim population, he had a better likelihood of acquiring a weapon there. It is part of the 1998 U.S. federal indictment, which claims that, "at various times from at least as early as 1993, Osama bin Laden and others known and unknown, made efforts to obtain the components of nuclear weapons."[8]

Like Aum, bin Laden's group also appears to have sought to build a nuclear-yield weapon.[9] In 1993, bin Laden's deputy, Mamdouh Mahmud Salim, approved the attempted purchase of enriched uranium "for the purpose of developing nuclear weapons," according to the criminal complaint lodged against Salim on 25 September 1998, although it is unclear whether the group succeeded in buying any nuclear material.[10] It appears that, as with several other prospective buyers of nuclear materials, Al Qaeda became the object of a fraudulent scheme to supply them with useless nuclear material that the vendors would claim was weapons-usable. In the case of Al Qaeda, the offered "red mercury" turned out to be radioactive rubbish. They were also offered "enriched uranium" that was really low-grade reactor fuel, unusable in a nuclear-yield weapon without extensive further enrichment.[11] This failure to acquire useful nuclear material is likely to have been a critical factor in Al Qaeda's increased short-term focus on chemical means, as their weapon of choice.

In February 2001, Jamal Ahmed Fadl, testified in the trial of the 1998 African embassy bombers that Al Qaeda was trying to acquire nuclear material from the early 1990s onwards. Fadl said that a bin Laden lieutenant ordered him to buy uranium from a former Sudanese Army officer, who offered to sell ore from South Africa for US$1.5 million. However, Fadl was unsure whether the material was authentic, although it was shipped to Afghanistan.[12] In November 2001, bin Laden told a Pakistani journalist from the Urdu-language *Ausaf* paper that his movement already had chemical and nuclear weapons. He stated, "I wish to declare that if America used chemical or nuclear weapons against us, then we may retort with chemical and nuclear weapons...We have the weapons as a deterrent."[13]

The discoveries after September 11 very clearly show, however, that Al Qaeda has continued to prioritize nuclear and radiological weapons and, it now appears, may be closer to the latter than to any other type of CBRN weapon. In August 2001, an Arab delegation met scientists from Kabul University and offered them financial assistance in exchange for help and advice in locating and mining uranium within Afghanistan.[14] Although Al Qaeda appears to have gained some material, usable in a nuclear-yield device, both the British and U.S. governments believe that the organization is incapable of producing such a weapon at present. However, they believe that Al Qaeda may have experimented with crude chemical weapons in Afghanistan.[15] In November, President Bush asserted that Al Qaeda "continued to seek chemical, biological and nuclear weapons."[16]

Al Qaeda's agents are supposed to have spent over £1 million in the search for enough material with which to build a radiological weapon.[17] United States intelligence reports noted a meeting in which an associate of bin Laden's wielded a canister allegedly containing radioactive material that could be disseminated with a conventional explosive. However, conclusive evidence that Al Qaeda has a radiological capability remains elusive. Although diagrams and documents relating to radiological weapons were found in Afghanistan in facilities abandoned by Al Qaeda, these were of a type readily available via the Internet and were apparently of an extremely poor quality that would be unlikely to work.[18] Likewise, detailed plans for a nuclear-yield device were discovered in one of the Kabul buildings abandoned by Al Qaeda. Written in Arabic, German, Urdu and English, the documents contained descriptions of how to use TNT to compress a sphere of plutonium into a critical mass, sparking a chain reaction.[19] However, these documents, although clearly showing an interest in nuclear-yield weapons, also contain information that is readily available in open literature. The theory of such a weapon design is well-known, the practical application of that information is more difficult, even assuming that the group could acquire the requisite quantity of fissile material.

In the wake of the September 11 attacks in the United States, it has emerged that Al Qaeda may have sought the means to build a "dirty bomb."[20] Although there have been previous allegations relating to the organization's attempts to acquire material to build a nuclear-yield bomb, the claims over a radiological weapon represent a significant departure. British intelligence forces are currently investigating allegations made by a Bulgarian businessman, Ivan Ivanov, that in April 2001, he was approached by a middleman for bin Laden, seeking to obtain radiological material. Ivanov allegedly had a series of meetings near the Pakistani border with Afghanistan, including one with bin Laden. He then met with a "chemical engineer," near Rawalpindi, and was offered US$200,000 to help the scientist acquire spent nuclear fuel rods from the Kozlodui nuclear electricity plant in Bulgaria. The plan would have involved buying the rods legally, through a newly established environmental front company that would deal with nuclear waste. Ivanov declined the opportunity and reported the contact once he returned to Europe.[21]

In 2001, customs officials seized 10 lead-lined containers on the border between Uzbekistan and Kazakhstan. The containers held a substantial quantity of radioactive material, ostensibly intended for a company in Quetta, Pakistan. The precise type of material remains unclear, but it seems unlikely to have been a legitimate shipment and it does seem possible that bin Laden's Al Qaeda was a potential end-user.[22] There must also be concerns that the main threat in this respect may not be "leakage" from the former Soviet Union, but assistance provided to Al Qaeda by Pakistani sources. In October, two former key members of Pakistan's nuclear program were detained as a result of their connections to the Taliban. Bashiruddin Mahmood was a project director before Pakistan's 1998 tests and has since been running a relief organization, Ummah Tameer-I-Nau (UTN), sympathetic to the Afghan regime. Abdul Majid was a director of the Pakistan Atomic Energy Commission in 1999.[23] Allegedly, they planned to use finely-milled uranium, obtained from Pakistan, around a core of explosives to create such a "dirty bomb," delivered either as an artillery shell or a mortar round. However, there was no evidence that either Mahmood and Majid, or Al Qaeda more generally, had been able to acquire such radioactive material.[24]

Al Qaeda appears to have attempted both to acquire chemical and biological weapons, and to manufacture their own. In March 1999, the London-based paper *Al-Sharq al-Awsat* revealed that associates of bin Laden, on trial in Egypt as part of the "Albanian Arabs" case, had allegedly been offered anthrax and other biological agents from a factory in East Asia for US$3,695 plus freight charges. They also supposedly received an offer from a laboratory in the Czech Republic to supply a deadly gas (possibly botulinum, although that is unlikely to be in a gaseous form) for US$7,500 per sample.[25] Ahmad Salama Mabrouk, a member of al-Jihad, the group to which the defendants belonged, and part of bin Laden's coalition of organizations, gave an interview to the London paper *al-Hayat*. In it, Mabrouk claimed that over the past two years, the group had acquired chemical and biological agents from Eastern Europe and the former Soviet Union, and that al-Jihad planned to use them against U.S. and Israeli targets.[26] Although the specific claims have been unverifiable, their general point was supported in June 1999 by anonymous U.S. intelligence sources that told ABC News that "there is mounting evidence that bin Laden's network has acquired ingredients for chemical or biological weapons through countries that were once part of the Soviet Union." The same sources further claimed that bin Laden had set up two crude weapons laboratories in Afghanistan, one near Khoust and the other near Jalalabad.[27]

In the aftermath of September 11, it has become increasingly obvious that Al Qaeda's interest in CBRN weaponry has continued until the present. Amongst the finds have been: material relating to chemical, biological and nuclear weapons from the Tarnak Farms site near Kandahar,[28] information on the dispersal of anthrax in a Ummah Tameer-I-Nau (UTN) house in Kabul,[29] information on producing ricin in another house in Kabul,[30] and the discovery of an Al Qaeda volume, distributed on CD-ROM, that contained chapters detailing the production methods for a range of chemical agents and the biological agents, botulinum and ricin.[31] The organization had a series of laboratories in Afghanistan, dedicated to the development of chemical and biological weapons. These used equipment that had been purchased abroad and then shipped to Afghanistan from countries such the United Arab Emirates and Ukraine.[32] The organization appears also to have sought the help of scientists within Afghanistan, to promote its pursuit of such weapons. Delegations of Pakistani scientists visited Kabul University six times from 1998, offering to provide funding for chemical weapons-related research and asking for help to obtain large quantities of sodium cyanide and thionyl chloride, both dual-use chemicals, but capable of being used to create crude chemical weapons. Thionyl chloride is a possible precursor for mustard gas and several nerve agents and sodium cyanide is usable in the formation of a cyanide weapon.[33] However, although Al Qaeda's interest in chemical and biological weapons is clear, the group's success in acquiring such agents is far less so, although there have been some unverified finds, such as the supposed discovery of 30 boxes, each containing 10 phials of a colourless liquid, with "Sarin/V-Gas" marked in Cyrillic lettering on the side of each box.[34]

More ominously, groups linked to Al Qaeda and operating in Europe appear to have been plotting to use chemical or biological weapons in their attacks. In December 2000, German police broke up an alleged plot by GSPC, an Algerian-based group operating in Europe and associated with Al Qaeda. It supposedly planned to attack the European Parliament in Strasbourg with sarin.[35] In 2001, an Italian-based cell planned to launch an attack in France, before being interdicted by Italian security services. For this attack, they discussed using "a suffocating gas" although precise plans for the attack, including its location were never clarified. One possibility was Notre Dame in Paris, as the group discussed "La Dame" as a potential target. The surveillance tapes made by the Italian security services reveal the cell's leader, "Saber," explaining his desire to acquire chemical weapons because plastic explosives are outmoded and gas is more effective because "it's a liquid ... as soon as it's opened, people suffocate." However, it is also obvious that the cell has made little progress towards acquiring such a weapon: "Saber" tells other members that he needs a formula for the poison gas that has been developed by a Libyan chemistry professor.[36]

Although there is an increased interest in chemical and biological weapons by Al Qaeda and associated groups, as shown by the finds in Afghanistan and the plots to attack targets in Europe, there appears still a major disconnection between the current position and an immediate threat. The evidence listed above suggests interest in such agents and plots for the possible use of CBRW, but offers little new evidence of a credible capability. The gap between desire and capability is a crucial one, although it would be unwise to dismiss the concept that a well-organized, well-funded, and well-connected group, such as Al Qaeda, could successfully acquire chemical and biological weapons and keep the fact hidden, especially given the diffuse global nature of the group. However, the open source evidence revealed in the past six months does no more than indicate an interest in, and desire to acquire, such weapons, something that governments and analysts have known for several years.

Other Groups' Use of CBRN Weapons

The overwhelming majority of incidents involving CBRN materials and sub-state groups are extremely small-scale events, rather than terrorist attacks. The "Database of Incidents Involving Chemical, Biological, Radiological, or Nuclear (CBRN) Materials, 1900–Present" at the Centre for Nonproliferation Studies, Monterey Institute of International Studies, lists around 680 incidents perpetrated between 1900 and 2002. Of those, only around half were classified as having been perpetrated by groups or individuals with political or ideological motivations (ideological being taken to include religious motivations), and which could thus be considered sub-state terrorism. The rest consist of criminally-motivated acts for economic gain, or were judged to be false (apocryphal) cases. However, of these, the overwhelming majority of incidents are important not because they represent a significant threat, but rather because they show a growing interest in non-conventional weaponry amongst such groups and individuals. Of the incidents listed between 1995 and 2000, a third were hoaxes and pranks and many others involved the attempted acquisition of such weapons, so the number of incidents that genuinely involve CBRN weapons is significantly smaller than might initially appear.[37] In 1999, 65 incidents involved the use or possession of an agent. Similarly, 113 incidents in 2000 involved the use or possession of an agent.[38] Of these, most incidents resulted in zero or very few fatalities. This is in large part due to the agents involved, the majority of which were non-warfare "household" agents. In 1999 and 2000, these included agents such as acid, pepper spray, chlorine, insecticide or pesticides, and rat poison. A few incidents did involve military-grade agents such as ricin, capable of causing an extensive number of casualties. However, where an agent was used, it was likely to be a low-end or household agent. In 1999, for example, over half of the incidents of agent-use involved tear gas. Although this cannot be considered a household agent, it is unlikely to cause fatalities and is certainly at the low end of the scale compared to anthrax, ricin or sarin, for example. Other uses of agents involved non-specific "poisons" or cyanide, for example, neither of which should be regarded as "high-end."[39] Clearly, however, such incidents are largely unrelated to WMD terrorism, except that the number of hoaxes and other such events reflect a widespread fear of WMD terrorism that can be exploited by almost anyone with the inclination.

However, a more ominous small-scale type of attack occurred shortly after September 11. The United States was confronted by the posting through the U.S. Mail of a series of letters containing anthrax. In these attacks, five people died from anthrax inhalation and 18 people were infected.[40] Although there have been hundreds of incidents in the United States since 1998 involving threats or hoaxes of packages containing anthrax, the attacks of that autumn were significant because the letters genuinely did contain the pathogen. More worrisome still, the anthrax had been milled to a fine powder and processed with chemical additives to make them more readily airborne and inhaled into the lungs of victims. This suggests that the perpetrators had access to specialized knowledge and technology relating to the weaponization of anthrax. It seems possible that the perpetrators may have acquired a small quantity of the powder on the black market.[41] A worrying alternative is that the perpetrators, who remain unidentified, have developed the means of manufacturing high-quality anthrax as a dried powder and could therefore launch further, possibly more widespread or more effectively delivered, attacks that endangered thousands of people.[42]

Although the attacks of that autumn were small-scale, and certainly not intended to cause mass casualties, they were indicative of an extremely troubling potential for further action. The letters accompanying the anthrax warned that an attack had occurred and stated the agent involved.[43] The primary intention of the attacks was therefore clearly to cause fear and disruption, an objective in which they were successful. Moreover, the attacks had a significant economic and especially psychological impact on U.S. society, and it is this that may encourage further, unrelated groups to identify small, but genuine, uses of biological agents as the best means of attaining their goals.[44] The attacks were especially effective psychologically, coming as they did so soon after the immensely traumatic attacks of September 11 and the possibility of further high-casualty terrorism. Moreover, the letters affected not only the intended recipient, but in some cases, a staff member responsible for opening mail or a postal worker who simply handled the letter in transit. In two cases, victims were fatally exposed to anthrax through cross-contamination of their post in the mailroom sorting office.[45] Therefore, the number of people who might have been exposed to anthrax was much higher than might have been expected from such a crude form of weapon delivery. The public fear reflected not only the uncertainty over who could have been exposed and thus possibly infected by the anthrax, but also the concern over the number of packages which could have been tainted and who might be the next recipient of such a letter. The disruption was increased because heightened public fears increased the number of false alarms of further anthrax attacks. By mid-October, the FBI and other agencies had had to respond to 2,300 scares, the vast majority of which were either practical jokes or legitimate mistakes over "suspicious" packages. The false alarms caused millions of dollars and ten of thousands of man-hours, as each had to be thoroughly checked and then investigated.[46]

Other significant incidents involving chemical or biological agents include the Rajneeshees, a religious cult that used salmonella to contaminate salad bars in The Dalles, Oregon, in 1984, with the intention of influencing a local election. In the process, the group sickened 751 people.[47] The Covenant, the Sword, and the Arm of the Lord (CSA), a U.S. group influenced by Christian identity beliefs in the mid-1980s, acquired a barrel of potassium cyanide, a toxin with widespread industrial uses, with the intention of poisoning U.S. urban water supplies to further the group's ideological and religious objectives. However, the CSA compound was surrounded and the group's members detained by the FBI before such an attack could occur.[48] Both the PKK and Liberation Tigers of Tamil Eelam, groups motivated by nationalism rather than religion, are alleged to have used chemical weapons on at least one occasion. It is important to note, however, that, in each case, the use of non-conventional weapons was for a small-scale tactical attack, not to attempt an act of mass-destructive terrorism. On March 28, 1992, the PKK poisoned three water tanks of a Turkish Air Force base outside Istanbul. The water was foamy, and, when tested, was found to be contaminated with cyanide. The tanks contained 50 milligrams of cyanide per litre, a lethal dose.[49] On August 27, 1996, detectives discovered a container of sarin and 20 containers of mustard gas in Istanbul. Emin Ekinci, a member of the PKK, was arrested for having the agents in his possession.[50] The Liberation Tigers of Tamil Eelam (LTTE) have also resorted to non-conventional weapons. On June 18, 1990, the Sri Lankan Army reported that the group had attacked a Sri Lankan Army encampment with canisters filled with an unidentified poison gas, later identified as chlorine.[51]

The most important sub-state use of radiological material occurred on 23 November, 1995, when Chechen guerilla leader, Shamyl Basayev, informed the Russian television network, NTV, that four cases of radioactive cesium had been hidden around Moscow. Russian officials largely dismissed the nuclear threat, claiming that the material was cesium-137.[52] Basayev was intent on displaying capability and on ensuring that his threats to launch further attacks against Moscow, unless Russia withdrew from Chechnya, were taken seriously.[53]

His warning was plausible because the state of the Russian nuclear industry made it impossible to rule out the possibility that the Chechens had indeed acquired dangerously radioactive material.

Aum Shinrikyo's attempted acquisition of a nuclear capability involved mining uranium in Western Australia and attempting to enrich the natural uranium using lasers, a technical choice that owed more to Shoko Asahara's fascination with such devices than a rational decision to use the most effective technique for a nascent proliferator. The cult initially sought to acquire an intact weapon from the former Soviet Union. It attempted also to purchase dual-use equipment in the U.S., actively recruited employees of Russia's premier nuclear research facility, the I. V. Kurchatov Institute (although Russian authorities deny that either of the known Aum members at the Institute had classified knowledge about nuclear weapons design),[54] and physicists from Moscow State University to join the cult, and in 1993, sought, but were denied, a meeting with Russian Energy Minister Viktor Mikhailov to discuss the purchase of a nuclear warhead.[55] Aum failed to acquire a nuclear bomb, although it is possible that they negotiated with intermediaries for such a purchase, as suggested by numerous entries, citing prices, in the diary of Kiyohide Hayakawa, who made several trips to Russia on weapons-buying expeditions.[56] The cult also developed links with Russia's military, political and scientific elite. During 1992 and 1993, they also approached Russian scientists for help with both their laser and nuclear programmes.[57]

Al Qaeda and Aum Shinrikyo are by no means the only terrorist organizations to seek, or claim to possess, nuclear weapons. Of the incidents that involve weapons, rather than simply nuclear material, the overwhelming majority have been hoaxes. The U.S. Department of Energy's Nuclear Emergency Search Team (NEST) has dealt with hundreds of such hoaxes in the thirty years since its creation. However, aside from plans to acquire nuclear weapons, hoaxes and the threatened use of such weapons, very few incidents have occurred that involve them, certainly when compared to chemical, biological or even radiological weapons.

Difficulties in Acquiring, Weaponizing and Delivering CBRN Weapons

There are two main reasons for the relative paucity of examples of major incidents involving terrorist use of CBRN weapons. First, as discussed earlier, there is the motivational factor: Many groups have simply not felt the need to acquire such weapons or have felt moral constraints about using such devices. Second, there are the problems associated with acquiring and using such devices, challenges that continue to exist. Mass destruction is not guaranteed, even if sought, from the terrorist acquisition of a CBRN capability. Aum Shinrikyo is the best example of this. The cult was well-financed, organized and connected, yet it largely failed in its objectives. As well as the sarin used in the attacks of June 1994 in Matsumoto and March 1995 in Tokyo, the cult also sought to acquire a range of other chemical and biological agents including anthrax, botulinum toxin, Q-fever, Ebola virus, VX and hydrogen cyanide.[58] Aum had difficulties developing virulent batches of the pathogens, and then in effectively delivering the agents. The sarin used in the March 20 attacks was contained in plastic bags that were placed on the floor of the subway car and then pierced with the sharpened point of an umbrella. The impurity of the sarin and the crude delivery method were both crucial in undermining the efficacy of Aum's attack.

One of the central challenges to effective deployment of either chemical or biological weapons is weaponization and delivery. Chemical weapons would be relatively easy to deliver in an enclosed space, but much harder to disperse in a way so as to cause high levels of casualties in an open space. Effective delivery of biological agents is more problematic. To be effective, biological agents would need to be dispersed in an aerosol cloud consisting of particles small enough (one to five microns) to be easily inhaled and retained in the lungs. This requirement poses significant hurdles for the terrorist attempting to use such pathogens to cause high casualties.[59] The efficacy of a biological agent would depend on several factors: the agent itself, the delivery system, the quantity of agent used, the efficacy of the aerosolization of the agent and the weather conditions at the time of release. For example, strong winds may affect the dispersal of the agent, and bright light, significant heat or dryness may all adversely affect the time the pathogen remains infectious after release. However, the degree to which a biological agent is affected by these factors varies: Anthrax, for example, is relatively hardy, a significant advantage for a terrorist.

The acquisition of chemical and biological agents varies enormously in difficulty. For example, while smallpox is supposedly held in just two sites in the world, some other biological pathogens are easier to acquire, notably ricin, for which the main ingredient is beans from the castor plant, and for which a plethora of publications, many originating with the radical right in the United States, provide instructions on production.[60] Both plague and anthrax are naturally available in some areas of the world in which they are endemic. However, a terrorist group would have to ensure that it held a virulent strain of the pathogen, if it acquired anthrax from soil samples, for example. Moreover, although the raw materials and production methods for making ricin are straightforward, and ricin is a highly lethal pathogen, this does not mean that producing a weapon capable of causing mass casualties is equally easy: there remains the issue of effective delivery. Several of the groups, such as the Minnesota Patriots' Council, that have produced ricin in this way have also produced only a very impure version of the pathogen.[61]

Both chemical and biological agents can be produced using dual-use technology, methods and equipment that have legitimate as well as illegitimate purposes. Fermenters can be used to grow pathogens but are also widely available for production in a range of legitimate industries from brewing and pharmaceuticals to biotechnology. Freeze-drying and milling machines, extremely helpful in the conversion of agents into a dry finely ground powder ideal for dispersion, are widely used in the pharmaceutical industry. Such usage makes it difficult to impose meaningful restrictions on access to weapons-usable equipment, particularly if the terrorist organization operates behind a front company to make its purchases.

Chemical agents, being compounds, may be acquired as a series of precursors, rather than as an entire agent. For obvious reasons, acquiring precursors is an easier route, although tight controls exist on some of these as well, through the Chemical Weapons Convention and Australia Group. In spite of this, groups seeking such precursors can use front companies and other evasive measures to circumvent such restrictions, particularly if a complicit supplier can be found. In other cases though, constituent chemicals are used so widely in industry that controlling them is all but impossible. Such chemicals can then be used to produce the chemical precursors or, ultimately, the chemical agent. Here, the problem for the terrorist lies not so much in acquiring most of the key ingredients, but in the process of manufacturing an effective agent from those ingredients. Although many "recipes" are readily available, either in open literature or on the Internet, the reliability of these recipes is often limited.[62]

A radiological device is likely to be the easiest type of CBRN weapon for terrorists to acquire. At its simplest, it requires no more than conventional explosives and a radioactive source, such as cesium-137 from a hospital X-ray machine. Such radioactive sources remain widespread and poorly protected, certainly compared to other types of nuclear materials. In spite of this, the disruptive potential of a radioactive weapon or "dirty bomb" is considerable.

A nuclear-yield weapon is likely to be the hardest type of CBRN device for terrorists to acquire. Terrorists intent on acquiring a nuclear-yield device have three options: steal or purchase an intact weapon; steal or purchase a sufficient quantity of weapons-usable materials and build a crude nuclear-yield device; or enrich enough weapons-grade material to build a device. In reality, the second option—to acquire enough weapons-usable material to build a nuclear-yield weapon—is widely regarded as the most credible of the three.

Most terrorist groups seem unlikely to follow the example of Aum Shinrikyo in attempting to enrich material to a weapons-usable state. The process is lengthy, costly and, for many of the cruder forms of enrichment, potentially easily discovered. Success is also far from assured: Many state programs spend millions and take years trying to enrich enough material for a viable nuclear weapons programme.

A group unwilling or unable to enrich its own weapons-usable nuclear material would have to rely on buying or stealing it. Another pathway to nuclear terrorism is to acquire nuclear material to construct a device, but acquiring sufficient nuclear material is likely to prove difficult. In spite of reports of nuclear "leakage" in the former Soviet Union, only a handful of cases involving weapons-significant materials are known, notably in the early 1990s. Never was the quantity involved sufficient to build a weapon. In late 2001, the International Atomic Energy Agency stated that it knew of 175 incidents involving weapons-significant material, but of those, only 18 involved highly-enriched uranium (HEU) or plutonium. Such a figure is not conclusive as it reflects only the incidents that are discovered, although it is indicative. Moreover, the need to acquire a considerable quantity of fissile material would seem to preclude all but the most affluent or state-sponsored groups.

Whether through enrichment or acquisition of enough fissile material for a nuclear-yield weapon, terrorists seeking to build a nuclear weapon then have a number of design options: constructing a gun-type weapon using HEU, or developing an implosion device using either HEU or plutonium. In terms of design, the crude gun-type device is significantly the easier of the two, requiring between 50 and 60 kilograms of HEU. An implosion device would require around 8 kilograms of plutonium. The difficulties of such a device arise in two areas: The sphere of plutonium needs to be minutely engineered, and the shock wave has to be simultaneous to the millionths of a second. If either condition is not met, there is a substantial risk of an unpredictable nuclear yield or, more likely, a failure to reach supercriticality. A gun-type assembly would have a high probability of achieving some nuclear yield without requiring testing of components and using open literature. An implosion device is likely to be more sophisticated, requiring a higher degree of technical competence. However, in each case, the crucial barrier is the acquisition of enough nuclear material for the device.[63]

The final method for terrorists to acquire a nuclear-yield device is to steal or purchase an intact weapon. Concerns over nuclear-yield terrorism heightened significantly after the Soviet Union's collapse, due largely to the fear over "loose nukes" and the opportunities for nuclear materials and nuclear expertise to leave the country and be exploited by rogue states or terrorists. That terrorists could acquire an intact nuclear weapon seems far-fetched; states obviously have a considerable stake in protecting their mass-destructive weapons generally.

Conclusion

The likelihood of terrorist use of CBRN weapons in the wake of September 11 remains extremely unclear. The scale of the attacks suggest that mass-destructive terrorism is now a fact and it thus seems unlikely that, given the option, Al Qaeda would avoid using CBRN weapons to cause mass casualties. However, although discoveries in Afghanistan and the disruption of plots in Europe continue to show that Al Qaeda and its associated groups are interested in CBRN weapons, these discoveries do not indicate that the organization has successfully acquired such weapons. Moreover, the evidence clearly shows that Al Qaeda has simply been trying to develop any type of weapon that might help its cause. The suggestion, therefore, would be that CBRN weapons are being pursued simply as part of a range of options, for instrumental purposes, rather than as an end in itself. The attacks of September 11 show that CBRN weapons are not necessary to cause mass casualties. CBRN weapons and WMD are not synonymous. Given the difficulty and expense of acquiring and effectively using such weapons, Al Qaeda may continue to seek CBRN weapons, but is not likely to rely on doing so successfully. The attacks of September 11, and the subsequent discoveries suggest a group that is pragmatic and has an instrumental approach to CBRN acquisition.

The implications of September 11 for other groups seeking CBRN weapons remains to be seen. Clearly, the level of fear and awareness of potential attacks with such weapons has risen to unprecedented levels. However, this does not necessarily equate to an increased likelihood of CBRN weapons being used by sub-state actors, except for disruptive purposes. The number of false incidents or hoaxes, for example, the use of anthrax in the United States, reflect that. The attacks of September 11 raised the bar for terrorist violence, but also showed that innovative use of conventional weapons can achieve this purpose. Due to the technical challenges posed in successfully using CBRN weapons, conventional weapons remain more likely instruments for terrorists intent on causing mass destruction, at least in the short term.

Notes

1   Richard Falkenrath, Robert Newman and Bradley Thayer, *America's Achilles Heel* (Cambridge, MA: MIT Press, 1999), p. 47.
2   Michael Bar-Zohar, *The Avengers*, (New York: Hawthorne Books, 1967), pp. 40–52.
3   Peter Chalk, "Re-thinking U.S. Counter-Terrorism Efforts," *RAND Op-Eds*, available at http://www.rand.org/hot/op-eds/092101SDUT.html.
4   Chalk, "Re-thinking U.S. Counter-Terrorism Efforts."
5   "US warning on terror weapons," *BBC News*, available at http://news.bbc.co.uk/hi/english/world/americas/newsid_2000000/2000784.stm, 22 May 2002.
6   *Ibid.*
7   Ukraine has strenuously denied any involvement with bin Laden or his organization and noted that the last tactical nuclear weapons left the state in 1992. See Volodymyr Vassylenko, "Bin Laden's weapons," *The Times* (London), available at http://web.lexis-nexis.com, 2 November 1998.
8   John J. Goldman and Ronald J. Ostrow, "U.S. Indicts Terror Suspect Bin Laden," *Los Angeles Times*, 5 November 1998, p. A1; "U.S. Indictment: 'Detonated an Explosive Device'," *The New York Times*, 5 November 1998, p. A8.
9   Although enriched uranium can be used in a Radiological Dispersal Device (RDD), other radioactive materials, such as cesium-137 or cobalt-60, are more likely to be used in a RDD. Therefore, Al Qaeda's attempted acquisition of enriched uranium is more likely to be indicative of a desire to construct a nuclear-yield weapon.
10   Michael Grunwald, "US Says Bin Laden Sought Nuclear Arms; Complaint Cites Alliance With Sudan, Iran," *The Washington Post*, 26 September 1998, p. A19;

Benjamin Weiser, "US Says Bin Laden Aide Tried To Get Nuclear Weapons," *The New York Times*, 26 September 1998, p. A3.

11 Douglas Waller, "Inside the Hunt for Osama," *Time*, 13 November 2001.

12 Daniel McGrory, "Al-Qaeda's $1 million hunt for atomic weapons," *The Times* (London), available at http://www.thetimes.co.uk/article/0,,2001390014-2001395984,00.html, 15 November 2001.

13 Bob Woodward, Robert G. Kaiser and David Ottaway, "US Fears Bin Laden Made Nuclear Strides: Concern Over 'Dirty Bomb' Affects Security," *The Washington Post*, 4 December 2001, p. A1; Stephen Farrell, "Bin Laden makes nuclear threat," *The Times* (London), available at http://www.thetimes.co.uk/article/0,,2001380020-2001391616,00.html, 10 November 2001.

14 Tom Walker, Stephen Grey and Nick Fielding, "Al-Qaeda's secrets: Bin Laden's camp reveal chemical weapon ambition," *The Sunday Times* (London), available at http://www.Sunday-times.co.uk/article/0,,9002-2001540887,00.html, 25 November 2001.

15 Zahid Hussain, "Bin Laden met nuclear scientists from Pakistan," *The Times* (London), available at http://www.thetimes.co.uk/article/0,,2001390003-2001392244,00.html, 12 November 2001.

16 "Bush: Bin Laden seeking nuclear bomb," *CNN*, available at http://www.cnn.com/2001/WORLD/europe/11/06/gen.europe.conf/index.html, 6 November 2001.

17 Anthony Lloyd, "Bin Laden's nuclear secrets found," *The Times* (London), available at http://www.thetimes.co.uk/article/0,,2001390014-2001395995,00.html, 15 November 2001 .

18 Woodward, Kaiser and Ottaway, "US Fears Bin Laden Made Nuclear Strides: Concern Over 'Dirty Bomb' Affects Security."

19 Lloyd, "Bin Laden's nuclear secrets found."

20 Philip Webster and Roland Watson, "Bin Laden's Nuclear Threat," *The Times* (London), 26 October 2001, p. 1.

21 Adam Nathan and David Leppard, "Al-Qaeda's men held secret meetings to build 'dirty bomb'," *The Sunday Times* (London), 14 October 2001, p. A5.

22 David Pugliese, "Police suspect bin Laden making 'dirty' nuclear bombs," *National Post*, available at http://www.nationalpost.com, 17 October 2001.

23 Webster and Watson, "Bin Laden's Nuclear Threat;" "Nuclear Network: The need for action against bin Laden is sharper still," *The Times* (London), 26 October 2001, p. 21.

24 Nick Fielding, Joe Laurier, Gareth Walsh, "Bin Laden 'almost had uranium bomb'," *The Sunday Times*, 3 March 2002, Section 1, p. 13.

25 Khalid Sharaf-al-Din, "Bin-Ladin Men Reportedly Possess Biological Weapons," *Al-Sharaq al-Awsat*, 6 March 1999 (FBIS Document ID: FTS19990306000273).

26 "Egypte: le Jihad affirme détenir des armes chimiques," *Agence France Presse*, available at http://web.lexis-nexis.com, 19 April 1999; "Egyptian militant says

Bin Laden's group possess deadly weapons," *Deutsche Presse-Agentur*, available at http://web.lexis-nexis.com, 19 April 1999; "Le Jihad a obtenu des armes chimiques et biologiques d'Europe de l'est," *Agence France Presse*, available at http://web.lexis-nexis.com, 20 April 1999; Buccianti Alexandre, "Des extremistes musulmans detiendraient des armes chimiques et bacteriologiques, selon un dirigeant islamiste," *Agence France Presse*, available at http://web.lexis-nexis.com, 21 April 1999.

27 John McWethy, "Bin Laden Set to Strike Again?" *ABC News*, available at http://www.abcnews.go.com/onair/WorldNewsTonight/wnt990616_binladen.html, 16 June 1999; CNN, "Bin Laden feared to be planning terrorist attack," available at http://cnn.com/US/9906/16/bin.laden.plot/, 16 June 1999.

28 "Suspect chemical war camp found," *CNN*, available at http://www.cnn.com/2001/WORLD/europe/12/16/ret.rumsfeld.afghan/index.html, 16 December 2001.

29 "In the house of anthrax: Chilling evidence in the ruins of Kabul," *The Economist*, available at http://www.economist.com/world/asia/PrinterFriendly.cfm?Story_ID=876941, 24 November 2001.

30 Anthony Lloyd and Martin Fletcher, "Bin Laden's poison manual," *The Times* (London), available at http://www.thetimes.co.uk/article/0,,2001390015-2001397104,00.html, 16 November 2001.

31 "Evidence suggests al Qaeda pursuit of biological, chemical weapons," *CNN*, available at http://www.cnn.com/2001/WORLD/asiapcf/central/11/14/chemical.bio/index.html, 14 November 2001.

32 "Evidence suggests al Qaeda pursuit of biological, chemical weapons," *CNN*, available at http://www.cnn.com/2001/WORLD/asiapcf/central/11/14/chemical.bio/index.html, 14 November 2001.

33 Walker, Grey and Fielding, "Al-Qaeda's secrets: Bin Laden's camp reveal chemical weapon ambition."

34 Walker, Grey and Fielding, "Al-Qaeda's secrets: Bin Laden's camp reveal chemical weapon ambition."

35 Charles Bremner and Daniel McGrory, "Bin Laden cell plotted French poison attack," *The Times* (London), available at http://www.thetimes.co.uk/article/0,,2001540010-2001553794,00.html, 30 November 2001.

36 Bremner and McGrory, "Bin Laden cell plotted French poison attack."

37 Figures to March 2002. I appreciate the assistance of Jason Pate of the Centre for Nonproliferation Studies in Monterey, California, for these numbers, based on the CNS Database of Incidents Involving Sub-National Actors & CBRN Materials.

38 Jason Pate, Gary Ackerman and Kimberley McCloud, "2000 WMD Terrorism Chronology: Incidents Involving Sub-National Actors and Chemical, Biological, Radiological, or Nuclear Materials," available at http://cns.miis.edu/pubs/reports/cbrn2k.htm, 12 March 2002.

39 Gavin Cameron, Jason Pate, Diana McCauley and Lindsay Defazio, "A Chronology of Sub-State Incidents Involving CBRN Materials, 1999," *The Nonproliferation Review*, Vol. 7, No. 2, (Summer 2000), pp. 157–174.

40 Javed Ali, "No clear pattern emerging in anthrax investigation," *CNN*, available at http://CNN.com, 25 December 2001.

41 Jonathan B. Tucker, "The Proliferation of Chemical and Biological Weapons Materials and Technologies to State and Sub-State Actors," Testimony before the Sub-Committee on International Security, Proliferation and Federal Services of the U.S. Senate Committee on Governmental Affairs, 7 November 2001.

42 Ali, "No clear pattern emerging in anthrax investigation."

43 Jason Pate, "Anthrax and Mass-Casualty Terrorism: What is the Bioterrorist Threat After September 11?" *US Foreign Policy Agenda*, available at http://usinfo.state.gov/journals/itps/1101/ijpe/pj63pate-2.htm, November 2001.

44 Tucker, "The Proliferation of Chemical and Biological Weapons Materials and Technologies to State and Sub-State Actors."

45 Guy Gugliotta, "Study: Anthrax tainted up to 5,000 letters: cross-contamination blamed for deaths of two women," *The Washington Post*, available at http://www.washingtonpost.com/wp-dyn/articles/A11611-2002May13.html, 14 May 2002, p. A02.

46 Damian Whitworth, "America paralysed by 2,300 anthrax scares," *The Times* (London), available at http://www.thetimes.co.uk/article/o,,2001350017-2001361611,00.html, 17 October 2001.

47 W. Seth Carus, "The Rajneeshees," in Jonathan B. Tucker (ed.), *Toxic Terror: Assessing Terrorist Use of Chemical and Biological Weapons* (Cambridge, MA: MIT Press, 2000), pp. 115–138.

48 Jessica Eve Stern, "The Covenant, the Sword, and the Arm of the Lord," in Tucker, *Toxic Terror*, pp. 139–158.

49 "Turks report attempt to poison Air Force unit," Reuters, 28 March 1992; Alexander Chelyshev, "Terrorists Poison Water in Turkish Army Cantonment," *TASS*, 29 March 1992.

50 "Sarin gas reportedly among mustard gas containers seized in Istanbul," *Hurriyet*, 27 August 1996, p. 18, cited in *BBC Summary of World Broadcasts*, 30 August 1996.

51 Bruce Hoffman, "The Debate Over Future Terrorist Use of Chemical, Biological, Nuclear and Radiological Weapons," in Brad Roberts (ed.), *Hype or Reality: The "New Terrorism" and Mass Casualty Attacks* (Alexandria, VA: The Chemical and Biological Arms Control Institute, 2000).

52 *Agence France Presse*, 23 November 1995; Mark Hibbs, "Chechen Separatists Take Credit For Moscow Cesium-137 Threat," *Nuclear Fuel*, Vol. 20, No. 25 (5 December 1995), p. 5.

53 Stephane Orjollet, "Nuke package raises fear of Chechen attacks—but how real are they?" *Agence France Presse*, 24 November 1995.

54 "Russian nuclear staff said to have contacts with Japanese sect," BBC Summary of World Broadcasts, available at http://web.lexis-nexis.com, 25 May 1995.

55 David E. Kaplan and Andrew Marshall, The Cult at the End of the World (New York: Crown, 1996), pp. 112, 190–192, 208; Falkenrath, Newman and Thayer, America's Achilles' Heel, pp. 20, 22; David Brackett, Holy Terror: Armageddon in Tokyo (New York: Weatherhill Inc., 1996), pp. 92–93.

56 Kaplan and Marshall, The Cult, pp. 191–192; Brackett, Holy Terror, p. 92.

57 Brackett, Holy Terror, p. 92.

58 Tucker, Toxic Terror, p. 251.

59 Tucker, "The Proliferation of Chemical and Biological Weapons Materials and Technologies to State and Sub-State Actors."

60 Tucker, "The Proliferation of Chemical and Biological Weapons Materials and Technologies to State and Sub-State Actors."

61 See Jonathan B. Tucker and Jason Pate, "The Minnesota Patriots Council," in Tucker, Toxic Terror, pp. 159–184.

62 Tucker, "The Proliferation of Chemical and Biological Weapons Materials and Technologies to State and Sub-State Actors."

63 Gavin Cameron, Nuclear Terrorism: A Threat Assessment for the 21st Century (Basingstoke: Macmillan Press, 1999), pp. 131–132.

CHAPTER 4

NETWORKS, NETWAR AND INFORMATION-AGE TERRORISM

Kevin A. O'Brien*

*Thanks to my colleagues in RAND and RAND Europe–including Andrew Rathmell and Lorenzo Valeri, Bruce Hoffman, John Arquilla and Greg Treverton–for their ground-breaking work in support of many of the ideas I have covered, as well as Joseph Nusbaum and Allison Van Lare for assistance with research contributed to this paper.

Introduction

Defining the Problem: Asymmetric Actors and Threats—The Place of Cyber-War

Since the end of the Cold War, much has been made regarding the changing security agenda and the emergence of new threats. In reality, most—if not all—of these threats to national and international security are evolutions of pre-existing threats, which have undergone modification brought about by numerous engines of change in today's world. The much-vaunted globalization, new liberalizations in formerly autocratic states, increasing privatization of state functions, and, most importantly, the revolution in computing, telecommunications, and data-transference capacities—commonly referred to as the Information Revolution—have all impacted strongly on the international security agenda and on the nature of the threat actors in today's world.

This has given rise, in the threat-perceptions environment, to the introduction of the term "asymmetric threat" to refer to those threats which have gained prevalence since 1990 and present non-traditional threat postures to (generally) Western governments, defence and national security communities. Generally speaking, these threats do not present the danger of major conventional war to the Developed World powers, but do present other equal (if not, in some cases, greater) dangers to the populations and governments of these states.

While this paper is not the place to summarize or explore the varied nature of asymmetric threats and actors, it will discuss two of the key pillars of asymmetry: notably, information operations and terrorism, including the links between the two. The proliferation of networked computers and telecommunications systems means that our physical infrastructure is now being overlaid by another layer: the national information infrastructure (NII). The NII has been defined as "that system of advanced computer systems, databases and telecommunications networks…that make electronic information widely available and accessible. This includes the Internet, the public switched network and cable, wireless and satellite communications." Given the reliance of modern society on this NII, any major disruption could impact on the national economy as well as on individual government departments or businesses. And yet, the NII has not been developed with security in mind. Specific portions of it are highly secure, notably some internal networks within government or in some financial institutions. However, overall, the NII is extremely vulnerable to disruption from either physical attack (arson, bombs, etc.) or logical attack (such as "malware" and other software programmes).

The U.S. government has taken the lead in studying threats to its NII from hackers, terrorists or foreign governments. Its Department of Defence warned last year that the insecurity of the NII had created a "tunnel of vulnerability previously unrealized in the history of conflict." The Central Intelligence Agency, meanwhile, has warned that it treats Information Warfare (IW) as one of the two main threats to American national security, the other being Nuclear, Biological and Chemical Weapons Warfare.

This is asymmetric warfare—but it is not all that novel nor all that new: as U.S. military analyst Colonel Charles J. Dunlap has stated, "In a way, seeking asymmetries is fundamental to all war-fighting. But in the modern context, symmetrical warfare emphasizes what are popularly perceived as unconventional or non-traditional methodologies."[1] In its most basic form, asymmetric warfare is an approach that tries to focus whatever may be one side's comparative advantages against its enemy's relative weaknesses. Generally, an asymmetric threat implies that an opponent is incapable, due either to his own capabilities or the strength of the force opposing him, of confronting an opponent (generally the Developed World, although this could include multinational corporations, transnational financial communities, or an international organization such as the UN) in a conventional manner using like means or weapons. Therefore, he chooses an asymmetric approach, using means (including the element of surprise, weapons and tactics in ways that are unplanned or unexpected) that will foil, off-set, reduce or circumvent the technological superiority of his opponent, or even give him the advantage over the opponent. As asymmetric attacks generally avoid strength and exploit vulnerabilities, an opponent could design a strategy that fundamentally alters the battle-space within which a conflict (generally low intensity but with high involvement) is fought.

These threats can manifest themselves in a number of different ways, forming part of both the ends to be achieved and the ways and means of achieving these. They can have tactical and strategic impacts. At the strategic level, they work to exploit the fears of the civilian population in order to either weaken support for the democratic process, undermine the government, or to compromise its alliances and partnerships; in this sense, the threats have a strong psychological, as well as physical, impact (for example, playing on the degree of comfort a population has with electronic commerce). In addition, the potential for attacks on international forces deployed regionally (witness the 1992–1993 UN operations in Somalia), or on citizens, property or territory of the major powers itself increases the requirement for a flexible and, sometimes, unconventional response to the security of deployed forces, peace support operations, and Western interests abroad. At the tactical level, they can force an actor to change course or tactics (for example, by playing on the modern fear of Western military forces to casualties), or carry out attacks that are difficult for Western forces to confront and prevent (for example, through terrorist activities or attacks, both physical and electronic, on critical national infrastructures). Threats deriving from terrorist activity, complex emergencies and peace support operations, economic disruption, civil disobedience and organized crime all represent an asymmetric approach to confronting a more powerful opponent.

Not only is it likely that many of the conflicts facing the West will be of an asymmetrical and devolving nature, it is also likely that these threats will come from diverse, differing and simultaneous vectors. For example, the possibility that transnational terrorism will be accompanied or compounded by cyber-/infrastructure attacks damaging vital commercial, military, and government information and communications systems is of great concern. In this sense, a major Western country could suffer greatly at the hands of an educated, equipped, and committed group of fewer than fifty people; such an attack could cause an effect vastly disproportionate to the resources expended to undertake it.[2] It should be noted that one of the open questions regarding the attacks of September 2001 is why—as will be explored here later—Al Qaeda did not use the cyber-tools and knowledge at its disposal to cause additional destruction and chaos alongside its real-world attacks.

All of these threats present the requirement for a massively-improved intelligence capability to warn against and provide support to operations against these threats. While the traditional intelligence process may not present the best options for timely and cost-effective collection, processing, analysis, assessment and dissemination of intelligence relating to these threats, it is clear that traditional intelligence-collection means—very technologically heavy and still driven by Cold War requirements—definitely do not present the best options for dealing with asymmetric threats. While technologically- or technically-based profiles (such as through intercepted electronic and communications traffic, or the use of orbital assets to determine the location of transnational terrorist bases in Afghanistan or delivery-system testing in North Korea, Iran or Pakistan) will continue to be of use to the intelligence collection process, the best assets for intelligence-gathering on asymmetric threats will be human and open-source.

Asymmetry and Information Operations

One of the central pillars of asymmetry is the use of information operations to counter your opponent; as will be noted throughout this paper, the linkages between this pillar and another—terrorism—leads to concerns about the ways in which today's terrorists can use cyberspace[3] to both plan and conduct their attacks. These "information-age terrorists" present potentially the single greatest threat (in terms of the potential to render mass destruction and death) to today's information-age societies.

The U.K. Ministry of Defence recognizes that "our increasing dependence on high technology to provide our battle-winning edge—and the widening disparity between our military capabilities and those of potential adversaries—

may lead potential aggressors to adopt alternative weapons or unconventional strategies [including] asymmetric warfare;" this is because "integration of information systems into military operations offers significant advantages but also introduces new vulnerabilities."[4] Under such a scenario, information warfare could be used to disable critical national infrastructures throughout Western states through attacks on computer networks, paralysing communications, transportation, power systems, and industrial enterprises; other information operations, including perception-management operations and psychological warfare, would allow opponents to exploit the international news media to weaken the resolve of Western decision-makers (as happened during the Kosovo conflict).

The recent U.S. Quadrennial Defence Review stated that a future adversary could "employ asymmetric methods to delay or deny U.S. access to critical facilities; disrupt our command, control, communications, and intelligence networks; or inflict higher than expected casualties in an attempt to weaken our national resolve."[5]

Future asymmetric actors will have a number of tools at their disposal; these include the use of cyber- or cyber-based warfare and the acquisition of selected high-technology sensors, communications, and weapons systems. This could be called the "strategy of the niche player," where cyber-weapons and tools would be used to disrupt military and civilian information technology (IT) systems, as well as launching attacks on NII and critical national infrastructures (CNI) in order to disrupt and destroy the information-based economies and infrastructures of Western states.[6] The threat is compounded by the selected acquisition of high-technology sensors, communications and weapons systems by rogue states and non-state actors such as transnational organized crime (TOC) groups. The exploitation of civilian sources such as the Internet and commercial satellite imagery, as well as the proliferation of advanced weapons, permit better operational planning, more accurate targeting and greater damage by the asymmetric actor.[7] Most ironically, the Developed World is making the asymmetric actor's job much easier through its over-reliance, increasing daily, on large volumes of information provided through a largely unregulated Internet. In most instances, the populations and governments of Western countries rely almost entirely on national critical information infrastructures (NCII) consisting of government and corporate computer servers, telecommunications facilities and Internet service providers. All of these present ready targets for any type of asymmetric attack discussed here; responding to a potentially devastating cyber- or cyber-based attack has become one of the key priorities of most Developed World governments today.[8]

Information Warfare and Netwar

Information Dominance and Information Superiority

As the "information spectrum" includes "data," "information" and "knowledge," in a manner of speaking, "information warfare" can include threats, protection and activities along each of these paths.[9] Information itself exists in different forms:

- Ground truth
- As sensed
- As perceived by an individual (direct or indirect observation)
- As shared by two or more individuals

"Deriving from information," "awareness" and "understanding" are the results of cognitive processes with these inputs. Thus, by attacking each of these points—or, indeed, defending each of them—one is engaging in the most basic form of information warfare. By defeating your opponent's awareness of the situation while maintaining yours, or by modifying his understanding of the facts and truth while enforcing your own (or, indeed, the view which you want your opponent to have of a situation), one is winning in information warfare.

These concepts translate fluidly across the whole spectrum of information operations (including elements such as computer network operations, psy-ops and propaganda, "netwar" or cyber-war, etc.): In any of these scenarios, you are attempting to change your opponent's awareness and understanding of the situation; even in circumstances where attack and defence parameters are used in support of cyber-terrorism, the aim is to defeat your opponent's systems—often by "taking them down," eliciting information from them, or modifying their contents in order to create a different impression or make a statement—and thereby his understanding of reality.

Where this changes is in the ability of terrorists, organized criminal groups or other sub-state malicious actors to use the date, information and knowledge resources available in the information society to plan and organize, finance and communicate, and ensure command and control (C^2)

over real-world operations; this was clearly demonstrated over the past eight years by Al Qaeda and other pan-Islamist terrorist organizations, and not simply a realization post-September 2001, as will be discussed later. Even in these situations, however, the terrorists used the information and communications technology (ICT) resources both at their disposal and—most importantly—at the disposal of their opponents in both Western and Asian intelligence services to defeat their opponent through "spoofing" their real intentions.

Information Operations, Computer Network Operations and Netwar

With the West leading the world in information technologies and the Information Revolution sweeping large parts of the globe, the vulnerability of these states to cyber-based information operations (IO), as well as to the more "traditional" aspects of IO such as psychological warfare and perception-management warfare, has increased markedly. Ironically, the more the world digitizes, the more vulnerable it becomes. In the military and government fields, this is becoming all the more worrying: computerized weapons systems are used for precision strikes, e-mail is used for military communications, and logistics processes have become digitized; insiders, rogue hackers, and foreign military jammers can exploit all of these.[10] In addition, the use of such non-technological IO means deployed against a much more capable and technologically-advanced conventional force was demonstrated more than adequately in the Kosovo campaign, where Belgrade easily "won" the psychological and perception IO war against NATO. But in a more worrying sector—that of cyber-based IO—the West is becoming increasingly vulnerable as it becomes increasingly capable. This is not only in the military sector, but also in the civilian and commercial sectors, as was aptly demonstrated by both the Distributed-Denial-of-Service (DDoS) attacks launched against the Internet-based companies Yahoo, Amazon and E-Bay during 1999–2000, and by the ILOVEYOU e-mail virus—estimated to have cost Western businesses US$7 billion (£4.7 billion) in damage[11]—launched seemingly as a practical joke from the Philippines by college students in 2000.

Information operations are "actions taken in support of objectives which influence decision-makers by affecting other's information and/or information systems, while exploiting and protecting one's own information and/or information systems."[12] Targets include the major elements of the national economy: the public telecommunications network, the financial and banking system, the electric power grid, the oil and gas networks, and the national transportation system (including the air transportation system). The conduct of offensive IO poses a clear asymmetric threat to the West, with its increased reliance on information and information systems as a vital component of decision-making, presenting the possibility of organizations, or individuals, with hostile or malicious intent, taking action to deny, disrupt or destroy capabilities in this area. This could have devastating consequences combined with WMD or terrorist activities: For instance, taking down a city's emergency telephone system through a cyber-attack while setting off terrorist bombs and interfering with the media could produce an asymmetric synergy, making the individual attacks much more effective than they would have been alone.[13] IO has been used to infiltrate or disrupt military or civilian information technology systems, including those used for command, control, communications and logistics, to modify or manipulate data, or to attack the national strategic infrastructure (i.e., by disrupting critical systems such as international air traffic control systems).[14]

Offensive IO can be divided into three principal categories:

a) *Attacks on infrastructure*, "activity that causes damage to information or information systems, or interferes with operations," involving a broad spectrum of operations—including activities such as computer network attack (CNA), electronic warfare and physical destruction—ranging from hacker vandalism of public Internet sites to coordinated reconnaissance, infiltration, data manipulations or DDoS attacks on corporate or government information systems.

b) *Deception*, "designed to mislead an enemy by manipulation, distortion, or falsification of evidence to induce him to react in a manner prejudicial to his interests," including manipulation of the open media, such as propaganda operations through public communication channels including television, radio and the Internet, as well as misinformation and hoaxes, sometimes taking advantage of new video and audio manipulation technologies and computer animation.[15]

c) *Psychological operations*, "ability to influence the will of another society," involving political or diplomatic positions, announcements, or communiqués, as well as the distribution of leaflets, radio or television broadcasts, and other means of transmitting information that promote fear or dissension, with its message reinforced through acts such as hostage-taking or the threat of mass casualties.[16]

Interestingly, cyber-terrorism is not only about damaging systems but also about intelligence-gathering. The intense focus on "shut down" scenarios ignores other more potentially effective uses of IT in terrorist warfare: intelligence-gathering, counter-intelligence and disinformation. In addition, conflict in the form of cyber-warfare that would blur conventional boundaries between crime and war might prove attractive to an opponent that sees no strategic benefit in a direct confrontation with the military of the West in a regional war.

Computer Network Operations and Cyber-War

As outlined by Andrew Rathmell in a forthcoming article,[17] computer network operations (CNO) are "a subset of a broader set of malicious computer-mediated activities." British military doctrine states that CNO comprises three key elements:

a) *Computer network exploitation* (CNE), namely, "the ability to gain access to information hosted on information systems and the ability to make use of the system itself,"

b) *Computer network attack* (CNA), namely, the "use of novel approaches to enter computer networks and attack the data, the processes or the hardware," and

c) *Computer network defence* (CND), which is "protection against the enemy's CNA and CNE and incorporates hardware and software approaches alongside people-based approaches."[18]

As outlined in a recent Centre for Strategic and International Studies (CSIS Washington) study, there is currently a lack of clarity as to the nature of cyber-war and what it means for those defending against such attacks. The CSIS study concluded that, in order to be able to defeat cyber-war, we need a clear picture of current and projected cyber-war options for attackers:

- Effective defence and response requires a full-scale net technical assessment of what attackers can really do, key vulnerabilities, and requirements for defence and response
- Exercising responses to assumptions about such attacks is not analysis or adequate planning
- Cyber-war can occur at a number of levels and in conjunction with other means of attack
- A covert cyber-war may be possible where the attacker cannot be identified quickly or at all
- Larger-scale cyber-war may involve clearly identifiable attackers[19]

CNO is one element of information operations (IO); another is "netwar."

Netwar

My colleagues within RAND—David Ronfeldt and John Arquilla—first introduced the term "netwar" several years ago to refer to "an emerging mode of conflict at societal levels, short of traditional military warfare, in which the protagonists use network forms of organization and related doctrines, strategies, and technologies attuned to the information age." The protagonists are likely to consist of dispersed small groups who communicate, coordinate, and conduct their campaigns in a networked manner, without a precise central command.[20] Ronfeldt and Arquilla believe that a network's strength depends on five levels of functioning: organizational (design level), narrative (story being told), doctrinal (strategies and methods), technological (information systems in use), and social (personal ties to assure loyalty and trust). As an example of "netwar," the Al Qaeda network functioned on all of these levels during the planning and execution of the attacks on the WTC. The network also makes the group appear leaderless, and thus makes it harder to find those responsible.

During confrontations with Iraq—even as far back as Operation *Desert Storm*—it is believed that CNO capabilities (such as computer viruses inserted into the Iraqi command-and-control computers) were used; in addition, during Operation *Restore Hope* in Haiti, the U.S. used hacking to exploit knowledge about Haitian government intentions and capabilities.[21] By the time of the 1999 Kosovo conflict, NATO and its member states were openly using CNO, distorting information perceived by Serbian air defence systems on their screens. Hackers disrupted and defaced Serb and NATO websites, and jammed computer messaging systems with "e-mail bombs;" U.S. hackers based in the CIA and NSA—following a Presidential Finding—burrowed into Serb government e-mail systems, while some infiltrated their way into the networked systems of banks around the world in search of accounts held by the Serbian leadership.[22]

It is perhaps not surprising that the U.S. military and government have advanced the furthest in developing concepts of netwar and IO for use in conflict. The U.S. now includes IO as a key component of national security strategy and doctrine; this emphasis has only been heightened since September 2001. The U.S. views information superiority (IS) as centring on three key areas: intelligence; command, control, communications and computers (C^4); and IO, which builds on the traditionally narrower activities of command-and-control warfare (C^2W) and information warfare. With components including deception, physical destruction, psychological operations, operational security, and electronic warfare—underpinned and bound together by a foundation of intelligence and communications—CNO (supported by the Joint Task Force–Computer Network Operations (JTF–CNO) under USSPACECOM), which has recently been added as the ability to logically interfere with an information system, has become of increasing relevance.

Outside the United States, IO is a relatively recent doctrinal construct not yet accepted by all NATO nations; even within the U.S. armed forces, it is viewed with scepticism by some. In the U.K., for example, the MoD recently established the Land Information Assurance Group (Volunteers), comprising a forty-person-strong Territorial Army unit, to develop effective counter-measures against cyber-attacks.

The Relationship Between Cyber-Crime, Cyber-Terrorism and Cyber-War

Legal Considerations of Information-Age Terrorism and Cyber-Terrorism

One of the starting points for considering the growing threat from cyber-terrorism, as well as the use of cyberspace by transnational terrorist organizations, is the legal basis for considering such activities. This provides not only a comparative international framework for understanding the approach that governments are taking to combat cyber-terrorism and cyber-based terrorists, but also an appreciation of how governments perceive the threat.

As noted in the U.K. government's 1998 "Legislation Against Terrorism: A Consultation Paper," the threat from cyber-terrorism, as well as the significant use of cyberspace, continues to grow exponentially:

> The advent of new technologies, advanced means of communication and ever-more sophisticated ways of moving money around have already influenced the way terrorists operate and will continue to do so. Terrorist organizers and fund-raisers no longer have to be in the same country as their target or indeed as each other. Their communications to each other can be encrypted. And there is the potential, if the right targets are hit (such as strategic computer systems running banking or air traffic control operations), to affect thousands or even millions of people. Such technologies could not have been envisaged when the existing counter-terrorist legislation was framed over 20 years ago, but the powers made available in future must be adequate—and flexible—enough to respond to the changing nature of the terrorist threat both now and in the years to come.[23]

The U.K.'s *Terrorism Act* (2000) designates "terrorism" as "the use or threat of action where...(b) the use or threat is designed to influence the government or to intimidate the public or a section of the public, and (c) the use or threat is made for the purpose of advancing a political, religious or ideological cause [and the action] (e) is designed seriously to interfere with or seriously to disrupt an electronic system." Significantly, the jurisdiction for such activities includes action "outside the United Kingdom" and includes reference to any person or to property "wherever situated," reference to the public includes "the public of a country other than the United Kingdom," and reference to the government includes "the government of the United Kingdom...or of a country other than the United Kingdom." Finally, section 5 states that "a reference to action taken for the purposes of terrorism includes a reference to action taken for the benefit of a proscribed organization."[24]

Overall, for the purposes of cyber-terrorism, this means that any individual engaged in, for example, the e-*Intifada* that has been on-going between supporters of the Israeli government and supporters of the Palestinian self-determination cause since October 2000 when the real-world *Intifada* kicked-off again—regardless of where in the world they are based—are subject to prosecution under this Act, whether a member of a proscribed terrorist organization or not. Significantly, at the moment, no cyber-based group (such as known "hacktivist" groups such as the notable Pakistani cracker group "G-Force Pakistan," a group active since February 2000 and which defaced 19 different sites within three days of the *Intifada* recommencing) has yet been added to any listing of proscribed (or even noted) international terrorist organizations.

In the United States, the *Uniting and Strengthening America by Providing Appropriate Tools Required to Intercept and Obstruct Terrorism Act*—or USAPATRIOT Act, as passed on 24 October 2001—includes an amendment to the *Immigration and Nationality Act* and U.S. Code to state that:

> (iv) ENGAGE IN TERRORIST ACTIVITY DEFINED: As used in this chapter, the term "engage in terrorist activity" means, in an individual capacity or as a member of an organization—(I) to commit or to incite to commit, under circumstances indicating an intention to cause death or serious bodily injury, a terrorist activity; (II) to prepare or plan a terrorist activity; (III) to gather information on potential targets for terrorist activity[25]

This—in conjunction with all of the points raised throughout USAPATRIOT relating to "electronic crime"—obviously alludes to the mounting evidence that Al Qaeda used the Internet to support its operations.

In Canada, the definition of "terrorist activity" defines terrorism as an action "taken or threatened for political, religious or ideological purposes and threatens the public or national security by killing, seriously harming or endangering a person, causing substantial property damage that is likely to seriously harm people or *by interfering with or disrupting an essential service, facility or system.*" The act must "intentionally (C) cause a serious risk to the health or safety of the public or any segment of the public,... or (E) causes serious interference with or serious disruption of an essential service, facility or system, whether public or private, other than as a result of advocacy, protest, dissent or stoppage of work that is not intended to result in...harm"—both of which clearly refer to cyber-terrorism.[26] This is applicable "either within or outside of Canada" and is carefully circumscribed to make it clear that disrupting an essential service is not a terrorist activity if it occurs during a lawful protest or a work strike and is not intended to cause serious harm to persons. Canada will also sign the Council of Europe Convention on Cyber-Crime.

Finally, under Australia's new *Security Legislation Amendment (Terrorism) Bill 2002*, terrorism acts are defined to include an act which "(d) creates a serious risk to the health or safety of the public or a section of the public; or (e) seriously interferes with, seriously disrupts, or destroys, an electronic system including, but not limited to (i) an information system; (ii) a telecommunications system; (iii) a financial system; (iv) a system used for the delivery of essential government services; (v) a system used for, or by, an essential public utility; or (vi) a system used for, or by, a transport system."[27]

Thus, it is clear that cyber-terrorism and cyber-based terrorist organizations are regarded in the same light as real-world terrorism; at the same time, national statutes and amendments to anti-terrorism laws are moving to confront the borderless nature of the cyber-terrorist threat—much in line with moves to deal with the transnational nature of the "new terrorism."

Threats and Actors: "Information-Age Terrorism"

The FBI defines terrorism as "the unlawful use of force or violence against persons or property to intimidate or coerce a government, the civilian population, or any segments thereof, in furtherance of political or social objectives." In the information age, terrorism has expanded its scope and found an increasingly prominent use for instruments such as the Internet to facilitate these efforts. Tim Thomas has coined the term "information terrorism" for this process of exploiting the Internet for terrorist purposes, defining it as (1) the nexus between criminal information system fraud or abuse, and the physical violence of terrorism and (2) the intentional abuse of a digital information system, network, or component toward an end that supports or facilitates a terrorist campaign or action. Computer attacks are the most often cited example of "the use of force or violence" in the information age because they are the attacks with which everyone has some familiarity. [28]

Amongst both governments and businesses, there is increasing concern that information security breaches and cyber-crime will undermine trust in the new economy and threaten the development of the information society. In the U.K., then-Foreign Secretary Robin Cook warned Parliament on 29 March 2001 that "a computer-based attack on the national infrastructure could cripple the nation more quickly than a military strike."[29] In the same month, the European Commission pointed out that "the information infrastructure has become a critical part of the backbone of our economies. Users should be able to rely on the availability of information services and have the confidence that their communications and data are safe from unauthorized access or modification. The take-up of electronic commerce and the full realization of Information Society depend on this."[30]

The commercial world is also paying increasing attention to the problem. Worldwide, computer network intrusions were estimated to have cost companies some US$15 billion in 2000. European companies alone lost some US$4.3 billion from information security breaches. This rising tide of crime is undermining consumer confidence and slowing the growth of e-business. In the U.S., the Federal Trade Commission estimates that 61 percent of Internet users do not buy online because of security fears; in Britain, the National Consumer Council found that over 45 percent of Internet users would spend more if they could be reassured about the security of e-commerce sites.

Transnational Terrorists and Cyberspace

In the wake of September 2001, it is clear that terrorists are using cyberspace for their own means. The capabilities and opportunities offered to terrorists include such things as using the Internet to gather detailed targeting information, gathering and moving money about to support activities—or even manipulating stocks to benefit the terrorist organizations (as is suspected from September 2001), coordinating and planning activities from around the world, and using it as a platform for propaganda and publicity (for example, terrorists leave messages of future or planned activities on websites or by e-mail, while publicizing accountability for acts of violence)—in a similar manner, the Internet can be used for psychological terrorism and rumour-mongering. It can also be used to conduct attacks against individuals, groups, or companies such as financial institutes, or to directly lobby decision-makers through extortion, brand-destruction, fraud and other means.

In addition to these concerns is the fact that the Internet has changed terrorist communications networks from those of strong central control to ones with no clear centre of control due to its networked nature. In this same sense, the Internet can be used for clandestine communications through virtual private networks, posting messages by e-mail and on electronic bulletin boards, as well as steganography (hiding messages within pictures and objects) and encryption.

Al Qaeda and Terrorism in Cyberspace

The cyber-trail of the attacks

One of the ways in which officials worldwide will develop new methods for critical infrastructure protection (CIP) is through an understanding of how the terrorists carried out this attack. Until as recently as last year, bin Laden used high-technology means (such as satellite telephones) to communicate with his followers. This stopped abruptly as bin Laden realized the potential threat this posed to him. However, although bin Laden may only use the lowest technological means—such as in-person communication with his subordinates—these subordinates are believed to use encrypted Internet messages to correspond with each other.

Currently, it is believed that Al Qaeda uses both high- and low-technology means to coordinate its activities: In organizing the attacks, the terrorists used active cyber-means—booking airline tickets online, exchanging hundreds of e-mails, using the Internet to learn about the aerial application of pesticides—to plan their attacks; they also protected their communications by using public computer terminals, anonymous e-mail services, and encryption or steganography on websites to relay information publicly. Much of this granted them the total anonymity that was essential to the preparations for these attacks. But it also left, in the aftermath, an electronic trail for investigators to follow.

In 2000, former FBI Director Louis Freeh highlighted this issue to the Senate: "Uncrackable encryption is allowing terrorists—Hamas, Hezbollah, Al Qaeda and others—to communicate about their criminal intentions without fear of outside intrusion." Indeed, bin Laden may actually have used technological means to "spoof" Western intelligence collection (such as SIGINT and IMINT) into believing that he was planning an attack "overseas" and not on the continental U.S., turning the West's intelligence means against it, and using human couriers to carry the real messages: According to Congressional sources, U.S. intelligence intercepted communications discussing such attacks, and other warnings since May 2001 pointed towards an overseas attack on U.S. interests, similar to the attack on the USS *Cole* in October 2000.

In the United States, the powers granted by the *Foreign Intelligence Surveillance Act* (FISA) has allowed officials to develop a clear picture of the terrorists' activities prior to the attacks: For example, one FISA search authorized authorities to monitor the Internet communications of a particular user, which has yielded hundreds of e-mails linked to the hijackers in English, Arabic and Urdu. According to the FBI, some messages have included operational details of the attack. Other officials have seized library log-in sheets and computer equipment, and issued search-warrants to AOL, Microsoft, Earthlink, Yahoo, Google, NetZero, Travelocity and many smaller providers. It is hoped that lessons will be learned from this which will contribute to future detection and deterrence of attacks.

In December 2001, the Canadian Office for Critical Infrastructure Protection and Emergency Preparedness (OCIPEP) released a report on the potential for Al Qaeda to regroup in cyberspace, based upon their long-demonstrated use of the Internet and ICT to support their operations. Warning of "a possible future cyber-attack by agents or sympathizers of Osama bin Laden's Al Qaeda terrorist organization," the report stated that "bin Laden's vast financial resources would enable him or his organization to purchase the equipment and expertise required for a cyber-attack and mount such an attack in very short order." While bin Laden himself may no longer have (assuming he is even alive) the ICT resources to call on which he has used over the past decade, the study does not rule out the possibility of Al Qaeda agents or sympathizers in other countries carrying out sophisticated and coordinated cyber-attacks against critical infrastructure facilities, such as the U.S. telecommunications grid, electric power facilities and oil and natural gas pipelines.[31]

Osama bin Laden demonstrated a sophisticated knowledge of ICT in the months between the August 1998 attacks in Africa and the September 2001 attacks in the U.S. A report released the day after the U.S. attacks stated that bin Laden may have deliberately used the West's intelligence capabilities against it by "spoofing" these intelligence services—and particularly their SIGINT assets—into believing that an attack was going to take place in Africa and not the U.S. Since May, there had been numerous warnings that bin Laden or another terrorist leader was preparing a major campaign against Americans, but all the intelligence suggested that any attacks would occur overseas. Osama bin Laden appears to have used the communications he knew the United States was monitoring to throw America's spies off his trail, instead using human couriers to carry his real messages and money.[32]

The Threat: The Rise of Non-Traditional Sub-State Actors

The spectrum of cyber-threats is commonly taken to range from recreational hackers at the bottom end to national intelligence services and armed forces at the top end. In between, in terms of capability, come sub-state entities such as semi-organized crackers, "hacktivists," organized criminals and terrorists. Cyber-threats emanating from such groups can be defined as "all forms of electronic attacks as well as physical attacks and threats to system integrity." The concern of such threats surrounds both those that may cause observable disruption (e.g., direct action, terrorism) and those that may be clandestine (e.g., espionage and crime). Such threats are directed both to the functioning of information infrastructures and to the information carried on such infrastructures (i.e., to the confidentiality, integrity and availability of information and information systems).[33]

In the study of international and corporate security, it has become axiomatic that organized sub-state actors, including terrorists and insurgents, organized criminals and activist movements, have become increasingly powerful actors in international affairs as a result of social, political and technological changes. As the authors of a Norwegian government study put it: "The coercive power of sub-state actors (i.e., the ability to influence state conduct through violence and sabotage or the threat to do so) is growing and will continue to grow in the future."[34]

A number of authors have championed the idea that evolutionary changes have led to the emergence of a "new terrorism" in the 1990s.[35] Proponents of the "new terrorism" thesis argue that political aims are being replaced by new motivations, ranging from those groups that aim to alter society at a fundamental level (millenialism) and those that are focused on single issues like abortion, the environment or animal rights.

"New terrorism" is also defined by its adoption of novel organizational structures and new patterns of group membership. One of the most common themes regarding this facet of "new terrorism" is that of flattened hierarchies. Traditional hierarchies have become increasingly unnecessary as advances in information technology have made communications easier to arrange. Such leaderless resistance is the natural consequence of ever-increasing levels of cellular disaggregation by sub-state actors. As Arquilla and Ronfeldt note, such organizations are a compromise between "collective diversity" and "coordinated anarchy," with modern communications technologies allowing discreet and minimal communications for consultancy and mobilization. Under this system, "subversive networking" undermines state power through the utilization of "semi-autonomous cellular structures." Examples of such activity include the networking of Mexican *Zapatistas* and U.S. "hacktivists" and the cellular organization of London's J18 anti-capitalist protests.[36]

Cyber-Crime versus Cyber-Terrorism

The 25 October 2000 cracking of Microsoft's internal data-sharing networks by persons unknown and the alleged theft of various Windows code has highlighted, more than ever, the threat posed by cyber-crime. Often referred to as computer crime or e-crime, cyber-crime is taking greater forms every week throughout the world. Exploited by traditional criminal organizations, such as the growing TOC elements operating around the world today, terrorist groups, both domestic and transnational, national governments and their intelligence services, and individuals, cyber-crime impacts on everything from banking systems to aviation authorities, security and customs organizations and telecommunications systems. Such TOC groups can be placed in different countries across the globe, all of which are linked by computers. In reality, cyber-crime can affect any individual or organization which uses a computer and networked communications to conduct their affairs.

Cyber-crime is quite strictly, as defined by various national computer crime statutes, criminal activity which requires knowledge of computers to succeed in the commissioning of offences such as hacking into a computer to alter or destroy files, or to gain information (known as "cracking") for personal benefit. This is distinct from other types of computer and networking criminal activity, such as computer-related crime in which computers are used as tools, but knowledge of computers is not necessary for the successful commission of the offences. Cyber-crime's relationship with the Internet can be divided into crimes which use the Internet, but which are simply an electronic extension of traditional crime (such as fraud, theft, smuggling, and distribution of obscene or racist material); there are crimes which have developed because of the very existence of the Internet, including attacks on the Internet itself through such means as hacking, DDoS attacks, and virus attacks; and there is the use of the Internet by the criminal as a means for communications or storage.

A February 2000 report in *Business Week* paints a vivid image of the damage that cyber-crime can inflict. In December 1999, 300,000 credit card numbers were snatched from online music retailer CD Universe. The previous March, the Melissa virus caused an estimated US$80 million in damage when it swept around the world, paralysing e-mail systems. That same month, hackers-for-hire pleaded guilty to breaking into phone giants AT&T, GTE, and Sprint for calling-card numbers that eventually made their way to organized crime gangs in Italy; the FBI estimated the costs to be US$2 million.[37]

According to a recent Australian Transaction Reports and Analysis Centre (Austrac) report, cyber-banking and cyber-crime will be the most important challenge of the twenty-first century. The Internet revolution has made money transfers across frontiers alarmingly easy, and the world's police forces have yet to catch up with criminals who are taking full advantage of the new information technology that is readily available in any neighbourhood computer store.

Cyber-crimes are perpetrated by a number of different actors. The overwhelming majority are carried out by internal sources (insiders), including past and present employees of companies and institutions; some even estimate that up to 90 percent of economic crime in this area is attributable to insiders. Other actors involved include hackers/crackers, virus writers, narcotics traffickers, paedophiles, fraudsters, organized criminal groups, terrorists, and foreign intelligence services. Increasingly, computers and the Internet are being used in a range of traditional crimes, including murder for hire and making criminal threats.

TOC is becoming more involved in cyber-theft and cyber-intrusion every month. In September 1999, the "Phonemaster," an international group of criminals who penetrated the computer systems of MCI, Sprint, AT&T, Equifax, and even the National Crime Information Centre, were convicted of theft and possession of unauthorized access devices, and unauthorized access to a federal computer. One suspect downloaded thousands of Sprint calling-card numbers, which he sold to a Canadian individual, who passed them on to someone in Ohio. These numbers made their way to an individual in Switzerland and eventually ended up in the hands of organized crime groups in Italy.[38] Even a number of transnational terrorist groups, such as the Peruvian Sendero Luminoso, are becoming more involved in cyber-crime to fund their activities. The Russian *mafiya* and other groups are moving away from drugs into the more profitable business of computer crime.

There is a wide variety of cyber-crimes, most of which mirror similar activities in the "real" world. These include computer and networking crimes such as:

a) *Computer network break-ins*, where hackers use software tools installed on a computer in a remote location to break into computer systems to steal data, plant viruses (such as the ILOVEYOU virus, which crashed millions of computers worldwide and caused an estimated US$10 billion damage)[39] or Trojan horses, or work mischief of a less serious sort by changing user names or passwords,

b) *Industrial espionage*, where networked systems provide opportunities for cyber-mercenaries to retrieve information regarding R&D and marketing strategies,

c) *Software piracy*, where as much as US$7.5 billion worth of software may be illegally copied and distributed worldwide annually,

d) *Child pornography*, where the acquisition of images of children, in varying stages of dress and performing a variety of sexual acts, through the Internet makes both the trading of such images and the establishment and networking of individuals involved in such activities much easier—and much easier to hide,

e) *Distributed-Denial-of-Service* (DDoS) attacks, in which computers are instructed to repeatedly send e-mail to a specified e-mail address, thereby overwhelming the recipient's account and potentially shutting down entire systems,

f) *Password sniffing*, the use of programmes which monitor and record the name and password of network users as they log in, jeopardizing security at a site, and *spoofing*, in which one computer is disguised to appear electronically to be another computer in order to gain access to a system that would normally be restricted, and

g) *Credit card fraud*, in which credit card information is stolen from companies' online databases and used over the Internet.[40]

With around 80 percent of a company's intellectual property in digital form today, spending on Internet security software has increased markedly: Last year, companies in the U.S. spent US$4.4 billion on such purchases, including firewalls, intrusion-detection programs, digital certificates, and authentication and authorization software; by 2003, those expenditures could total US$8.3 billion. A 2000 FBI/Computer Security Institute survey noted that, of the 520 companies and institutions surveyed, more than 60 percent reported unauthorized use of computer systems throughout 1999, up from 50 percent in 1997, while 57 percent of all break-ins involved the Internet, up from 45 percent in 1998. Less than 15 percent of these cases were reported to the authorities.[41]

DDoS attacks are particularly worrying, as they are not technically illegal in most countries. This was brought home when Yahoo was taken down on 6 February 2000, then retailer Buy.com was hit the next day, only hours after going public. By that evening, E-Bay, Amazon.com, and CNN had all been struck. The following morning, online broker E*Trade and others were frozen out by attacks. The software to conduct these attacks is simple to use and readily available at underground hacker sites throughout the Internet. There are currently an estimated 1,900 websites that offer digital tools giving individuals the power to crash computers, hijack control of a machine, or retrieve a copy of every keystroke.[42]

In 2000, the U.K.'s Serious Fraud Office noted that Internet and telephone fraud alone amounted to £30 million. More worrying is the increase in telephone-related hacking, in which an 0800 facility is used by crackers, who have the technology and general awareness to cross the telephone system and come out on a public telephone line. The average cost from this activity (from a Friday afternoon to a Monday morning) to the telephone bill of a company is about £12,000 a day. Ironically, one of the biggest victims of this has been the Metropolitan Police Service, who had their telephone system hacked into, with an estimated loss of approximately £500 million.[43]

Cyber-Fraud and E-Crime

In many senses, the Internet is already its own global state, with its own economy and finances. Direct Internet sales are expected to reach US$5 trillion in the U.S. and Europe by 2005.[44] As e-commerce continues to grow, the Internet provides a seemingly helpful tool for investors due to its convenience and the inexpensive cost of researching investment opportunities; unfortunately, it has also become an excellent tool for perpetrators of fraud.

Auctions were the most prevalent cyber-fraud in 1999, largely due to the fact that many online auctions are run by individuals. The National Consumer League's Internet Fraud Watch concluded that auctions constituted 87 percent of all online frauds in 1999 (up from 68 percent in 1998 and 26 percent in 1997), followed by general merchandising frauds at 7 percent, Internet access service frauds at 2 percent, company equipment and software frauds at 1.3 percent, work-at-home frauds at 0.9 percent, and advance-fee loans, magazines, adult services, travel/vacations, and pyramid scheme frauds at around 0.1–0.2 percent each. Consumers lost over US$3.2 million to cyber-fraud, with an average loss per consumer of US$580 for online purchases of computer equipment or software, and US$465 for general merchandise sales. The average loss per consumer to online auction sales was US$293.[45] The Federal Trade Commission, which responds to consumer complaints regarding Internet fraud, filed 61 suits in 1999, up from 1 in 1994. Thus far, these actions have resulted in the collection of more than

US$20 million in payments to consumers and the end of schemes with annual estimated sales of over US$250 million.[46]

Total frauds reported rose from 689 in 1996 to 10,660 in 1999, with the Internet (at 90 percent) and e-mail (at 5 percent) being the primary contact methods for initiating the fraudulent action. Examples of fraud include *pyramid schemes* in which participants attempt to make money solely by recruiting new participants into the programme; *pump and dump* schemes, in which readers are urged to buy a stock quickly before the price falls, following which the fraudsters sell their shares and stop hyping the stock, resulting in the price plummeting and the investors losing their money; and other investment schemes in which spectacular profits or guaranteed returns are offered, such as extraordinarily high bank deposit rates, promises of free stocks, get-rich-quick e-mail opportunities, or stock that is artificially inflated. Interestingly, the overwhelming majority of fraudulent payments (93 percent) were made offline by cheque or money order sent to the fraudulent company.[47]

Attempts at cracking stock market and banking financial assets have also increased; an example was the attempt by Russian TOC to use crackers to make 40 illegal transfers from Citibank in an attempt to steal US$10 million. In addition, online investment fraud is increasing. In the U.S., the Securities and Exchange Commission (SEC) receives around 250 complaints per day of suspected cyber-fraud, totalling more than 54,000 in one year, an increase of 50 percent from five years ago. Attempts to crack down on violators appear to meet with little result; this may be partly because the number of investors trading online grew by 2.2 million to more than 5.2 million in 1999, with more than 25 percent of all stock trades occurring over the Internet. Many of these individuals are new to online trading and thus prone to such frauds. One recent cyber-fraud took in US$6.3 million before the SEC was able to stop it.[48]

One famous example is of two individuals in Los Angeles who were convicted in December 1999 of securities fraud for artificially inflating a company's stock price by posting false information about the firm on Internet bulletin boards. The pair, using public computers at the University of California which made tracing them much more difficult, made US$370,000 by purchasing shares of a company called NEI Web World at 13 cents a share then selling them for as much as US$15 after claiming on bulletin boards that LCG Wireless Inc. planned to buy NEI Web World. The case is similar to that of PairGain, believed to be the first instance of Internet-based stock manipulation, in which a former employee of PairGain Technologies Inc. directed bulletin board visitors to a false Bloomberg story that said the company was a takeover target. PairGain stock soared by 31 percent before dropping back down; the employee pleaded guilty in June 1999.[49]

One of the biggest frauds ever perpetrated on the Internet was the fictitious "Dominion of Melchizedek," in which a fake "country" was established by California-based cyber-fraudsters as a "tax haven," and offers made to incorporate banks, insurance companies, trusts and private corporations for a few thousand dollars. "Melchizedek" claimed to have "embassies" and other "legations" in Washington, Canberra, Budapest, Lima and Sao Paulo, and "trade centres and liaison offices" in Singapore and Lagos. The group was caught in 1998 and 1999 through international law enforcement efforts.[50]

Currently, the FBI estimates that cyber-crimes are running at approximately US$10 billion a year. More than 90 percent of all companies have reported breaches, while 74 percent reported theft of proprietary information, financial fraud, system penetration by outsiders, data or network sabotage, or Denial-of-Service (DoS) attacks. Information theft and financial fraud caused the most severe financial losses, at US$68 million and US$56 million respectively, while losses traced to DoS attacks were only US$77,000 in 1998, and by 1999, had risen to just US$116,250. All this may be contributing to a decreasing public confidence in e-commerce. A spring 2000 poll conducted by the Information Technology Association of America found that 61 percent of those surveyed said that rising cyber-crime made them less likely to do business over the Internet, while 62 percent said they did not believe enough was being done to protect consumers against cyber-crime.[51]

In March 2000, then-FBI Director Louis Freeh reported that cyber-attacks in the U.S. had doubled in the last year.[52] In addition, there exists the threat that, during a foreign intervention, asymmetric opponents may use IO strategically (in both the cyber and psycho-political arenas) to cause mass disruption to civil society and introduce a cyber-war that would slow the decision-making process of the governments involved. While amateur hackers receive most publicity, the real threat comes from the professionals or "cyber-mercenaries." This term refers to highly-skilled and trained products of government agencies or corporate intelligence branches working on the open market. The Colombian drug cartels hired cyber-mercenaries to install and run a sophisticated secure communications system, while Amsterdam-based gangs used professional hackers to monitor and disrupt the communications and information systems of police surveillance teams. While amateur hackers have little reason to move around, the professionals can be very mobile; for this reason, links with TOC groups are of great interest. The Russian and Eastern bloc governments produced numerous trained hackers as well as IW weapons. Bulgaria is notorious as a virus factory while portable Directed Energy weapons (which will fry unshielded electronic circuitry) can be purchased openly in the Baltic states. Finally, an asymmetric opponent could also conduct a slow-motion strategic economic warfare campaign against private economic interests in the West, through attacks by a high-performance criminal organization on a wide range of e-payment or electronic currency systems that facilitate the global transition to e-commerce. In these situations, there appears—at first—little that Western governments and the international community can do to defeat these threats.

However, such attacks may not be as easy as it would (at first) seem. In order to launch a sophisticated attack against a hardened target, an actor will most likely have three to four years of practice in C, C++, Perl and Java (computer languages) programming and general UNIX and NT systems (types of computer platform) administration, knowledge of LAN/WAN theory, remote access and common security protocols (network skills), and a lot of free time. On top of these technical nuts and bolts, there are certain skills that must be acquired within the cracker community.

Other forms of attack (in addition to penetration or "cracking" attacks) are becoming more prevalent. Both DoS and DDoS attacks have grown in strength since the February 2000 attack on U.S.-based e-commerce sites. At the moment, a coordinated attack to bring down a government's or a corporation's computer systems cannot be maintained long enough to be little more than a nuisance. Yet, while only annoying at the moment, as interconnectivity increases and the importance of the online economy becomes manifest, such exploits will have serious financial implications.

Cyber-terrorism is not only about damaging systems but also about intelligence-gathering. The focus on "shut down" scenarios and analogies to physically violent techniques ignore other more potentially effective uses of IT in terrorist warfare: intelligence-gathering, counter-intelligence and disinformation. In addition, concomitant cyber-attacks with real-world terrorist incidents (as alluded to in the September 2001 attacks) could potentially multiply the disastrous consequences massively. Attacking an information system would be a good way to either distract the target or otherwise enable the terrorist to perform a physical attack: For example, had Aum Shinrikyo been able to crack the Tokyo power system and stop the subways, trapping passengers on the trains, the number of casualties caused by their 1995 sarin gas attack might have been significantly larger.[53]

Other concerns include "cracking" attacks whose aim are not to gather information but rather to erase or modify existing data within an information system. For example, U.K. and U.S. interbank transactions are backed up daily with multiple remote tapes, so any cracker wanting to destroy the interbank market will cause the loss of at most one day's transactions. However, consequences could rebound on consumer confidence in the banking system were exploits to be publicized. Similarly, "spoofing"—which includes attempts to create phoney records or phoney messages in a system (such as creating false bank accounts), or attempts to give phoney instructions to the processing system—can also cause systems to fail.

Competitor Governments and Cyber-War

Most interestingly, the perception that asymmetric threats are posed solely by those opponents of the West who possess little strength in any sector is quickly dismissed by the fact that the Chinese People's Liberation Army (PLA) has published recently a number of studies in which asymmetric warfare and tactics are seen as the key in any future conflict, whether military or otherwise, with the West (particularly the U.S.). Stating that "hacking into websites, targeting financial institutions, terrorism, assassinating U.S. financiers, using the media and conducting urban warfare" are among the methods considered by the PLA, these studies are driven by the efforts of the PLA to modernize their IW/IO capabilities. Recognizing that it cannot match the West in either conventional or nuclear weapons, the PLA has begun to emphasize the development of new information and cyber-war technologies, including viruses and similar cyber-threats, to neutralize or at least erode any enemy's political, economic and military information and command-and-control infrastructures.[54] Designating this practice as "Unrestricted Warfare," the PLA argues that China can outmanoeuvre Western high-tech sensors, electronic counter-measures and weaponry by employing different methods entirely. "If [China] secretly musters large amounts of capital without the enemy nation being aware of this at all and launches a sneak attack against its financial markets," they write, "then after causing a financial crisis, buries a computer virus and hacker detachment in the opponent's computer system in advance, while at the same time carrying out a network attack against the enemy so that the civilian electricity network, traffic-dispatching network, financial transaction network, telephone communications network and mass media network are completely paralysed, this will cause the enemy nation to fall into social panic, street riots and a political crisis."[55]

Indeed, the Chinese government and PLA may be behind the most sophisticated on-going cyber-war today. Known collectively as "Solar Sunrise" (February 1998) and "Moonlight Maze" (on-going since mid-1999), this series of increasingly sophisticated cyber-attacks and attempts at penetrating U.S. government systems has been traced to sources in both China and Russia, but no clear perpetrators have come to light. While "Solar Sunrise" exploited lax computer security in the DoD (and was ultimately believed to be the work of two California teenagers), "Moonlight Maze" was suspected of having links to both the Chinese PLA and the Russian Academy of Sciences; the hackers accessed sensitive DoD science and technology information.[56]

Such concerns were enhanced when—following the downing of the U.S. EP-3 by Chinese fighters—a number of U.S. government websites were taken over and defaced by suspected Chinese hackers in the days following the incident. On one site at the Department of Labour, a hacker posted a tribute to Wang Wei, the Chinese pilot who was killed in a collision with the EP-3 on 1 April. By the end of the week, the so-called "Honker Union of China"— an informal network of Chinese hackers—claimed that they had defaced more than 1,000 U.S. websites; one message said, "Don't sell weapons to Taiwan, which is a province of China." American hackers responded with their own methods: For example, web-portal Sina.com was struck by a series of DoS attacks on the evening before 1 May.[57]

Thomas has also noted that, with regard to the Internet, a terrorist attempts to succeed by using the Internet's open promise of an integrated and cooperative world to discredit governments, degrade user confidence, and corrupt or disrupt key systems through the insertion of data errors or by causing intermittent shutdowns. This produces, in many cases, fear or alarm and thus is a modern-day supplement to traditional terrorism.[58]

One asymmetric response to military weakness is to seek the use of international legal instruments to restrain vertical proliferation on the part of a rival; hence the Russian gambit at the UN. Russia's attempts to ban IO make strategic sense and mirror its efforts to restrict nuclear weapons in the early years of the Cold War. Russia recognizes that, as it struggles to rebuild its economy, it is vulnerable to the advanced tools and doctrines of IO that its Western rivals are developing. Unable to counter in kind, or to afford comprehensive defensive measures, Russia is seeking to use international law to reduce America's military advantage. In this sense, the West will need to pay particular attention to this most pressing of new concerns.

Defending Against Cyber-Terrorism: Critical Infrastructure Protection and Information Assurance

By 2001, European and U.S. policymakers at the highest levels were expressing their concerns that insecure information systems threatened economic growth and national security. President Bush's National Security Advisor, Condoleezza Rice, noted in March 2001 that "it is a paradox of our times that the very technology that makes our economy so dynamic and our military forces so dominating also makes us more vulnerable." She warned, "Corrupt [the information] networks, and you disrupt this nation."[59] As a result of these concerns, a complex and overlapping web of national, regional and multilateral initiatives has emerged.[60] A common theme behind these initiatives is the recognition of the inadequacy of existing state-centric policing and legislative structures to police international networks and the importance of ensuring that private networks are secured against disruption. One way of grouping these initiatives is to use the standard information security paradigm of deterrence, prevention, detection and reaction.

a)   *Deterrence*: Multilateral initiatives to deter CNA include harmonizing cyber-crime legislation to promote tougher criminal penalties and better e-commerce legislation (Council of Europe Convention, UNCITRAL).

b)   *Prevention*: Multilateral initiatives to prevent CNA centre around promoting the design and use of more secure information systems (e.g., R&D initiatives between the U.S. and EU; Common Criteria) and better information security management in both public and private sectors (e.g., ISO and OECD standards and guidelines initiatives). Other measures include legal and technological initiatives such as the promotion of security mechanisms (e.g., electronic signature legislation in Europe).

c)   *Detection*: Multilateral initiatives to detect CNA include the creation of enhanced cooperative policing mechanisms (e.g., G-8 national points of contact for cyber-crime). Another important area is the effort to provide early warning of cyber-attack through exchanging information between the public and private sectors (e.g., U.S. Information Sharing and Analysis Centres, FIRST, European Early Warning and Information System).

d) *Reaction*: Multilateral initiatives to react to CNA include efforts to design robust and survivable information infrastructures, development of crisis management systems, and improvement in coordination of policing and criminal justice efforts.

Overall, these initiatives involve significant investments of time and effort from a variety of government departments in many nations, from numerous international organizations and from numerous companies, large and small. Many initiatives are pre-existing, many are being pursued in isolation. Nonetheless, there has emerged a coherent and effective set of initiatives involving states and businesses, not to mention some NGOs, that is focused upon improving the security of the emerging global information environment.

Notes

1   Michael Evans, "Conventional Deterrence in the Australian Strategic Context," Land Warfare Studies Centre Working Paper No. 103, available at http://www.defence.gov.au/lwsc/wp103.html, May 1999.

2   See http://www.emergency.com/asymetrc.htm.

3   The term "cyberspace" is used here to refer to any and all aspects of the Internet and World Wide Web (including communications and informational means), as well as any networked system or systems which are connected to other systems outside of themselves.

4   See http://www.dti.gov.uk/ost/forwardlook99/states/mod/text.htm#section02.

5   See http://forum.ra.utk.edu/summer99/asymmetric.htm.

6   Robert H. Allen, *Asymmetric Warfare: Is The Army Ready?* Army Management Staff College, Seminar 14, Class 97-3, available at http://www.amsc.belvoir.army.mil/asymmetric_warfare.htm, 1997.

7   Government of Canada—Department of National Defence, *Threat Definition: Asymmetric Threats and Weapons of Mass Destruction* (3000-1 (DNB CD) April 2000), p. 17.

8   Government of Canada—Department of National Defence, p. 18.

9   David S. Alberts, "Information Superiority & Network-Centric Warfare," Presentation for Research and Strategic Planning, OASD (C3I), 19 June 2000.

10 See http://www.amsc.belvoir.army.mil/ecampus/pme/research/Prof_Articles/1997/asymmetric_warfare.htm.

11 See http://www.zdnet.com/zdnn/stories/news/0,4586,2570175,00.html.

12 Government of Canada—Department of National Defence, p. 12.

13 Joseph C. Cyrulik, "Asymmetric Warfare and the Threat to the American Homeland," *Landpower Essay Series* 99-8, Institute of Land Warfare, Association of the U.S. Army, November 1999.

14 Government of Canada—Department of National Defence, p. 12.

15 Cyrulik, "Asymmetric Warfare and the Threat to the American Homeland."

16 Government of Canada—Department of National Defence, p. 12.

17 Andrew Rathmell, "Controlling Computer Network Operations," *Information & Security Journal*, special issue on "The Internet and the Changing Face of International Relations and Security," forthcoming.

18 Government of the U.K.—Ministry of Defence, *Draft Doctrine for Information Operations: Joint Doctrine Pamphlet XX-01*, Joint Doctrine and Concepts Centre, Shrivenham, 1 March 2001, p. 8.

19 Centre for Strategic and International Studies, *Asymmetric Warfare and Homeland Defense* (8 December 2000), p. 39.

20 John Arquilla, David Ronfeldt and Michele Zanini, "Networks, Netwar and Information-Age Terrorism," in Ian O. Lesser, Bruce Hoffman, John Arquilla, Brian Jenkins, David Ronfeldt and Michele Zanini (eds.), *Countering the New Terrorism* (Santa Monica, CA: RAND, 1999), p. 47.

21 William M Arkin, "The Cyberbomb in Yugoslavia," *The Washington Post*, 25 October 1999.

22 "Pentagon Sets Up New Center for Waging Cyberwarfare," *Military and C4I*, available at http://www.infowar.com/MIL_C4I/99/mil_c4I_1000999a_j.shtml (accessed 9 March 2000).

23 Presented to Parliament by the Secretary of State for the Home Department and the Secretary of State for Northern Ireland by Command of Her Majesty, available at http://www.archive.official-documents.co.uk/document/cm41/4178/4178.htm, December 1998.

24 Government of the United Kingdom and Northern Ireland, *Terrorism Act* (2000) s1(1-5) "Definitions."

25 Government of the United States, *Uniting and Strengthening America by Providing Appropriate Tools Required to Intercept and Obstruct Terrorism Act* (25 October 2001), HR 3162 RDS (107th CONGRESS, 1st Session): SEC. 411. "DEFINITIONS RELATING TO TERRORISM – Amendment to Section 212(a)(3) of the Immigration and Nationality Act (8 U.S.C. 1182(a)(3))," available at http://frwebgate.access.gpo.gov/cgi-bin/getdoc.cgi?dbname=107_cong_public_laws&docid=f:publ056.107.

26 Government of Canada, *Anti-terrorism Act*, Bill C-36: s83.01 (1)(b)(ii), available at http://www.parl.gc.ca/37/1/parlbus/chambus/house/bills/government/C-36/C-36_4/C-36TOCE.html, 18 December 2001.

27 Government of Australia, *Security Legislation Amendment (Terrorism) Bill 2002*, Part 5.3:100.1(2) "Definitions," available at http://search.aph.gov.au/search/ParlInfo.ASP?action=view&item=0&from=browse&path=Legislation/Current+Bills+by+Title/Security+Legislation+Amendment+(Terrorism)+Bill+2002+[No.+2]/Text+of+the+bill&items=1, 13 March 2002.

28 Timothy L. Thomas, *Deterring Asymmetric Terrorist Threats to Society in the Information Age*, available at http://www.waaf.ru/31.htm, October 2001.

29 Hansard, 29 March 2001: Column 1125.

30 Commission of the European Communities, *Creating a Safer Information Society by Improving the Security of Information Infrastructures and Combating Computer-Related Crime*, COM(2000) 890 final (26 January 2001).

31 Dan Verton, "Report warns of al-Qaeda's potential cybercapabilities," *The New York Times*, 4 January 2002.

32 "How al-Qaeda Spoofed the West—Bin Laden may have tricked spies: Officials say their intelligence pointed to an attack overseas," *Seattle Times*, 12 September 2001.

33 As defined by the Information Assurance Advisory Council (IAAC) Threat Assessment Working Group; see http://www.iaac.org.uk.

34 Lia Brynjar and Annika S. Hansen, *An Analytical Framework for the Study of Terrorism and Asymmetric Warfare* (Kjeller: Norwegian Defence Research Establishment, 1999), p. 10.

35 Bruce Hoffman, *Inside Terrorism* (New York: Columbia University Press, 1998); and Ian O. Lesser *et al.* (eds.), *Countering the New Terrorism*. Also see Walter Laqueur, *The New Terrorism: Fanaticism and the Arms of Mass Destruction* (Oxford and New York: Oxford University Press, 1999).

36 John Arquilla and David Ronfeldt, *The Advent of Netwar* (National Defence Research Institute, Santa Monica: RAND, 1996), pp. 67–75; Richard Reeves, Nicole Veash and John Arlidge, "Virtual Chaos Baffles Police," *The Observer*, 20 June 1999.

37 Ira Sager *et al.*, "Cyber Crime: First Yahoo! Then eBay. The Net's vulnerability threatens e-commerce—and you," *Business Week*, 21 February 2000.

38 Statement for the Record of Guadalupe Gonzalez (Special Agent in Charge, Phoenix Field Division, FBI) on Cybercrime Before a Special Field Hearing Senate Committee on Judiciary Sub-Committee on Technology, Terrorism, and Government Information, Washington, D.C., 21 April 2000.

39 Gary Fields, "Poll: Cybercrime deters shoppers—61% say viruses, other attacks make them less likely to spend on the Net," *USA TODAY*, 20 June 2000, p. 5A.

40 Natalie D. Voss, "Crime on the Internet," *Jones International and Jones Digital*

Century, available at http://www.digitalcentury.com/encyclo/update/crime.html, 1999.

41 Sager *et al.*, "Cyber Crime."

42 Sager *et al.*, "Cyber Crime."

43 Detective Inspector James O'Connell (Metropolitan Police Computer Crime Unit), "Strategies to Defeat Crime: Policing Cybercrime," *Cityforum Conference Transcripts*, available at http://www.cityforum.ltd.uk/c_oconnell.htm, 9 May 2000.

44 "Foreword and Summary," *Cybercrime... Cyberterrorism... Cyberwarfare...* (Washington, D.C: Centre for Strategic and International Studies, 2001).

45 "National Consumers League Warns Consumers Millions are Lost to Internet Fraud," *NCL* (16 February 2000).

46 Sager *et al.*, "Cyber Crime."

47 "Going once, going twice...scammed!" *Internet Fraud Watch*, 23 February 1999.

48 Andrew Fraser, "Regulators Struggle to Keep Up With Explosion of Online Fraud," *The Wall Street Journal Interactive Edition*, 1 March 1999.

49 Lisa M. Bowman, "L.A. pair charged over cyberfraud," *ZDNN*, available at http://www.zdnet.com/zdnn/stories/news/0,4586,2410171,00.html, 15 December 1999.

50 "Cyberfraud—The Fictitious 'Dominion Of Melchizedek'," *The Nation* (Bangkok), 30 May 1999.

51 Fields, "Poll: Cybercrime...".

52 "FBI Chief says Cyber Attacks Doubled in a Year," *Newsbytes*, available at http://www.infowar.com, 28 March 2000.

53 Johan J. Ingles-le Nobel, "Cyberterrorism hype," *Jane's Intelligence Review*, Vol. 11, No. 12 (December 1999).

54 See http://www.insightmag.com/archive/200002063.shtml.

55 See http://www.insightmag.com/archive/200002063.shtml.

56 "DoD Official Says Hackers Are More Sophisticated Since Solar Sunrise," *Hacker Sitings and News*, available at http://www.infowar.com/hacker/99/hack_102599b_j.shtml, 25 October 1999.

57 "Chinese Hackers Invade 2 Official U.S. Web Sites," *The New York Times*, 28 April 2001; "Hackers Report a Truce," *Reuters*, 10 May 2001.

58 Thomas, *Deterring Asymmetric Terrorist Threats*.

59 AP, "National Security Adviser sees cyberterrorist threat," 26 March 2001

60 An overview of such activities is included in Andrew Rathmell and Kevin O'Brien (eds.), *Information Operations: A Global Perspective* (Coulsden: Jane's Information Group, 2000).

TRENDS IN TERRORISM

CHAPTER 5

AL QAEDA AND ITS LINKS TO
TERRORIST GROUPS IN ASIA

Peter Chalk*

*The opinions and conclusions expressed in this paper are derived entirely from the author's own personal research into Asian terrorism and unconventional security over the past eight years. They should not be interpreted as representing those of RAND or the sponsors of any of the Corporation's work.

International attention on the threat of Asian Islamic extremism has escalated markedly since Al Qaeda launched its devastating attacks against the United States on September 11.[1] Not only is this part of the heightened global awareness of terrorism in general, it also reflects the fact that groups and militants based in the region are known either to have passed through training camps formerly under the charge of the Taliban or to have established links with Osama bin Laden and his global terror network.

This paper examines the principal Islamic entities in Asia that have been linked to Afghan extremism and terrorism. The paper first briefly examines the organizational dynamics and motives of Al Qaeda and discusses its former interaction with the Taliban. It then goes on to explore the extent of the contacts that have been established between the network and groups based in Asia, focusing its analysis on organizations in Kashmir, the southern Philippines and Indonesia.

Al Qaeda

Organizational Dynamics

Al Qaeda's origins can be traced back to the 1990/91 Persian Gulf War and the deployment of U.S. troops on Saudi soil, although 1998 marked the group's first real emergence as a concrete entity. It was in this year that bin Laden issued his now-famous *fatwa*, which specifically affirmed the killing of Americans and their civilian and military allies to be religious duty for each and every Muslim to be carried out whenever and wherever it was possible.[2]

Al Qaeda—literally the "Base"—operates both on its own and through an interlocking complex of overseas terrorist organizations and cells that is thought to link extremists in at least 40 countries. Osama bin Laden, who heads the network as emir-general, oversees a consultative council (*Shura majlis*) of five committees—military, religious, legal, finance and media.[3] Organizationally, Al Qaeda appears to function in an extremely fluid manner, adopting and switching between both tightly-centralized and loosely-constituted structures. High profile actions, such as the 1998 U.S. embassy bombings in Kenya and Tanzania and the 2001 strikes against the World Trade Centre and Pentagon exhibit characteristics of utmost operational security, long-term planning and vertically-integrated leadership. On the other hand, more opportunist attacks, such as the planned millennium bombings in Jordan and Los Angeles seem to be organized on a "venture capitalist" basis with Al Qaeda providing money, but only the loosest form of centralized control and direction.

Prior to the U.S. military campaign that was launched against the Taliban in October 2001, Al Qaeda maintained at least six dedicated terrorist training camps in Afghanistan—at Khost, Mahavia, Kabul, Jalabad, Kunar and Kandahar—plus two subsidiary depots in Tora Bora and Liza. In addition to these facilities, the group is known to own safe-houses, training facilities and guest-houses in Pakistan, the Sudan, Somalia and Kenya.[4] Most of Al Qaeda's dedicated fighters are veterans of the anti-Soviet war in Afghanistan, many of who were inducted into the so-called 055 Brigade from a huge *mujahideen* recruitment database created by bin Laden during the 1980s.[5]

While Al Qaeda operates on a truly global scale, between 1996 and 2001 the movement was headquartered and sustained out of Afghanistan, where it enjoyed the active backing of the ruling Taliban militia. The relationship between these two entities is now one of record and basically stemmed from a reciprocal arrangement of mutual self-interest. In return for basing privileges in Afghanistan, bin Laden provided the Taliban with both troops (in the guise of the 055 Brigade) and finance (reportedly as much as US$100 million over six years) to prosecute the war against the Northern Alliance (NA). [6] The Afghan haven provided Al Qaeda with a secure location in which to train its operatives and plan its attacks, while money and personnel from bin Laden allowed the Taliban to rapidly overrun and marginalize the NA. It is in this context that one former Afghan government official has remarked that the Taliban and bin Laden are "two sides of the same coin: Osama cannot exist in Afghanistan without the Taliban and the Taliban cannot exist without Osama."[7]

Ideological Base

Al Qaeda's ideological base essentially revolves around bin Laden's self-defined *jihad* against the U.S., its allies and regimes infused with Western values and precepts. The core of much of Al Qaeda's aggression has been Washington, which bin Laden views as the main instigator of all that is wrong in society—from crime to greed and materialism—and as hell-bent on imposing a dysfunctional and immoral way of life across the planet. More intrinsically, he regards American hegemony as an evil aberration that has prevented Islam from taking up its rightful position as the world's greatest and pre-eminent religion and culture. Sponsoring global attacks against U.S. interests is regarded as both a necessary and just means for overcoming this adverse state of affairs.[8]

The overall thrust of bin Laden's ideological hatred extends beyond the West and the U.S. to include moderate, secular Muslim governments, which he interprets as integral to the subversion of true Islamic ideals and interests. One state that has been particularly singled out in this regard is Saudi Arabia, both on account of Riyadh's willingness to supply oil to the West and the modern orientation of the ruling royal family as well as the fact that American troops have been endorsed on the soil of one of Islam's most sacred heartlands.[9]

Nor has bin Laden drawn the line at moderate Muslim governments. Indeed his vision of the global *jihad* necessarily affirms the need to support *any* organization that is dedicated to furthering fundamentalist goals and objectives. For bin Laden, the ultimate objective is to foment a worldwide pan-Islamic revolution. Seen in this context, there can be no respite until the United States and all those that support and adhere to its values are destroyed.

In pursuit of his internationalist ambitions, bin Laden has fostered pragmatic and tactical alliances with groups that literally span the globe. In undertaking such an endeavour, the Saudi renegade has demonstrated a remarkable ability to bridge personal rivalries and ideological differences, creating a breadth of connections that is unprecedented in the history of modern terrorism. It is the extent of this transnationalism that sets bin Laden apart from other exporters of cross-border violence and is one of the main factors accounting for the perceived strategic threat that he is seen to pose, not only to the United States, but to the international system in general.[10]

Principal Asian Groups Linked to Al Qaeda

Al Qaeda support has been extended to three main types of groups. First, entities opposed to Muslim governments that are deemed to be morally bankrupt and complicit in the suppression of true Islamic ideals and interests. Second, organizations fighting against regimes that are perceived to be oppressing their internal Muslim populace. Third, groups striving to create and maintain an independent Islamic state.[11] In Asia, this backing has coalesced most visibly in Kashmir, the southern Philippines and Indonesia, although at least in logistical terms, there are growing indications that Malaysia is also being integrated into Al Qaeda's overall terror network.

Kashmir

Kashmir has been the scene of intense tension since the late 1980s when the Jammu and Kashmir Liberation Front (JKLF) launched its armed campaign to separate the predominantly Muslim province from India and unite with Pakistan. Originally, the insurgency in Kashmir was fought almost exclusively along indigenous and nationalist lines. However, during the 1990s, the nature of the conflict changed and is now overwhelmingly mercenary and religiously based. This transformation is owed, in large part, to the intervention of Islamabad's Inter-Services Intelligence (ISI) Directorate, which has explicitly sought to replicate the success of the anti-Soviet *mujahideen* campaign it coordinated in Afghanistan by exhorting foreign Islamists to participate in a *jihad* that is being fought on behalf and in the name of oppressed co-religionists. It is in this context that Kashmiri links to Al Qaeda have emerged.[12]

Although several militant groups exist in Kashmir, two have been most directly connected to Afghanistan and bin Laden: Laskar-e-Tayyeba (LeT), literally "Army of the Pious," and Jaish-e-Muhammad (JeM), literally "Soldiers of Muhammad."[13] LeT initiated violent operations in 1993 and acts as the armed wing of the *Markaz-ad-Da'awa-wal-Irshad madrasah* in Pakistan; JeM emerged in 2000 following the negotiated release of several Islamic militants jailed in India, including Masood Azhar, the ultra fundamentalist cleric who founded the group and formerly led the Harakat-ul-Mujahideen (HuM).[14]

Both LeT and JeM define their objectives in local and global terms, with the rhetorical enemy specified as any state that is perceived to be anti-Islamic. The annual diary of *Markaz-ad-Da'awa*, for instance, specifically asserts its intention to bring the *jihad* to the United States, Israel, Russia, the United Kingdom and France, announcing plans to "plant Islamic flags in Delhi, Tel Aviv, Washington, Paris and London." In a similar vein, JeM boasts pictures of burning American effigies on the group's calendars and posters.[15] Indeed the group's leader, Masood Azhar, has specifically declared that no Muslim should rest in peace until India and America are annihilated.[16]

The two organizations are known to enjoy the active backing of the ISI. The Directorate has provided materiel as well as financial support— allegedly to the tune of US$4 million a month—and are believed to run training courses in camps located near to the disputed Line of Control (LoC).[17] Somewhat more seriously have been Indian and U.S. assertions that elements within the ISI have used their influence in Afghanistan to help foster tactical links between JeM, LeT and Al Qaeda in an attempt to spark a wider Islamic revolution across the sub-continent.[18] According to this theory, the long-term aim is to create a block of Pakistani-led Muslim nations that links Central Asia, through Afghanistan, to the Indian Ocean.[19] While these claims almost certainly reflect an opportunistic attempt to mobilize international opinion in favour of Delhi's position on Kashmir, there are signs suggesting that JeM and LeT have established tactical links with bin Laden and his global terror network.[20]

The first real indication that such contacts exist became clear in August 1998 following U.S. cruise missile strikes in Afghanistan that were launched in retaliation for the attacks against Washington's embassies in Kenya and Tanzania. At least two dozen of the militants that were killed in Al Qaeda camps were subsequently identified as affiliates of HuM (the precursor to JeM and similarly led by Azhar) and LeT.[21] The existence of these activists almost certainly reflected training agreements that had been established between the two groups and bin Laden—connections which, in the case of HuM, Indian and Western intelligence sources strongly believe have since been carried over to JeM. Indeed, LeT members have specifically stated that most of their senior members have had the privilege of "working with Muslim heroes such as Osama bin Laden."[22]

Many of the LeT militants that have been killed or captured in Kashmir have been linked to radicals that have been trained in Afghan camps run by either Al Qaeda or the Taliban.[23] Interrogated members describe largely similar experiences at these facilities, typically detailing courses that run for three weeks and cover basic weapons-handling in everything from anti-aircraft guns and rocket-propelled grenades (RPGs) to AK-47 rifles and pistols. Upon completion, they are generally sent to ISI "graduate schools" where they learn advanced skills in such things as escape-and-evasion, ambush techniques, intelligence and field communications.[24]

Apart from training, Indian sources claim that Al Qaeda has supplied both JeM and LeT with money, weapons and ammunition.[25] This materiel, combined with the logistical support of the ISI, has been linked to several high-profile operations in Indian territory over the last two years, including a major car bombing in Srinagar in April 2000 (claimed by JeM), a series of massacres in Jammu and Kashmir in August 2000 (blamed on LeT), a suicide strike against the Srinagar State legislature in October 2001 (again claimed by JeM), a direct assault on the country's national Parliament in December 2001 (attributed to both LeT and JeM) and, most recently, an attack on the U.S. Kolkata Cultural Centre in January 2002.[26]

LeT and JeM suicide attacks, which in the Kashmiri context are largely unique to these two organizations, have additionally been portrayed as reflecting Al Qaeda's influence and explicit endorsement of *fidayeen* martyr squads. Certainly this style of attack has become more frequent over the last three years and may well reflect the style of fanatical absolutism that has come to characterize many of bin Laden's closest adherents.[27]

The Southern Philippines

Two main Islamic groups are currently fighting in the southern Philippines: the Moro Islamic Liberation Front (MILF) and the Abu Sayyaf Group (ASG, literally the "Bearer of the Sword"). While the former does retain a large cadre of militants at its disposal, is known to have established a Special

Operations Group (SOG) to carry out urban sabotage missions (including, allegedly a series of bombings in Metro Manila during December 2000 that left more than 20 people dead)[28] and includes elements that have been linked to local, regional and international Islamists, it is the latter that is generally recognized as posing the greatest threat in terms of terrorism and extremist links to Al Qaeda.[29] This is particularly true among U.S. policymakers (see below).

The ASG first emerged in 1989 under the leadership of Abdurajak Janjalini. The group is committed to the establishment of an exclusive, independent Islamic Theocratic State of Mindanao (MIS) and is infused with a highly intolerant religious credo that calls for the deliberate and systematic targeting of all southern Filipino Christians. In pursuit of this objective, the ASG has explicitly defined its ideological and operational agenda as intimately tied to an integrated effort aimed at asserting the global dominance of Islam through armed struggle.[30]

Abu Sayyaf cells are known to have established links with bin Laden's Al Qaeda network, receiving financial as well as materiel support. Philippine and Western intelligence sources maintain that the bulk of this assistance has been channelled to the group via a series of front organizations originally created by Jamal al-Khalifa, the Saudi renegade's brother-in-law. Prior to his arrest in San Francisco in December 1994, Khalifa doubled as the President of the Philippine Chapter of the International Islamic Relief Organization (IIRO) and Director of the World Muslim League (WML).[31] Financial investigations conducted in the wake of the September 11 attacks in New York and Washington have identified both of these bodies as providing key logistical conduits that have been established (or at least abused) for the explicit use of international terrorist operations.

In addition to facilitating its own record of domestic-based terrorism—which has included bombings, assassinations, international kidnappings and civilian massacres (such as the 1995 Ipil attack, which left 54 Christians dead)—the ASG has used its foreign contacts to help with the creation of local logistics for international Islamic organizations wishing to operate out of the Philippines. Concrete evidence of these transnational ties first emerged in 1995 when the ASG was linked to a multi-pronged plot to bomb Washington's embassies in Manila and Bangkok, assassinate President Clinton during the 1996 Asia-Pacific Economic Cooperation (APEC) summit meeting in Subic Bay and destroy U.S. airliners flying trans-Pacific routes from American west coast cities (Operation *Bojinka*). The plan was developed by

Ramzi Yousef—the convicted mastermind of the 1993 attack against the World Trade Centre in New York—who had been despatched to the Philippines as a personal emissary of bin Laden to establish a tactical working relationship with the ASG.[32]

It is not known exactly how extensive ASG links with transnational extremists have been since 1995. However, operatives are believed to have attended terrorist training courses in Afghanistan, travelling to Al Qaeda and Taliban bases under the pretext of attending theological courses in Pakistani *madrasahs*. In addition, the Philippine government claims that bin Laden continues to channel money to the group via the front organizations established by Khalifa and that these finances have been used both to purchase weapons smuggled across the porous Malaysian border in Sabah as well as to stage terrorist attacks in Mindanao and Metro Manila.[33]

While there have been signs of an internal rupturing of the ASG along criminal lines since the 1998 death of its radically fundamentalist founder, Janjalini, the group continues to exhibit a strong identification with the goals and rhetoric of global Islamic extremism.[34] The string of Western kidnappings staged by the group in 2000, for instance, while undoubtedly motivated by financial imperatives, were also aimed at securing the release of Yousef, Sheik Omar Abdul Rahman (similarly convicted for the 1993 World Trade Centre bombing) and other Muslims imprisoned in the U.S. on terrorism charges.[35]

This internationalist orientation, which appears to have been further inspired by the ferocity of the Fall 2001 American military campaign in Afghanistan, may well prove critical in availing any logistical relocation of Al Qaeda forces that occurs post-Taliban.[36] Certainly it is this latter dimension that most U.S. commentators continue to stress and is one that they largely agree gives the ASG relevance and a threat quotient far beyond the 300–500 hardcore activists that the group is currently able to mobilize in the southern Philippine theatre.[37] Very much indicative of this perception has been the decision to initiate joint military exercises and training missions with Filipino Special Forces in Mindanao. The manoeuvres, which commenced in February 2002 and involve 650 American troops (in a non-combat role), are aimed at enhancing Manila's overall ability to root out and eliminate all ASG cells in the south, particularly in their traditional strongholds of Basilan and Sulu. Known collectively as *Balikitan-02-I*, the operations are viewed as an integral component of President Bush's on-going global war against terrorism and will run until at least July 2002.[38]

Indonesia

In Indonesia, Islamic extremism has emerged as an increasingly salient threat since the overthrow of President Suharto in 1998. Almost overnight, the Republic moved to shed the vestiges of nearly four decades of authoritarian rule in favour of an open political system based on democratic principles. Successfully achieving such a transition was always going to be fraught with difficulties; the increasingly critical state of the country's financial health, however, combined with a succession of poor leaders, have dramatically escalated the latent risks associated with this transformation.[39] Not only have poverty, inflation and unemployment interacted with a more fluid domestic environment to produce major outbursts of civil protest and violence, general dissatisfaction with the administrative performance of Jakarta has galvanized a re-awakening of atavistic Muslim identity that has further entrenched and radicalized popular sentiment across the archipelago.

Currently, the most visible threat in terms of global Islamic extremism and links to Al Qaeda exists in the guise of Laskar Jihad (LJ).[40] The group acts as the paramilitary division of the Forum *Komunikasi Ahlus Sunnah wal Jama'ah* (*Sunni* Communication Forum), which seeks to "promote true Islamic values" in Indonesia. It was formally established on 30 January 2000 in response to what the FKAWJ saw as the deliberate persecution of Muslims in the Moluccas. Thousands of activists were subsequently despatched to the islands to support their co-religionists, with 2000 officially declared as the Year of the Jihad against Christian "kafirs."[41]

LJ is led by Jafa Umar Thalib, a veteran of Afghanistan's war against the Soviet Union, and is headquartered near Yogyakarta on Java. The group believes there is a worldwide Jewish and Christian conspiracy to undermine Islam and specifically blames the West and Indonesia's current democratic polity for all the problems plaguing the Republic.[42] It is committed to the institution of *shariah* law across the entire archipelago and has called on all "true Muslims" to participate in a *jihad* aimed at liberating the country from the influence of the U.S. and its "infidel" cohorts. The movement has been involved in several large-scale civilian massacres in the Moluccas (especially on the island of Ambon) and, during 2001, has also been linked to atrocities in central Sulawesi.[43]

LJ is well-organized and retains a large cadre of armed militants. In addition, it is believed to receive backing from factions of the Indonesian Armed Forces (TNI), some of whom have been filmed directly participating in anti-Christian attacks. In interviews conducted during early 2001, senior LJ members specifically boasted of their group's relationship with the TNI, with Thalib actually claiming to have a direct hotline to the Army's former commander, Admiral Widodo.[44]

Of most concern, however, are indications that the group has established logistical and tactical links with Al Qaeda. Although Thalib has spoken disparagingly of bin Laden in the past, both on account of his explicit endorsement of suicide bombers and poor grasp of Islam, the LJ leader explicitly endorsed the 2001 attacks against the World Trade Centre and Pentagon, affirming them as an "important lesson for America to change its attitude of hostility towards Muslims."[45] Indonesian intelligence sources have also claimed that Al Qaeda operatives, including Kumpulan Mujahideen Malaysia (KMM)/Jemiah Islamiah affiliates based in Malaysia which have participated in LJ attacks in the Moluccas and Sulawesi as well as bombings in Central and Eastern Jakarta (see below), have helped to establish an international paramilitary facility in Sulawesi (near to the port city of Poso) to train Muslim extremists dedicated to the creation of a hard-line Islamic state comprising Indonesia, Malaysia, the southern Philippines, Singapore and Brunei[46] and are now working to establish "sleeper" cells across the rest of the country.[47]

Western sources have similarly pointed to the existence of some sort of LJ–Al Qaeda association. As with the Philippines, one of the main fears is that this tactical relationship, combined with the general internal chaos in Indonesia, will avail former Afghan-based terrorists with an alternative safe haven from which to radicalize Islamic sentiment, both within the Republic as well as more generally across the Asia-Pacific as a whole.[48] Expressing these concerns, Deputy Defence Secretary Paul Wolfowitz has remarked: "Going after Al Qaeda in Indonesia is not something that should wait until after Al Qaeda has been uprooted from Afghanistan."[49]

Malaysia

The threat emanating from Malaysia is more diffuse and less easily discerned than that in Kashmir, the Philippines and Indonesia. Although no concerted radical Islamic insurgent groupings exist *per se*, the country is known to contain extremist elements that have formed the basis for a loose logistical network that has figured prominently in the activities of Muslim militants, both regionally and internationally.[50]

The Philippines and Indonesia have both linked Malaysia to the activities of transnational Islamic militants operating in their respective states. Manila has long alleged, for instance, that weapons and logistics bound for the ASG (and originating in South Asia) have been smuggled via the porous Sabah border and that indigenously-based expatriates and militants have availed these movements.[51] Equally, Indonesia has periodically claimed Malaysian-based associates of bin Laden have worked in conjunction with LJ, implicating these militants in a string of church bombings that took place in Central and Eastern Jakarta during mid-2001 as well as generalized civil violence in the Moluccas and Sulawesi over the last two years.[52]

There are suggestions that international terrorist camps exist in Negri Sembilan and that these facilities are being used to train regional and transnational militants. These claims have never been formally substantiated, although captured ASG members have frequently alluded to the existence of operational facilities in Malaysia, including one notable testimony provided by Edwin Angeles, the group's former intelligence chief.[53]

The Central Intelligence Organization (CIA) also claims to have video evidence that an Al Qaeda operatives' meeting took place took place at a condominium in Kajang, Selangor during January 2000 in which plans for several anti-American attacks were discussed. It is now known that Khalid al-Midhar and Nawaf Al Hazmi, two of the terrorists involved in the September 11 strikes, attended this gathering and that Zacarias Moussaoui, the so-called "14th hijacker" currently standing trial in the United States, was also in the country later that year.[54]

More recently, extremists with links to Malaysia were implicated in a wider Al Qaeda plan to attack several high-profile Western targets in Singapore, including the island-nation's deep-water Navy port at Changi, the Ministry of Defence, a shuttle bus serving the Sembawang Wharves and Yishun subway, the U.S. and Israeli embassies, the British and Australian High Commissions and commercial complexes housing American firms. The plot first came to light following the seizure of a videotape and notes detailing reconnaissance of potential targets in Singapore from an Al Qaeda leader's house in Afghanistan.[55] The attacks were allegedly to have been carried out under the auspices of JI, a hitherto largely unknown entity that has now been identified in at least four

Southeast Asian countries, including Malaysia, the Philippines, Indonesia and Singapore.[56] The largest cell exists in Malaysia (with 200 members, this group is thought to act as a regionally-based leadership consultative council) and has been linked to the KMM—a group that appears to have been heavily influenced by the radical Islamic teachings and world-view of bin Laden.[57]

Western sources have focused increased attention on Malaysia since the attacks on the World Trade Centre and Pentagon, particularly after PAS leaders expressed vocal support for a countrywide *jihad* in support of the Taliban. There is little doubt that Kuala Lumpur's emphasis on modernization has encouraged a growing tide of religious revivalism throughout the country (reflected by hard-line Islamic electoral gains in Kelantan and, more recently, Terengganu).[58] As the examples of Pakistan, Saudi Arabia and Egypt well illustrate, such contexts can easily be subverted by outside fanatics and exploited to avail their own nefarious purposes. At the time of writing, some 47 militants with suspected links to Al Qaeda affiliates, the September 11 attacks against the United States and the plot in Singapore have been arrested in Malaysia.[59]

Conclusion

As this paper has outlined, there are strong indications that Al Qaeda has established concerted links in Asia and that bin Laden's extremist Islamic network is metastasising to this part of the world. Certainly there are aspects of the region that make it acutely vulnerable to this type of penetration and general exploitation as a springboard for local and wider international terrorist attacks. Not only is Asia characterized by highly porous land and sea borders that are well-suited to the smuggling of arms and personnel, many governments also retain close links with the West—notably Singapore, Thailand and the Philippines—which make them ideal as substitute targets for anti-American aggression.

In addition, there exists a substantial Islamic demographic milieu that extremists can quickly disappear into (Indonesia, for example, currently boasts the world's largest Muslim population), while political corruption and general economic mismanagement both mitigate against effective internal security provisions and provide fertile ground for the fundamentalist rhetoric of outside demagogues. The region's status as a global commercial and tourist hub has also provided a highly-developed transport and finance infrastructure that can be used as effectively for illicit as licit purposes (something that is readily reflected by years of drug smuggling). Finally, there is a highly active underground remittance (*hawala*) system in place in Southeast Asia, which is well-suited to the rapid transmission of funds in a largely untraceable manner. A similar network in South Asia is known to have formed a crucial financial conduit for Al Qaeda when it was based out of Afghanistan.[60]

If Asian governments are to effectively deal with the future threat of terrorism in the region—both dependent and independent of Al Qaeda—it is essential that they develop an effective and rigorous framework for coordinating collaborative action. The Association of Southeast Asian Nations' (ASEAN) Regional Forum (ARF), which remains the pre-eminent multilateral security regime in the Asia-Pacific, represents the logical mechanism through which to achieve such institutionalized cooperation. Certainly several member states (notably the Philippines, Malaysia, Singapore, Indonesia and Thailand) are now talking more explicitly about the need to enhance functional and procedural cooperation in the intelligence and communication areas, pledging to sign an ARF agreement of intent as soon as possible.[61] Thus far, however, the Forum has proven to be less than effective in terms of security deliberations, largely because of its preference for consensual and non-intrusive decision-making. Resolutions are generally not adopted unless they are unanimous and typically never allude or make reference to the internal policies of another member state.[62]

While these types of modalities may be conducive to furthering the appearance of harmonious regional relations, they are hardly suited to the type of frank and honest discussion needed for effectively dealing with national and international terrorism—particularly in a region where internally-based actors can so easily transcend and impact across national frontiers. Confronting the non-state challenges of the twenty-first century —of which political and religious extremism is but one manifestation—will require the region's polities to move away from these dysfunctional collaborative predilections and accept normative patterns that are no longer tied to, or embedded in what is rapidly becoming a largely irrelevant sixteenth century conception of national sovereignty.

Notes

1   The attacks launched against the United States were the largest and most lethal the world has seen. Altogether, four American internal flights were seized. Two planes were flown into the twin towers of the World Trade Centre in New York, precipitating the collapse of both structures. The third jet smashed into the Pentagon in Virginia, while the fourth crashed into a field in Pennsylvania after passengers resisted the hijackers; the intended target of the plane is not known, although there is speculation that it was bound either for Camp David in Maryland or the White House or Capitol Building in Washington D.C. The official death toll from the various attacks has been estimated around 3,500.

2   See, for instance, *Responsibility for the Terrorist Atrocities in the United States*, 11 September 2001, statement by Prime Minister Tony Blair before the British Parliament, available at http://www.number-10.gov.uk/text/evidence.htm, 4 October 2001; Ahmed Rashid, *Taliban: Islam, Oil and the New Great Game in Central Asia* (London: I.B. Tauris, 2000), p. 134; and Simon Reeve, *The New Jackals* (London: Andre Deutsch, 1999), p. 194. The *fatwa* was signed and issued in Khost (initially under the aegis of the International Islamic Front for Jihad Against Jews and Crusaders) and is generally seen as one of the clearest statements of bin Laden's anti-Western beliefs and global intentions.

3   Rohan Gunaratna, "Blowback," *Jane's Intelligence Review* (August 2001), p. 43.

4   See, for instance, Rashid, *Taliban*, Chapter 10; Gunaratna, "Blowback," pp. 42–45; "The Spider in the Web," *The Economist*, 22 September 2001; "One Man and a Global Web of Violence," *The New York Times*, 14 January 2001; "Borderless Network of Terror," *The Washington Post*, 23 September 2001.

5   Gunaratna, "Blowback," p. 43.

6   "Bin Laden Said to 'Own' the Taliban," *The Washington Post*, 11 October 2001; "Honoured Guest," *The Economist*, 22 September 2001.

7   *Responsibility for the Terrorist Atrocities in the United States*, 11 September 2001, p. 4.

8   Rashid, *Taliban*, Chapter 10; *Responsibility for the Terrorist Atrocities in the United States*, 11 September 2001, pp. 4–6; "One Man and a Global Web of Violence," *The New York Times*, 14 January 2001; "The Spider in the Web," *The Economist*, 22 September 2001.

9   Rashid, *Taliban*, Chapter 10; Gunaratna, "Blowback," p. 43; "The Double Act Wears Thin," *The Economist*, 29 September 2001.

10   "The Spider in the Web," *The Economist*, 22 September 2001.

11   Gunaratna, "Blowback," p. 43.

12   Author interview, Institute for Conflict Management, New Delhi, February 2001.

13   Additional groups include al-Badr, Harakat-ul-Mujahideen (HuM) and Hizbul Mujahideen (HM). The latter organization is the only entity that is still largely constituted by indigenous Kashmiris.

14 The Islamists were freed in order to secure the safe return of 155 hostages hijacked on an Air India flight to Khandahar. Although HuM carried out the operation in order to obtain the release of Azhar, the former leader moved to establish a more hard-line, fundamentalist organization on his return to Pakistan. The result was JeM which has since supplanted HuM both in terms of numbers and activities.

15 Author interview, New Delhi, February 2001. See also Jessica Stern, "Pakistan's Jihad Culture," *Foreign Affairs*, Vol. 79, No. 6 (2000), p.124.

16 Masood Azhar, quoted in "Militant Freed in Hijacking Vows to Destroy U.S., India," *Seattle Times* (U.S.), 5 January 2000.

17 Author interview, New Delhi, February 2001. See also Rashid, *Taliban*, pp.189–195; Stern, "Pakistan's Jihad Culture," p. 120; Roger Howard, "Probing the Ties that Bind Militant Islam," *Jane's Intelligence Review* (February 2000), p. 37; and "Pakistan Funds Islamic Terror," *The Sunday Telegraph* (U.K.), 16 May 1999.

18 Author interview, New Delhi and Srinagar, February 2001; "Pakistani Intelligence Had Ties to Al Qaeda, U.S. Officials Say," *The New York Times*, 29 October 2001. According to U.S. officials, much of this activity stemmed from the independent policies of hard-line ISI officers, including the Directorate's former Director General, Mahmood Ahmed (removed from his post by President Pervez Musharraf in the wake of the fall-out from the September 11 attacks), who had increasingly become a power to themselves, operating almost as a "government within a government."

19 Author interview, Paris, February 2001. Senior analysts emphasized similar rationalizations during interviews at the Institute for Conflict Management, New Delhi, February 2001. See also Rashid, *Taliban*, p. 195.

20 It needs to be noted that in the wake of the September 11 attacks against the U.S. and the suicide assault on India's Parliament in Delhi, Pakistan's President, Pervez Musharraf, has moved to crack down on Islamic extremists based in the country as well as reign in the more hard-line elements of the intelligence services. Among the more noticeable steps taken have been decrees banning both the JeM and LeT as well as three other groups (Tehrik-e-Nifaz-e-Shariat Mohammad/TNSM, Tehrik-e-Jaffria Pakistan/TJP and Sipha-e-Sehaba Pakistan/SSP); the arrest of 2010 militants across the country, including the leaders of JeM and LeT; an internal re-shuffling of the ISI and removal of the Directorate's former Director General, Lieutenant-General Mahmood Ahmed; and the initiation of reforms to prevent the abuse of mosques and *madrasahs*. See "Pakistani Intelligence Had Ties to al Qaeda, U.S. Officials Say," *The New York Times*, 29 October 2001; "Pakistan Arrests Scores of Islamic Radicals," *The Washington Post*, 5 January 2002; "Pakistani Militants Forced Underground," *The Washington Post*, 14 January 2002; and "Musharraf Visit Marks Turning Point in US Ties," *The Financial Times*, 12 February 2002.

21 Peter Bergen, *Holy War, Inc.: Inside the Secret World of Osama bin Laden* (New York: The Free Press, 2001), p. 208; "Over a Dozen Harakat Members Missing

Since US Attacks," *The News* (Pakistan), 26 August 1998; "Pakistani Intelligence Had Ties to Al Qaeda, U.S. Officials Say," *The New York Times*, 29 October 2001; and "Pak Cries Foul Over US Revenge Strike," *The Indian Express*, 22 August 1998.

22 Cited in *The News* (Pakistan), 7 March 1999.

23 The LeT is thought to have provided several hundred Afghan-trained militants to fight alongside the Taliban and Al Qaeda following the launch of U.S. military operations in October 2001.

24 Author interview, Srinagar, February 2001. See also Bergen, *Holy War, Inc.*, pp. 216–217.

25 Indian sources maintain that over three quarters of HuM's membership has now defected to JeM and that funding provided by bin Laden is the principal cause of this cross-group movement. See Praveen Swami, "The Tanzeems and their Leaders," *Frontline*, Vol. 17, No. 7 (August–September 2000).

26 "New Delhi Lays Blame," *The Washington Post*, 29 December 2001; "Kashmir Suicide Bombing Group Linked to Osama bin Laden: India," *Agence France Presse*, 2 October 2001; and "Delhi Tracks Al Qaida, Jaish Links," *Gulf News* (Dubai), 11 October 2001.

27 Author interviews, New Delhi, Jammu City and Srinagar, February 2001.

28 It is thought that the bombings were carried out by Father Rohman al-Ghozi. Following his arrest on 16 January 2002, Ghozi (who also uses the alias "Freedom Fighter") admitted to links with both MILF's SOG and Al Qaeda.

29 The bulk of the MILF activities have tended to take the form of traditional guerilla warfare directed against the Philippine Armed Forces (AFP). The group's leadership, under the central direction of Hashim Salamat, has also exhibited a willingness to enter into periodic peace-talks with Manila and has repeatedly portrayed itself as a tolerant entity that is ready to co-exist with members of other religious faiths. As noted in the text, however, there do appear to be renegade elements within the MILF that favour more hard-line tactics and who are believed to "moonlight" between the Front and more extreme groups. According to the AFP, these so-called "lost commands" retain residual tactical alliances both with prominent ASG members and regional Islamists, providing instruction and operational assistance in everything from random terrorist bombings to fully-fledged sabotage and demolition techniques. The August 2000 bombing of the Philippine embassy in Jakarta, for instance, has been interpreted as an Indonesian "thank you" note to the MILF for training provided in its Tawi-Tawi camp. Philippine officials also assert that MILF has received financial support from bin Laden and that elements within the Front are actively working in conjunction with Al Qaeda. Indeed one of the key members of the alleged Jemiah Islamiah (JI) terror plot in Singapore (see section on Malaysia) was a foreigner known as "Mike," whom intelligence sources now believe is a senior bomb-maker and trainer

in MILF. Mike allegedly arrived in Singapore in October 2001 to procure 17 tons of ammonium nitrate for the attacks and help local JI cells conduct surveillance of targets. Despite these various charges, it remains unclear whether these links are the product of sanctioned directives from the Front's central leadership or merely reflect individual contacts that have been incorporated into the group structure on an ad-hoc basis. Author interview, Hawaii, February 2002.

30 Mark Turner, "Terrorism and Secession in the Southern Philippines: The Rise of the Abu Sayyaf," *Contemporary Southeast Asia*, Vol. 17, No. 1 (June 1995), p. 15; Concepcion Clamor, "Terrorism in the Philippines," paper presented before the Council for Security Cooperation in the Asia-Pacific's (CSCAP) Working Group on Transnational Crime (WGTNC), Manila, May 1998, p. 5; "Validation of the Existence of the ASG," internal document prepared for the Philippine National Intelligence Coordinating Agency (NICA), 14 February 1997; and "Separatist Rebellion in the southern Philippines," *IISS Strategic Comments*, Vol. 6, No. 4 (May 2000), p. 2.

31 Author interview, Manila, June 1998. See also Peter Chalk, "The Abu Sayyaf Group and Osama Bin Laden: An Unholy Alliance," *Jane's Intelligence Review Pointer* (December 1998); John Cooley, *Unholy Wars: Afghanistan, America and International Terrorism* (London: Pluto Press, 2000), pp. 255–256; "Validation of the Existence of the ASG," p. 3; and "Master of Terror," *The Courier-Mail* (Australia), 29 August 1998. Khalifa was arrested for illegally trying to enter the United States. He was extradited to Jordan to face terrorism charges but was acquitted and has since remained in Saudi Arabia.

32 See, for instance, Turner, "Terrorism and Secession in the Southern Philippines," p. 8; "Disparate Pieces of Terrorist Puzzle Fit Together," *The Washington Post*, 23 September 2001; "Muslim Militants Threaten Ramos Vision of Summit Glory," *The Australian*, 13 January 1996; and "The Man Who Wasn't There," *Time*, 20 February 1995.

33 Author interview, Manila, June 1998. See also Chalk, "The Abu Sayyaf Group and Osama Bin Laden;" "US Enemy No. 1 Sighted in Mindanao," *The Philippine Daily Inquirer*, 23 August 1998; "RP Tightens Security vs. Extremists," *The Manila Times*, 25 August 1998; and "Master of Terror," *The Courier-Mail*, 29 August 1998.

34 Two main ASG factions currently exist: a Basilan group, which is led by Commander Robot and probably constitutes no more than 80 operatives; and a far more prominent Sulu group, which is led by Khaddafi Janjalini (the brother of Abdurajak) and numbers between 300 and 500 cadres. Author interview, Manila, February 2002.

35 Cooley, *Unholy Wars*, p. 256; "A Hostage Crisis Confronts Estrada," *The Economist*, 5 June 2000; "Philippine Military Begins Assault on Muslim Rebels," *CNN Interactive World Wide News*, 22 April 2000; "Philippine Forces Hit Rebel Stronghold," *The Washington Post*, 24 April 2000; "Gunmen Take Foreigners

Hostage in Malaysia," *The Washington Post*, 25 April 2000; and "Military Finds 2 Beheaded by Philippine Rebels," *The Washington Post*, 7 May 2000.

36 In December 2001, Philippine authorities arrested three suspected affiliates of bin Laden in Mindanao and Manila, accusing them of producing false passports and travel documents to aid the exodus of Al Qaeda members from Afghanistan. "Three More Foreign Terrorists Arrested," *The Philippine Star*, 7 January 2002.

37 See, for instance, "Attack Altering Politics Across Southeast Asia," *The Washington Post*, 11 October 2001; and "Disparate Pieces of Terrorist Puzzle Fit Together," *The Washington Post*, 23 September 2001.

38 "Grumblings Surface During 'Balikatan'," *The Philippine Daily Inquirer*, 3 February 2002; "Are We Losing Our Sovereignty (2)?" *The Philippine Daily Inquirer*, 3 February 2002; "Game Na?" *The Philippine Daily Inquirer*, 4 February 2002.

39 Good overviews of Indonesia's recent internal problems can be found in Paul Dibb, "Indonesia: The Key to South-East Asia's Security," *International Affairs*, Vol. 77, No. 4 (2001); Donald Emerson, "Will Indonesia Survive?" *Foreign Affairs*, Vol. 79, No. 3 (May/June 2000); Kerry Collison, "Indonesia: Disintegration of the Last Great Colonial Power?" *Defense and Foreign Affairs Strategic Policy*, Vol. XXVIII, No. 10 (2000); and "Indonesia is in Danger of Coming Apart," *The Australian*, 12 August 2000.

40 It should be noted that the Islamic Defenders Forces/Laskar Pembela Islam (LPI), which acts as the armed wing of the Islam Defenders Front (FPI), has also come under scrutiny for having links with Al Qaeda. However, the evidence in this case is spurious to say the least, consisting mainly of heresy and speculation, much of it drawing off LPI comments to "sweep" all American influence out of Indonesia. Certainly the group has not exhibited the same sort of threat potential as LJ. The bulk of its members are armed only with long sticks (which are generally never used) and the main focus of their activities appears to be directed at disrupting the operations of Jakarta-based businesses that are considered to be *haram* (unclean), such as bars, massage parlours, karaoke lounges and gambling dens. In addition to the LPI, other ad-hoc organizations also exist, such as the Indonesian Mujahideen Council, although, again, they do not appear (at least yet) to have a significant independent operational potential.

41 Greg Fealy, "Inside the Laskar Jihad," *Inside Indonesia*, available at http://www.insideindonesia.org/edit65/fealy.htm, January–March 2001. See also "Who are the Laskar Jihad?" *BBC Interactive News*, 20 June 2000; "Attack Altering Politics Across Southeast Asia," *The Washington Post*, 11 October 2001; "Java's Angry Young Muslims," *The Economist*, 20 October 2001; "Holy War in the Spice Islands," *The Economist*, 17 March 2001; and "The Black Bats Strike Back," *The Economist*, 11 August 2001.

42 According to Thalib: "The hostility by the Jews and the Christians toward Islam began at the time Allah's prophet was sent. This condition continues until the

end of this age, even now since the group (Jews and Christians) is led by the USA, the winner of the Cold War. This war was always covered up by all kinds of camouflage to make it look as if it were not a religious war. The truth of the fact is, it is a war against Islam and all Muslims." Jafar Thalib, quoted in "Indonesia: Jihad in Indonesia," *International Christian Concern*, available at http:// www.persecution.org/concern/2001/02.

43 *Ibid.*

44 Fealy, "Inside the Laskar Jihad;" "Java's Angry Young Muslims," *The Economist*, 20 October 2001.

45 Jafar Thalib, cited in "Indonesian Extremist Backs Terror," *Los Angeles Times*, 23 September 2001.

46 Authorities were first alerted to the possible existence of an international camp in Sulawesi after Spanish police arrested an Indonesian citizen, Parlindungan Siregar, who was allegedly in charge of organizing the training for foreigners at the Poso facility. According to the Spanish daily *El Pais*, some 3,000 fighters of various nationalities have already undergone insurgent instruction in Indonesia. Intelligence sources in Jakarta reject that an international facility exists in Sulawesi—insisting that it is merely a Muslim refugee camp. They do concede, however, that LJ militants did go to Poso in an attempt to indoctrinate "residents" with a fundamentalist, anti-Western view of Islam. Author interview, Hawaii, February 2002. See also "Spain Holds 8 Linked to Sept. 11 Plot," *The Washington Post*, 19 November 2001; and Paul Wolfowitz, "Al Qaeda Feared to Be Lurking in Indonesia," *The Washington Post*, 11 January 2002.

47 "Qaeda Moving Into Indonesia, Officials Fear," *The New York Times*, 22 January 2002; "Indonesia Confirms al-Qaeda Presence," *BBC Interactive News*, 12 December 2001; Wolfowitz, "Al Qaeda Feared to be Lurking in Indonesia;" "Indonesia Base for al-Qaeda," *The Daily Telegraph* (Australia), 12 January 2002; "Al Qaeda's Southeast Asian Reach; Group Operating in 4 Nations Believed Tied to Sept. 11 Hijackers," *The Washington Post*, 3 February 2002; and "Osama bin Laden and Indonesia," *Laksamana Foundation*, available at http:// www.laksamana.net/vnews.cfm?news_id=175.

48 For the past two years, Indonesia has no internal subversion law that can be used to make pre-emptive arrests of suspected terrorists and individuals deemed to pose a potential threat to national security (largely due to military excesses in Aceh, East Timor and Irian Jaya under Suharto). Intelligence officials, however, confirm that provision for such statutory legislation is once again being actively considered. Author interview, Hawaii, February 2002.

49 Wolfowitz, "Al Qaeda Feared to be Lurking in Indonesia."

50 Prior to the September 11 attacks against the United States, the clearest indication of a Malaysian connection to the activities of regional extremists was the example

of the Pattani United Liberation Organization (PULO) and the smaller New PULO—two Islamic separatist groups that were active in southern Thailand for much of the 1990s. Both groups are known to have retained operational and logistical bases in the northern Malaysian state of Kelantan, allegedly supplied with the active sanction of the province's ruling hard-line Parti Islam Se-Malaysia (PAS). This assistance is widely acknowledged as one of the main factors that allowed the Pattani insurgency to continue for so long. The Thai government also believes it was critical in allowing the perpetration of several high-profile civilian attacks, including a string of 33 bombings and assassinations in late 1997 that targeted state officials, law enforcement personnel, school teachers and other perceived symbols of Buddhist repression. Intelligence sources in Bangkok firmly believe that assaults such as these could not have taken place in the absence of sustained external Malaysian support. For further details, see Peter Chalk, "The Islamic Factor in Southern Thailand, Mindanao and Aceh," *Studies in Conflict and Terrorism*, Vol. 24 (2001), pp. 241–269; "Minister: 'Southern Separatists Receive Foreign Training,'" *The Nation* (Thailand), 6 January 1995; "Malaysia Denies Thai Terrorist Claims," *The Australian*, 6 January 1998; and "Malaysia 'Not Training Ground for Thai Rebels'," *The Straits Times* (Singapore), 5 January 1998. Good overviews of Malay-Muslim separatism in southern Thailand can be found in Omar Farouk, "The Historical and Transnational Dimensions of Malay-Muslim Separatism in Southern Thailand," in Lim Joo Jock and S. Vani (eds.), *Armed Separatism in Southeast Asia* (Singapore: ISEAS, 1984); Muthiah Alagappa, *The National Security of Developing States: Lessons from Thailand* (MA: Acorn House, 1987); R. J. May, "The Religious Factor in Three Minority Movements," *Contemporary Southeast Asia*, Vol. 13, No. 4 (1992), pp. 403–405; and David Brown, *State and Ethnic Politics in Southeast Asia* (London: Routledge, 1994), pp. 16–70.

51 Author interviews, Canberra, November 1999. See also "Worse to Come," *The Far Eastern Economic Review*, 29 July 1999; and "Malaysia Denies Supporting Separatists in Indonesia," *CNN Interactive World Wide News*, 20 July 1999.

52 "Osama bin Laden and Indonesia," *Laksamana Foundation*, available at http://www.laksamana.net/vnews.cfm?/news_id=175; "Al Qaeda's Southeast Asian Reach; Group Operating in 4 Nations Believed Tied to Sept. 11 Hijackers," *The Washington Post*, 3 February 2002.

53 Peter Chalk, *Grey-Area Phenomena in Southeast Asia: Piracy, Drug Trafficking and Political Terrorism* (Canberra: Strategic and Defence Studies Centre, 1997), p. 74; "13 Suspected of Sept. 11 Links," *The Washington Post*, 5 January 2002.

54 "Suspected al-Qaeda Agent Held; Saudi Arrested," *The Washington Post*, 5 November 2001; "Suspect Held in Al-Qaeda Terror Attacks," *The Associated Press*, 5 November 2001; "Malaysian Mujahideen Group Has Links with Al Qaeda," *Deutsche Presse-Agentur*, 5 January 2002; "Militants Will Be Hunted Down, Says Mahathir," *The Straits Times* (Singapore), 7 January 2002.

55 "Singapore Arrests Suspected Militants," *The Washington Post*, 6 January 2002; "Qaeda Moving Into Indonesia, Officials Fear," *The New York Times*, 23 January 2002; "Exclusive: Terror Plot on US Carrier Foiled," *Associated Press*, 28 December 2001; "Singapore Accuses Islamists of Bomb Plan," *The New York Times*, 7 January 2002; "Singapore Terror Group Had Plan to Bomb US Warships," *The South China Morning Post*, 12 January 2002; "A Tale with Many Beginnings," *The Straits Times* (Singapore), 11 January 2002; and "Suspects in Singapore are Linked to Al Qaeda and Plans for Anti-U.S. Attacks," *The New York Times*, 12 January 2002. The plot, which allegedly was to have been carried out by a hitherto unknown group calling itself Jemiah Islamiah, first came to light following the seizure of a videotape and notes detailing reconnaissance of potential targets in Singapore from an Al Qaeda leader's house in Afghanistan.

56 All four groups were allegedly involved in the Singapore plot. According to Philippine intelligence, they operate in much the same way as the Al Qaeda operational cells that carried out the U.S. African embassy bombings in 1998 and the suicide attacks on the World Trade Centre and Pentagon on September 11. Author interview, Hawaii, February 2002.

57 "Eye of the Storm," *Time*, 11 February 2002; "A Terror Network Unraveled in Singapore," *International Herald Tribune*, 23 January 2002; "Al Qaeda's Southeast Asian Reach; Group Operating in 4 Nations Believed Tied to Sept. 11 Hijackers," *The Washington Post*, 3 February 2002; "S.E. Asian Terror Group Tracked," *The Associated Press*, 10 February 2002; "Suspect Calls Malaysia a Staging Area for Terror Attacks," *The New York Times*, 31 January 2002. KMM is jointly led by two Indonesian clerics, Abubakar Ba'aysir and Riduan "Hambali" Isamuddin, and has established branches in all nine states of Peninsular Malaysia. The group advocates a radical new vision of Islam and is alleged to have facilitated numerous meetings for Al Qaeda operatives and associated businessmen, traders and bankers in exchange for liberal injections of financial assistance. Mahathir has also accused the group of seeking the violent overthrow of the Kuala Lumpur government.

58 See, for instance, "Mahathir's September Bonus," *The Economist*, 1 December 2001.

59 "13 Suspected of Sept. 11 Links," *The Washington Post*, 5 January 2002; "50 Malaysians 'Linked to Al-Qaeda'," *BBC News* (Internet version), 12 January 2002. On 10 January, Mahathir claimed that intelligence authorities had identified "about 50 Malaysians with links to al-Qaeda."

60 In the informal *hawala* or "trust" system no money is ever wired, nor are the names, accounts or records of senders/recipients kept. With commissions of only 1–2 percent (compared to average bank transfer fees that can run to as high as 15 percent), it is also the transfer medium of choice throughout most of Asia. In Southeast Asia, the system is used extensively in the Philippines (a product of the large number of overseas Filipino workers), Singapore and Malaysia. Author interview, Hawaii, February 2002. See also "Money Transfer Systems, Hawala

Style," *CBC News Online*, 13 November 2001; "Muslim World Moves Money Without Trace," *The Washington Post*, 10 November 2001; and "Cheap and Trusted," *The Economist*, 24 November 2002.

61 "Southeast Asia Alliance to Fight Terrorism," *Honolulu Advertiser*, 22 February 2002.

62 See, for instance, Mohamed Jawar Hassan, "Terrorism: Southeast Asia's Response," *PacNet*, 1 January 2002; "ASEAN Way Prevails in Tea Party's Polite Talk," *The Australian*, 30 July 1998; "Minutes of the Calamity Club," *The Economist*, 29 July 2000; "Ties That Bind," *The Far Eastern Economic Review*, 10 August 2000; and "Putting Regionalism in its Place," *The South China Morning Post*, 8 February 2002.

6

TERRORIST TRENDS AND PATTERNS IN THE ASIA-PACIFIC REGION

Rohan Gunaratna[1]

Throughout the 1990s, the centre of gravity of terrorism shifted from the Middle East (primarily, Lebanon and Syria) to the Asia-Pacific.[2] Within the latter region, terrorist elements diffused into parts of Central Asia (Tajikistan, Afghanistan), South Asia (Kashmir, Pakistan) and Southeast Asia (Philippines and Indonesia), increasing the potential for terrorist attacks both within and outside the region. In the early twenty-first century, the Asia-Pacific region is both an active and tacit host to a rich array of foreign and indigenous groups—Islamist Sunni (such as Al Qaeda) and Shiite (Hezbollah) groups as well as ideological and ethno-nationalist groups. This paper seeks to survey terrorist and guerilla trends and patterns in the Asia-Pacific.

The Asia-Pacific security environment has witnessed a range of new threats, technologies, and actors over the course of the past decade. While some Cold War threats continued, new threats throughout the 1990s have changed the security outlook of the Asia-Pacific. Events in the region contributed to international insecurity by setting many precedents. At the threshold of the twenty-first century, terrorist groups that did not receive significant attention by the terrorism research community of the West emerged as main players on the international stage: a religious cult, Aum Shinrikyo, employed sarin nerve gas against Japanese citizens in 1994 and 1995; an ethno-nationalist group, the Liberation Tigers of Tamil Eelam (LTTE)—based in the U.S.—waged cyber-warfare against Sri Lankan diplomatic missions in 1996; and an Afghan-based transnational Islamist group, Al Qaeda, conducted long-range suicide operations against U.S. targets in East Africa in 1998.[3] These unanticipated developments demonstrated a qualitative shift in the post-Cold War threat environment in the Asia-Pacific.

Nonetheless, the international community did little to control and contain these transnational groups, whether they were Islamist or ethno-nationalist. Except for post-Soko Asahara Aum pledging to abandon violence and follow a peaceful path to reach its goals, both Al Qaeda—a group with a presence in at least 94 countries—and the LTTE—a group with a presence in 54 countries—continued to function effectively. Although Al Qaeda has existed since March 1988,[4] the U.S. government started to fight Al Qaeda seriously only after the group conducted coordinated simultaneous airborne attacks against America's most outstanding targets in 2001. With the importance of Asia receding and the U.S. downsizing its human intelligence operations at the end of the Cold War, America lacked the high-quality intelligence as well as the support of pivotal states such as Pakistan to aggressively pursue Al Qaeda and its associated groups.

To the Afghan *mujahideen*, conquerors of the Soviet Red Army by 1989, America's policy of isolationism and disengagement after Mogadishu in 1993 made her appear weak as a global power. Taking advantage of its global reach, Al Qaeda survived a U.S. cruise missile attack in response to the East Africa bombings and launched a maritime attack against the USS *Cole* in October 2000. Subsequently, in September 2001, the Al Qaeda leadership based in Afghanistan used two launching pads—Hamburg, Germany and Kuala Lumpur, Malaysia—to strike the continental U.S. The loss of 3,000 lives provided the U.S. with the international mandate to intervene in Afghanistan and the conditions to construct a global coalition to fight the international alliance of Al Qaeda—the World Islamic Front for Jihad Against the Jews and the Crusaders. Nonetheless, exploiting the loopholes of the international system, gaps in international law enforcement cooperation, and weaknesses of the international intelligence community, post-Taliban Al Qaeda has struck or attempted to strike targets in the U.S., Europe, Balkans, Middle East, and in Asia.

With the post-September 11 disruption of the Al Qaeda network in North America and Western Europe, the group is stepping up operations in the Asia-Pacific, especially in Southeast Asia, America's second front against terrorism. As long as the public is alert and there is unprecedented international security, intelligence and law enforcement cooperation, it would be difficult for Al Qaeda to mount an operation on the scale of 9-11 that requires long-term planning and preparation. However, Al Qaeda and its associate groups can be expected to mount medium to small-scale operations worldwide until the international community develops, and more importantly, sustains, a multi-pronged, multidimensional, multi-agency and a multinational response. If the fight against the contemporary wave of terrorism is to succeed, a far-reaching approach against Islamism, Islamist terrorism, and terrorism of all typologies is essential. A norm must be set and an ethic must be built to abhor terrorism as a tool—as a means of political expression, protest, and seeking political power.

The Context

With the collapse of the Soviet Empire, the sweeping changes that we witnessed throughout the 1990s altered the behaviour of both state and non-state actors. The post-Cold War environment witnessed a steadfast remission of support by patron states for client groups. Previously, the patron-client relationship of employing terrorist and guerilla groups as state proxies limited conflict escalation from a Cold to a Hot War. In contrast, the post-Cold War terrorist groups are unrestrained both in their choice of weapons and target selection. With the termination of support from superpowers and their satellite states, only the imaginative and creative groups have survived the transition. They were groups that generated funds through organized crime: legal (trade, investments), quasi-legal and illegal (financial fraud; trafficking narcotics, humans; and CD, video piracy) businesses. Without a patron state, but with resources, the conduct of contemporary groups, especially extra-territorial groups, remains a law unto themselves. Although the nature, thinking, and conduct of terrorist groups were all transformed by the end of the Cold War, state intelligence, security and law enforcement authorities were slow to adapt to the new environment. Governed by national self-interest, the approach of states to the terrorist threat remained unchanged from the Cold War to the post-Cold War period. The frequency and magnitude of 9-11 has forced international security, intelligence and law enforcement authorities to cooperate and coordinate their activities to meet the existing and emerging threat. In spite of the heightened terrorist threat, some states in the Asia-Pacific, driven by narrow self-interest, are still reluctant to develop counter-measures and offensive action.

Since the beginning of contemporary terrorism in the Middle East in 1969, the world has witnessed two generations of terrorist groups. The second-generation terrorist groups of the post-Cold War environment differ from the first-generation groups of the Cold War. On the one hand, the geographic reach and strategic depth of contemporary groups have increased due to the communications revolution and international travel. As a result, rag-tag terrorist groups, including those groups in the Asia-Pacific, have been transformed into sophisticated entities. Moreover, proliferation of information technologies—satellite TV, fax, Internet, mobile phone—and unprecedented migration enhanced terrorist command, control, communication and information (C^3I) operations with their members and supporters domestically and worldwide. The quality of the threat also changed due to the privatization of security: the availability of both security personnel for hire and easy access to the weapons market. With the ending of U.S.- and Soviet-supported proxy wars in Asia, Africa, the Middle East and Latin America, the international arms market became saturated. With the economic decline in the former Soviet bloc countries, financial rather than security considerations determined the sale of weapons. As a result, some Asia-Pacific terrorist groups gained access to automatic weapons (AK-47, T-56, G-3, M-16, M-203), including stand-off weapons (RPG, LAW, SAM, TOW, mortars, artillery) and explosives (RDX, TNT), at competitive prices. Similarly, access to dual technologies—GPS, satellite imagery, land sat, radar, secure communication, computers, close-circuit scuba, sea scooters, speed boats, micro-lights—has empowered terrorist groups to challenge previously formidable land and naval forces. Accessibility to sophisticated weapons and dual technologies transformed violent political conflicts to low-intensity conflicts, and low-intensity conflicts to high-intensity conflicts.[5] The potential for escalation of terrorist and guerilla conflicts is high.[6]

Although the overall number of terrorist incidents has declined, both the number of conflicts and the intensity of most conflicts have increased. Today, guerilla and terrorist groups seek to acquire more sophisticated conventional and unconventional weapons and invest more in the planning and preparation phases, in order to inflict greater damage to infrastructure and to kill more people. In Asia, too, the number of terrorist operations has decreased, but terrorist lethality has increased due to easier access to weapons and better training. In Asia, terrorist groups have expressed an interest to acquire and use chemical, biological, radiological and nuclear (CBRN) material or develop expertise in production, possibly through criminal organizations operating in the former U.S.S.R. For instance, in June 1990, the LTTE staged a chlorine gas attack and Al Qaeda attempted to acquire, develop and use CBRN material from 1993. The terrorist acquisition of strategic material is hence the biggest threat facing states today. Moreover, most terrorist groups are becoming undeterred by the threat of punishment. By investing in the training of suicide terrorists, they defy the criminal justice and prison system. In addition, more than ever before, ideological indoctrination ensures that terrorists of all typologies are willing to kill and die. Suicide terrorism is emerging as one of the most popular tactics with Asian groups, with the LTTE especially conducting two-thirds of all suicide attacks. Terrorist groups like Al Qaeda, on the other hand, are interested in quality targeting. They seek, first, to conduct fewer attacks but with great precision and accuracy with the intention of killing and injuring more people, and second, to inspire and instigate its associate and affiliate groups to follow "their way." Integration of the suicide dimension to a CBRN attack can ease, if not overcome, problems of delivery.

Most major Asia-Pacific terrorist groups have assumed a multidimensional character. To advance their political aims and objectives, they simultaneously engage in activities other than terrorism such as guerilla warfare, political assassination, sabotage, ethnic cleansing, and electoral politics. By penetrating diaspora and migrant communities in the West, for instance, Asia-Pacific terrorist groups have developed state-of-the-art international support infrastructures outside the region for disseminating propaganda, raising funds, training, procuring weapons, and shipping. Using their support networks in Africa, the Middle East, Balkans, Caucuses, Western Europe and North America, some groups have conducted long-range and deep-penetration terrorist operational and support activities. Furthermore, access to global communications has enabled Asian ideological, secular and religious organizations spouting virulent ideologies to network with transnational constituencies as well as organizations with compatible aims and objectives. Like governments, contemporary terrorist groups also cooperate. In addition to learning from one another's operational efforts, successes and failures, some terrorist groups have developed closer cooperation at political, economic and military levels to share technology, personnel and intelligence.[7]

Of the three types of groups—ideological, ethno-nationalist and religious—the Islamist category poses the biggest challenge today and in the foreseeable future. Tens of thousands of Afghan-trained *mujahideen*, driven by the ideals of holy war (*jihad*), are fighting or have fought in Kashmir, Afghanistan, Tajikistan, Chechnya, Philippines, Bosnia, Kosovo, Algeria, Egypt, and southern Lebanon, etc. Some of these volunteers or their supporters—ranging from Saudi Arabia, Sudan, Albania, Pakistan, and Bangladesh—perceiving the West as evil, have either destroyed or attempted to destroy Western targets. The core of the "free-floating" conglomerate of terrorists are Asian, Middle Eastern, Caucasian, Balkan, African, American and European Muslims who participated in the semi-covert multinational and anti-Soviet Afghan campaign in the 1980s. Under the leadership of Dr Abdullah Azzam, the mentor of Osama bin Laden, the Maktab-il-Khidamat (Afghan Service Bureau) evolved as Al Qaeda Al Sulbha in early 1988. Although Al Qaeda is a small group of only 3,000 members dedicated to fighting the West, Al Qaeda and the Afghan-based Taliban regime trained over 110,000 Muslims to provide support to disparate groups active from the Philippines to Algeria, all aiming to establish Islamic states. As terrorist groups continue to forge ties and learn from one another, it is axiomatic that reducing the threat of terrorism requires us to develop a better understanding of all the groups that use political violence in the region.

The Conflict Landscape

Geographically, the Asia-Pacific extends from Hawaii to Armenia and occupies 29.6 percent of the world's land area. But, excluding Asiatic Russia, 61 percent or over 3.5 billion of the world's total population live in the Asia-Pacific.[8] The overwhelming characteristic of the Asia-Pacific region is its vulnerability to armed conflict. At the turn of the millennium, of the 16 high-intensity conflicts in the world, six were in the Asia-Pacific region: Assam (India), Bihar (India), Kashmir, Sri Lanka, Afghanistan and Myanmar.[9] Of the 23 high-intensity conflicts in 2001, eight were in the Asia-Pacific: Afghanistan, Sri Lanka, Kashmir, Aceh (Indonesia) and Maluku (Indonesia), Shiites-Sunni (Pakistan), Sindh (Pakistan) and the Philippines.[10] While the number of low-intensity conflicts increased from 17 to 29, violent political conflicts increased from 35 to 58 between 1998 and 2001.[11]

All the high-intensity conflicts are internal conflicts, except the international dispute between India and Pakistan over Kashmir and the conflict in Afghanistan. In response to 9-11, U.S., Allied and Coalition intervention in Afghanistan in October 2001 is likely to lead to a protracted conflict. Operating out of the 1,500-mile Pakistan–Afghanistan border, Al

Qaeda and Taliban are laying the groundwork for waging a sustained campaign to disrupt the restoration of the civil administration in Afghanistan and to oust President Musharraf from office in Pakistan. Two Al Qaeda associate groups—Harakat-ul-Mujahideen and Jaish-e-Muhammad—have intensified attacks both in Kashmir and elsewhere in India. This led to increasing India–Pakistan border tensions, in turn compelling Pakistan to redeploy its troops from the Afghan to the Indian border. This enabled Al Qaeda to re-establish lines of communications with Pakistani elements, along which fresh recruits and supplies have flowed. Meanwhile, despite a ceasefire in Sri Lanka since January 2002, the LTTE is building its strength to return to war with the Sri Lankan state. In South Asia, two principal state sponsors—India and Pakistan—provide sanctuary, weapons and training to some of the groups to target inimical states. All high-intensity conflicts in the Asia-Pacific region are in South Asia, excluding Indonesia and the Philippines. The on-going high-intensity conflicts in the Asia-Pacific have killed about two million combatants and non-combatants. Of the fatalities, 1.5 million were in Afghanistan, where *mujahideen* groups were provided with an abundance of weapons, training and finance by an anti-Soviet multinational coalition.[12]

Although only six countries in the Asia-Pacific region currently experience high-intensity conflict, the potential for low-intensity as well as for violent political conflict to escalate is high. Of the 17 low-intensity conflicts in the Asia-Pacific at the turn of the millennium, 11 were located in South Asia and the rest in Southeast Asia and the Far East. Of the 28 low-intensity conflicts located in the Asia-Pacific in 2001–2, 14 are located in South Asia, three in Central Asia and 10 in Southeast Asia. In South Asia, all but two low-intensity conflicts were in the Indian states of Andhara, Bihar, Assam, Haryana, Madhya Pradesh, Maharashtra, Nagaland, Punjab, Tripura, Uttar Pradesh, West Bengal and in the Siachen glacier in Kashmir. The other low-intensity South Asian conflicts were in Pakistan (intertribal in the Northwest Frontier Province), Nepal (Maoists) Bangladesh (communists in Kushtia). In Central Asia, the three conflicts are in Kyrgyzstan (Islamists in the Sokh enclave), Uzbekistan (Islamic Movement of Uzbekistan and the Hezb-ut-Tehrir) and Tajikistan (Kyurgan-Tyube, warlords). The low-intensity Southeast Asian conflicts are in the Philippines, Indonesia and Myanmar. In the Philippines, security forces clashed with the Abu Sayyaf Group in Mindanao and the New People's Army in Luzon. In Indonesia, clashes were between Nadhnat-ul Ulema and Golkar in Java, Christians and Muslims in Sulawesi,

Dayaks and Madurese in West Kalimantan, and Organasasi Papua Merdeka (OPM: Free Papua Movement) and the security forces. With the creation of East Timor, the first new state of the twenty-first century, the violence ended in early 2002. Both the Bougainville Revolutionary Army in Indonesia and the Patani United Liberation Organization in Thailand ceased violence by 2001. In addition to Shan and Karen guerillas in the north and in Taninthayi in Myanmar, Karen guerillas on the Thai border and Wa guerillas on the PRC border clashed.

Violent political conflicts could be active at a very low level or be dormant, but they retain the potential to graduate to the level of a low-intensity conflict. Of the 35 violent political conflicts at the turn of the millennium, 17 conflicts were located in South Asia and the rest in Southeast Asia, Northeast Asia and Oceania. Of the 58 violent political conflicts active in 2002, 36 were in South Asia, 13 in Southeast Asia, 6 in Northeast Asia, two in Oceania and one in Central Asia. South Asia's violent political conflicts occurred in India in Andhara Pradesh (People's War Group in Telengana), Aunachal Pradesh (Nationalist Socialist Council of Nagalim), Assam (Bodos versus Santhal), Assam (Karbi National Volunteers versus United People's Democratic Solidarity), Gujarat (Hindus versus Christians), Jharkhand (Maoist Communist Centre), Karanataka (People's War Group, Veerappan Gang) Maharasthra (People's War Group), Manipur (Pathei versus Waife), Manipur (Kuki versus Zomi), Meghalaya (Garo National Front), Mizoram (Reang), Orissa (Hindus versus Christians), Rajasthan (Brahmin versus Dalits), Siliguri Darjeeling Hill (Gurkha National Liberation Front), Tamil Nadu (Tamil National Liberation Army), Uttaranchal (gang warfare), Uttar Pradesh (Uttarkhand), Uttar Pradesh (Jaish-e-Muhammad), and North Bengal (Kamatapur Liberation Organization, United Liberation Front of Assam); in Pakistan, Baluchistan (intertribal), Khaipur (intertribal), Punjab (Kalabagh Dam), South Waziristan (intertribal) and Sukkur (intertribal); in Bangladesh, Shanthi Bahini in the Chittagong Hill tracts (Islamic Student Front (Chhatra Shibir), Jamaat-e-Islami Bangladesh National Party versus Awami League and Rohingiyas); and in Bhutan (Ngalong). Southeast Asia's violent political conflicts in Myanmar are in Arakan (Muslims versus Buddhists), Upper Sagaing (United Liberation of Assam, Nationalist Socialist Council of Nagalim), and Shin State (Chin National Force); in the Philippines, Cordillera (indigenous people); in Malaysia, Kedah (Muslims versus Indians); and in Indonesia, Bali (Kuta), Sumatra (Riau) and Sumba (Loli versus

Wewera); in Cambodia (Cambodian Freedom Fighters, Khmer Rouge); in Laos, Hmong (Chao Fa); in Vietnam, Central Highlands (United Front for the Liberation of the Oppressed Races); and in Thailand, Yala (Muslim separatists). In Northeast Asia, in the PRC, there is political violence in Tibet (Khampas) and Xinjiang (Uighurs). In more than one Chinese state, there are collective protests, gang warfare and conflicts with the Falun Gong. In Central Asia, the only violent political conflict is in the Djambul region between the Islamists and the security forces.

As opposed to internal conflicts, the worldwide threat of international conflict has receded in the 1990s.[13] Nonetheless, the interstate disputes in the Asia-Pacific remain unresolved. The two violent interstate political conflicts are between India and Pakistan over Kashmir and the Siachen glacier, the highest battlefield in the world, and between the two Koreas. There is potential for conflict between PRC and Taiwan. Next to Sub-Saharan Africa, the Asia-Pacific is the region most affected by conflict. In the mid-term, the Asia-Pacific region is more likely to be affected by both internal and international armed conflict.

South Asia

The scale of conflict in South Asia is the largest, followed by Southeast Asia and then Northeast Asia. As the most culturally diverse and the most densely-populated sub-region, South Asia is prone to conflict. At the end of the twentieth century, South Asia ranked among the most insecure geographic regions of the world.[14] Nonetheless, it is the fastest growing region in the world. In 1995–1996 alone, more U.S. companies have invested in India than in any period since 1947. Nonetheless, India is facing multiple conflicts—primarily, separatist violence in the northeast and in the north. However, the very size and diversity of India is likely to hold the world's largest democracy together. Except for the Kashmir issue, India has managed its conflict well. President Clinton's visit to India in early 2000, the first visit by a U.S. president in 22 years, demonstrated that the sub-region had been an internationally neglected geographic area. The region's importance grew only after U.S. intervention in Afghanistan in October 2001. Today, Israel and the U.S. are working closely with India in the global fight against terrorism.

India's arch-foe, Pakistan, has remained a safe haven for many Afghan veterans at the end of the anti-Soviet Afghan campaign. Following its status as a frontline state in the fight against the Soviets, the U.S. abandoned Pakistan after the defeat of the Soviet military in Afghanistan and the break-up of the Soviet Empire. As a result, the Islamist influence grew rapidly in Pakistan and Islamist terrorists used the country as a centre for ideological training.[15] In addition, some Arab countries refused to take the *mujahideen* back, others imprisoned them and many *mujahideen* retreated to Kashmir. As a result, in Kashmir, incomplete decolonization and international neglect has generated sustained violence since 1989. With the inflow of Afghan Arabs, moreover, the scale of violence increased. Al Qaeda's doctrine of kidnapping and murdering Western nationals, suicide attacks, and attacking the centre gradually influenced the Kashmiri groups. Of six Western hostages kidnapped in July 1995, only one American hostage escaped. As a result, the group responsible, Harakat-ul-Ansar (HUA, also known as Al Faran), was designated a foreign terrorist organization by the U.S. government. By 1999, Laskar-e-Tayyeba (LeT) had emerged as the most powerful Kashmiri group. Both HUA, known as Harakat-ul-Mujahideen (following the U.S. designation), and its splinter, Jaish-e-Muhammad, shared common terrorist training facilities in Afghanistan. With the emergence of Islamist groups, the activity and strength of the Pakhtunistan Movement, Al Zulficar organization, Jaye Sind Movement and even the Muttahida Quami Movement (MQM, previously Mohajir Quami Movement) declined. To access landlocked Afghanistan, Al Qaeda used Pakistan as a transit route for its recruits and supplies.

Contrary to popular perception, Pakistan's Inter-Services Intelligence (ISI) did not assist Al Qaeda directly. Although Al Qaeda benefited from the Taliban, the group operated clandestinely even as far as its host. Al Qaeda not only conducted its own operations, it also instigated and inspired a number of other groups to conduct terrorist operations. In November 1997, four U.S. employees of Union Texas Petroleum and their Pakistani driver were murdered in Karachi when their vehicle was attacked one mile from the U.S. consulate in Karachi. The Aimal Khufia Action Committee and Islami Inqilabi Mahaz, a Lahore-based group of Afghan veterans, claimed responsibility for the killings.[16] The motive for the attack was the conviction of Mir Aimal Kansi, a Pakistani national who had been tried in the United States in November for the murder of two CIA employees and the wounding of three others outside CIA Headquarters, Virginia, in 1993. Kansi was found guilty and sentenced to death. While Osama bin Laden publicly praised Kansi, Pakistani agencies collaborated with their U.S. counterparts to find the assassin. Similarly, an Al Qaeda terrorist, Ramzi Ahmed Yousef, was extradited from Pakistan to the United States in 1995, and was convicted in New York in November 1997 for his role in the 1993 World Trade Centre bombing in New York City. Although Al Qaeda maintained ties with Iranian-financed Hezbollah, a Shiite group, it also worked with the Taliban, an anti-Shiite and anti-Iranian group. Although Osama bin Laden actively discouraged Shiite–Sunni in-fighting, the Taliban trained several Sunni groups. As a result, Shiite–Sunni clashes continued in Pakistan. For instance, five Iranian Air Force technicians were killed in September 1997 in Rawalpindi. Laskar-i-Jhangvi, a violent offshoot of the anti-Shiite Sunni group, Sipah-i-Shahaba-Pakistan, claimed responsibility. The Iranian government-controlled press held Pakistan responsible for failing to stop the attack and accused the United States of "conspiring in the murders." Similarly, two Iranian construction engineers were killed in Karachi in February 1998. Islamism is not monolithic[17] but a lack of understanding prevented the U.S. from developing a far-reaching response to secure U.S. and allied interests, especially in the Middle East. In addition to Al Qaeda infiltrating the West, several Islamist groups, including Jamaat ul-Fugra – (established in the early 1980s), seeking to purify Islam through violence and led by Pakistani-based cleric Shaykh Mubarik Ali Gilani, infiltrated North America and the Caribbean.[18] Due to the presence of Muslim migrants and diaspora in the U.S. and in Western Europe, the West faces a continuous threat from Islamist terrorism.

The performance of the U.S.-led anti-terrorist Coalition has been effective in the short term but weak in the long term. While the U.S., its allies and Coalition partners continue to fight Al Qaeda and its associate and affiliated groups militarily, the Islamists are replenishing their human losses by sustained recruitment, and material wastage by fund-raising. The post-Taliban trajectory of Al Qaeda includes attempts to destroy U.S., U.K., Australian and Israeli diplomatic targets in Singapore, a U.S. warship in the Straits of Malacca, U.S. and British warships in the Straits of Gibraltar; poison the water supply to the U.S. embassy in Rome; bomb the U.S. embassy and American cultural centre in Paris; attack the U.S. naval base in Sarajevo; and fire a Stinger missile at a U.S. warplane taking off from the Prince Sultan air base in Saudi Arabia. To instigate Islamists to strike worldwide Jewish targets, an Al Qaeda suicide bomber attacked Africa's oldest Jewish synagogue, killing 11 German tourists, including one child, and five Tunisians in Djerba, Tunisia. After mounting surveillance on the

Sheraton hotel and the bus route used by French naval engineers and technicians working on the submarine project in Karachi, a suicide bomber of Harakat-ul-Mujahideen-al-Aalami, an Al Qaeda associate group, killed 11 Frenchmen on May 18, 2002. The same group also injured one U.S. marine and killed 11 Pakistanis in a suicide bomb attack against the U.S. consulate in Karachi on June 14, 2002, where a Suzuki vehicle laden with 500 kilograms of explosives was used. Al Qaeda associate groups have also staged a number of attacks including the kidnapping and murder of Daniel Pearl and bombing of a church in Islamabad, killing a U.S. diplomat's wife and daughter. Al Qaeda also targeted President Musharraf on April 26, but the remote control for detonating the explosives-laden vehicle failed to activate. As installing a pro-Al Qaeda or at least neutral regime in Pakistan is paramount to the survival of Al Qaeda and its associate groups, they are likely to target Musharraf again.

The irritants between India and its neighbours do not augur well for Indian as well as regional security. The long and porous border between India and the Kingdom of Nepal makes the Nepali economy adjunct to the Indian economy. Relations deteriorated between India and Nepal when India accused Nepal of providing sanctuary to the Gurukha National Liberation Front (GNLF) campaigning for Gurukha state in West Bengal in late 1987. Nepal's procurement of anti-aircraft and other weapons from the PRC further antagonized New Delhi. In mid-1988, Indian personnel violated Nepali territory. In early 1989, India did not renew the two treaties determining trade and transit and closed 13 of the 15 transit points of trade into Nepal. India used the upheaval in Nepal—precipitated by dependency, unemployment, underemployment, low productivity, illiteracy, poverty and malnutrition—to return a pro-India party to power. In mid-1995, there were the first signs of a communist insurgency in Nepal. The Maoist leaders were operating from India but as of early 2000, there was no indication of Indian covert support.[19] However, the Maoists had established political and military training camps inside India. Nepali intelligence believes that the Maoists have established links with a number of political, guerilla and terrorist organizations in the region and beyond.[20] The Maoist rebellion is likely to spread with time and destroy the economy of the country in the short and mid-term.

With the LTTE using the period of peace negotiations to strengthen itself militarily, there is a fragile peace in Sri Lanka. In addition to providing trainers to a number of terrorist groups, the LTTE has provided terrorist technologies to several groups in the region and beyond. As long as Prabhakaran, a proclaimed offender in the Rajiv Gandhi assassination is head of the LTTE, the group is unlikely to enter the political mainstream. As the Sri Lankan government is unprepared to meet the LTTE threat, the country is likely to suffer significant damage and destruction from terrorist bombings, sabotage of infrastructure, political assassinations, and guerilla attacks, when the conflict resumes.

Central Asia

The break-up of the Soviet Union provided opportunities for both India and Pakistan to establish close relations with Soviet Central Asia— Kazakhstan, Tajikistan, Turkmenistan, Uzbekistan and Kyrgyzstan.[21] The Middle East—notably Saudi Arabia, Iran and Turkey—have also developed strong political and economic ties with this Muslim majority region.[22] The conflict in Tajikistan came to an end with the establishment of a national reconciliation government in 1997. In 1998 and 1999, with the support of Moscow, Tehran and Islamabad, opposition parties were brought in, strengthening the peace initiatives.

Nevertheless, the instability in Afghanistan, the gateway to Soviet Central Asia, affected the rest of Central Asia. Several Islamist parties from Soviet Central Asia, notably Uzbekistan, received military training in Afghanistan. Furthermore, propaganda originating in Afghanistan and Pakistan was distributed outside mosques in the Soviet Central Asian countries. As a result, the Ferghana valley, linking Uzbekistan, Kyrgyzstan and Tajikistan, is the centre for Islamist ideological training. The terrorist threat has been low except for the attempted assassination of the Uzbek President, Islam Karimov, in Tashkent in February 1999, two abortive raids, and a wave of kidnappings—Japanese geologists, security forces personnel, U.S. mountain climbers, etc. The flow of narcotics from Afghanistan, enjoying a common border with Tajikistan, Uzbekistan and Turkmenistan, remains another security concern. As of late 1999, opium cultivation in northern Afghanistan had spread into Tajikistan and beyond, and into the Uzbekistan border. Until the core and penultimate leadership of Al Qaeda and the Taliban is destroyed, the international community is unlikely to restore a civil administration in Afghanistan.

Southeast Asia

Unlike Western Europe, Southeast Asia after World War II was the theatre of war against the communists. Contending forces of colonialism and nationalism were witnessed in the sub-region until the 1970s. With the proxy wars coming to an end in the 1980s, the region experienced unprecedented economic growth. Unlike the South Asian Association for Regional Cooperation (SAARC), the 10-member Association of Southeast Asian Nations (ASEAN) has "developed a corporate culture of close consultation and cooperation which has begun to influence and attract other states in the region."[23] Southeast Asia is a sub-region of half a billion people located between two giants—India and the PRC. Both militarily and economically, the ASEAN states—until the Asian crisis of 1997—were growing rapidly, and in competition with one other. Although varying degrees of post-crisis economic growth has reinforced regional security, terrorism, crime, narcotics, piracy, ethno-nationalism, religious fundamentalism, migration, refugees and the proliferation of light arms have contributed an element of instability. As of 2002, Southeast Asia is recording the highest incidents of piracy and regional governments are taking the threat seriously, and have scored partial successes against fighting crime and narcotics. Nevertheless, all threats, except guerilla warfare and terrorism, are at manageable levels.[24] Incidents of terrorism have increased since 1997 but government agencies have begun to develop multi-agency approaches to combat the phenomenon. Worryingly, Afghanistan and Middle Eastern-trained Islamists and philanthropists visited the region in the last decade, establishing links with domestic political and violent groups, and affecting Southeast Asia's stability. Countries in the region with Muslim populations—Thailand, Malaysia, Philippines and Indonesia—have become recruitment targets of these foreign groups. Some Asian Muslims, in fact, participate in the international Islamist networks of both Shiite and Sunni groups.

Thailand has emerged as a safe haven for a number of terrorist and criminal groups. For over a decade, the Lebanese Hezbollah has operated in Thailand. Furthermore, Hezbollah is using Thailand to conduct terrorist support operations in the region. Muslim separatist groups in southern Thailand re-emerged in the late 1990s, carrying out a series of bombings and other violent activities beginning 1997. Bomb attacks in October 1997 killed seven persons, and a bombing of a Chinese religious festival in December 1997 killed three and wounded 15. Government authorities credited separatist groups with assassinating 11 policemen in a two-month period and blowing up a railroad in May 1997. Since December 2001, southern Thailand has been witnessing a fresh wave of violence.

PULO, a group consisting of Sunni Muslims that has spearheaded most of the separatist violence, established links with Shiite Muslim groups forming an umbrella organization—Bersatu.[25] In 1995, a PULO splinter group, Barman National Baru persuaded youths to undergo terrorist training in Syria in exchange for a four-year membership card that guaranteed access to jobs and security in Malaysia.[26] Another splinter—New PULO—and a dissident group, too, have also been militarily active.[27] With economic development and the granting of autonomy by the Thai authorities in the south, support for separatism has declined. Sustained stability, however, is likely to depend on the willingness of the Thai government to accommodate the new demands of the parties in the south and to disrupt the operation of foreign terrorist groups on Thai soil.

The Islamist terrorist network in Malaysia spilled over to Singapore in the early 1990s. In December 2001, the Singaporean authorities detected and disrupted the infrastructure of Al Qaeda's Southeast Asian arm, Jemiah Islamiah (JI), in Singapore. The timely intervention prevented JI from conducting a series of attacks against U.S. and Allied targets in Singapore. The Singapore arrests paved the way for arrests in Malaysia and the Philippines. Kuala Lumpur took steps to ban terrorist organizations, notably the LTTE, which was engaging in training and fund-raising, and Al-Arqam.

Both the Abu Sayyaf Group (ASG) and the Moro Islamic Liberation Front (MILF), campaigning to establish an Islamic state in the southern Philippines, have been infiltrated by Al Qaeda. Formed after a split from the Moro National Liberation Front (MNLF) in 1991, ASG conducts kidnappings, bombings and assassinations. Its members are mostly younger Muslims, many of whom have studied or worked in the Gulf countries, where they were exposed to Islamist ideology. Despite stepped-up efforts by the armed forces of the Philippines in 1998 and 1999, the ASG remained a threat to the security of the state. On March 20, 2000, ASG attacked an army outpost and seized students, teachers, priests and others from two schools in Basilan. In return for 29 hostages, ASG requested the U.S. to release Ramzi Ahmed Yousef, convicted mastermind of the 1993 World Trade Centre bombing, and Sheikh Omar Abdul Rahman, who was convicted of conspiring to destroy New York City landmarks such as the UN building. In October 1997, the U.S. government designated ASG as a foreign terrorist organization and in December 2001, tasked U.S. advisors and troops with destroying the group. In the long term, it is likely that the government will be able to draw the MILF into the political mainstream but not the ASG. In addition to Hezbollah and Hamas, there are a few secular groups operating in the Philippines. Activities of the LTTE in the Philippines include human smuggling, drug trafficking, and illegal shipments of other logistical supplies.[28] As a matter of policy, the Philippine government considers all terrorist actions, regardless of motivation, as criminal acts. Therefore, the Philippine government undertakes all lawful measures to prevent terrorism and bring to justice those who commit terrorist acts. The government is committed to using force in a judicious manner in preventing, responding to and deterring terrorist attacks.

Indonesia, with the largest Muslim population in the world, is host to the Southeast Asian leadership of JI. Until July 2001, Al Qaeda ran a training camp for JI recruits in Poso, Sulawesi. As Indonesia is reluctant to act against groups that preach hatred and violence, there are a dozen small Islamist groups that are gathering momentum. The vast majority of Indonesians are peace-loving and do not perceive these groups as posing a significant threat to Indonesia's future stability. The Indonesian military is engaged in fighting two secular insurgencies—the Free Aceh Movement (GAM) in Sumatra and the Free Papua Movement (OPM) in Irian Jaya.

By negotiating one-on-one with two dozen separatist groups, the military government in Myanmar has managed the threat posed by their insurgencies quite well. Although some of the groups continue to engage in the cultivation and trafficking of narcotics and other contraband, the threat posed by these groups has markedly diminished. In the foreseeable future, it is likely that the government will continue with attempts to negotiate with the few groups that continue to defy the military regime. Many of the groups that have signed agreements with the military regime are likely to return to violence, if there is a regime change. Therefore, during the transition from military to civilian rule, the responsible body must ensure that the insurgent groups/new political parties are not marginalized. Efforts by the U.S. and EU to isolate the military regime in Myanmar have been counter-productive; the ending of technical assistance from the West to control and contain the cultivation and trafficking of narcotics has been especially unhelpful.

Northeast Asia

Both Aum Shinrikyo and the Japanese Red Army have publicly announced that they are abandoning violence. However, the threat to Japan and to Japanese interests overseas has not decreased. Japanese nationals continue to be kidnapped by terrorist groups from Columbia to Tajikistan. Furthermore, foreign terrorist groups such as Babbar Khalsa International and the LTTE continue to raise funds on Japanese soil. As there is no Muslim population in Japan, Islamist groups such as Al Qaeda, Hezbollah and Hamas have failed to establish a permanent presence in that country. Nonetheless, Al Qaeda procurement officers have purchased communication equipment and other dual technologies from Japan. Japan became one of the first victims of Al Qaeda terrorism when a Japanese national was killed and 11 injured when Ramzi Ahmed Yousef planted a test bomb on a Japan-bound Philippine Airlines flight in December 1994. The terrorist threat to Japan increased after the government of Japan extended support to the U.S. in the fight against terrorism.

The developments in Muslim Central Asia have had a major impact on the Uighur claim for independence from PRC.[29] Uighur separatists concentrated their initial spate of attacks in the Xinjiang Autonomous Region but gradually struck targets both in Beijing and elsewhere. The Uighurs, of Turkish origin, have a presence extending from Turkey to Kazakhstan. Since late 1996, there has been a wave of attacks by Afghan-trained Uighurs.[30] Uighur Islamists have also established strong links with the Islamists in Afghanistan and Pakistan. Furthermore, they have established a presence in the Ferghana valley, and conducted both demonstrations and terrorist attacks in Kyrgyzstan and Kazakhstan as well. Many Islamist groups in the Middle East and Central Asia are likely to continue its support for the Uighurs in the mid- to long term. Similar to the way it contained the rebellion in Tibet, Beijing will militarily contain the Uighur separatists. The U.S. is cooperating with the PRC to monitor the Eastern Turkistan Islamic Movement, an Al Qaeda associate group, active in PRC, Afghanistan and Central Asia.[31]

North Korea is the only Asia-Pacific country that remains on the U.S. State Department's list of state sponsors of terrorism. The main reason for

North Korea remaining on the list is because since 1979, it has been harbouring members of the Japanese Red Army who had hijacked a Japanese plane in 1970 and also attempted to assassinate the South Korean cabinet. Although North Korea's role in sponsoring international terrorism has declined, it continues to provide missile technologies to other state sponsors of terrorism. One of the few surviving Communist regimes, North Korea remains in economic shambles. The U.S. failure to draw North Korea out of its international isolation has been counter-productive.

Oceania

Oceania is the sub-region least affected by political violence. Its geographic isolation offers it relative insulation from violent conflicts in Southeast Asia. Nonetheless, the region is rich in two categories of groups—support networks for foreign guerilla and terrorist groups, and indigenous groups. The foreign groups operate in the two most developed countries in the region—Australia and New Zealand. Except for Al Qaeda and other associated Islamist groups, none of the foreign guerilla and terrorist groups directly threaten either Australia or New Zealand. In the Solomon Islands located in the South Pacific, two indigenous groups, the Isatabu Freedom Movement (IFM) and Malaitian Eagle Force (MEF) use stone-age weapons—sticks, bows, arrows, spears, swords and knives.

Despite several coup attempts in Fiji, which is also in the South Pacific, the scale of interracial and religious violence is low, despite the fact that Al Qaeda has attempted to infiltrate or infiltrated the Muslim community in Fiji. There is peace in the rest of the South Pacific—French Polynesia, Kiribati, Marshall Islands, Nauru, Samoa, Tonga, Vanuatu, American Samoa, Cook Islands, Federated States of Micronesia, Guam, Niue, Norfolk Island, Northern Mariana Islands, Pitcairn Island, Tuvalu and Wallis and Futuna Islands.

Response

Terrorism is a vicious by-product of protracted socio-economic and political conflict. To regulate the existing and emerging terrorist threat in the Asia-Pacific region, it is necessary to develop a comprehensive range of policy responses. To meet the immediate threat, it is critical to develop exceptionally good counter-terrorism intelligence. The approach of punishing individuals for their crimes, but permitting groups that have perpetrated violence to exist, is highly counter-productive. Governments must target terrorist organizations, especially their propaganda, recruitment, training, fund-raising, procurement and transportation infrastructures. Furthermore, target governments must develop arrangements with host states to disrupt terrorist support networks and assist affected states by sharing intelligence and exchanging personnel to fight transnational terrorist support and operational networks. Al Qaeda is only one organization active in the Asia-Pacific. The focus on Al Qaeda and other Islamist groups—the category of groups posing the greatest threat to international security—is creating space for numerous other groups to grow. While targeting Al Qaeda as a priority, the international community, especially Asia-Pacific governments, must focus on militarily pressurizing and politically drawing these groups into their democratic mainstreams.

Terrorist groups can be effectively crushed only at an early stage. The failure to fight efficiently and ethically—especially against an ethnically- and religiously-empowered group—can lead to indiscriminate violence that can favour the terrorist group. With time, most conflicts can gather momentum, thereby generating substantial popular support. In such instances, a political solution over a military solution should be considered. Often, devolving regional autonomy or power sharing has been the most effective strategy but works mostly only in the formative phases of a conflict. The process requires close supervision, particularly during the implementation phase. A politico-military approach is to politically isolate a group in order to stem support and recruits and simultaneously offer political and economic incentives to militarily pressurize it to join the mainstream. Often, links with foreign groups, state sponsors, or diaspora migrant support can provide the confidence to fight on. Transnational networks make such groups more resilient. While some of these threats can be resolved unilaterally by states, most require bilateral and multilateral arrangements. Intractable conflicts with an international dimension such as Kashmir cannot be resolved bilaterally—it will require third-party mediation. Impediments to the regulation of these threats lie not in the lack of strength at the domestic and international level but the lack of political will and political capital. Some of the threats can be regulated at a sub-regional and others at a regional level. Some of the threats are new, others are old but have assumed a renewed dimension. Therefore, new institutions often capable of delivering multi-pronged responses, especially non-military responses, are essential for regulating extant and emerging threats.

Conclusion

The existing and emerging threats after the end of the Cold War have transcended the territorial boundaries of the nation-state. The phenomenon of globalization—the increase in porosity of the boundaries, enhanced communication, rapid movement and migration of people, free flow of information, and greater access and transfer of lethal technology—has added a new dimension to the security of the Asia-Pacific region. Today, even to address a local or a national problem, security planners must think regionally and globally. As such, inter-agency and intra-agency cooperation at national and international levels is at the heart of fighting terrorism. The simmering-away of East-West tensions has created the space and opportunity to end many conflicts. Throughout the 1990s, many regional conflicts—born during the Cold War and fuelled by East-West tensions—have either ended or escalated. While a few have ended through domestic mediation and third-party intervention, others have escalated. The escalation in conflicts is largely attributed to the resurgence of ethnicity and religiosity. The nature of the post-Cold War conflict scenario is that almost all conflicts are intrastate but with serious interstate implications.[32] Since the end of the Cold War, the science and the art of conflict resolution and confidence-building has enhanced significantly. Of all the regions of the world, South Asia is most resistant to negotiated resolution of conflicts.[33]

Terrorism has replaced the nuclear threat during the Cold War. What is clear is that the number of internal armed conflicts that spawn terrorism has exponentially increased during the last decade. In the Asia-Pacific region, as in the rest of the world, terrorism is largely a by-product of armed conflicts. Ethnic and religious politics fuel as many as 70 percent of armed campaigns today. Unlike the ideologically driven Cold War terrorist groups, the bulk of contemporary terrorist groups and political movements benefit from the post-1990 worldwide resurgence of ethnicity and religiosity. What is certain is that there has been an emergence of nationalist, separatist and irredentist conflicts as a primary post-Cold War security threat to the international system. These ethno-political and religious conflicts produce the highest level of fatalities and casualties, the largest internal displacements and refugee flows, and the greatest human rights violations.[34]

As the challenges posed by contemporary terrorist groups are the product of a new environment, they differ markedly from the threats posed by Cold War groups. Since World War II, domestic and international institutions were largely structured to manage Cold War issues. Currently, governments and international organizations are developing strategies and mechanisms to address these new challenges, especially terrorism, narcotics and organized crime.

Like the rise of Islamic fundamentalism in the Middle East, partially triggered by Western intervention in the Gulf campaign, Islamic fundamentalism is on the rise in the Asia-Pacific, largely due to the U.S. intervention in Afghanistan. As in South Asia, the Islamist threat is likely to fuel many domestic conflicts in Southeast Asia. Of all the conflicts, the dispute over Kashmir between two undeclared nuclear powers poses the single biggest threat to Asian security. Traditionally, nuclear empowerment deterred open confrontation. But in the sub-continent, two nuclear powers are next to each other, and already engaged in an insurgency. With India insisting on bilateral talks over the UN-disputed territory of Kashmir, the root cause of tension, it is likely that the conflict will remain unresolved. South Asia is entering a new arms race in the Asia-Pacific. Although the most serious threat to the globe throughout the 1990s stemmed from international conflict, internal conflicts and transnational threats—especially terrorism and organized crime—will gather greater momentum in the early twenty-first century.

Traditionally, superpowers or regional powers have been prepared to fight other states or intervene in states. For instance, the U.S. forces prepared for regional contingencies to meet challenges posed by the Arab-Israeli conflict, and conflicts in the Persian Gulf, Korean peninsula, India and Pakistan and possibly PRC and Taiwan.[35] With internal conflicts assuming a new dimension, states will have to reorient their forces and doctrines, and develop political, military, legal and international instruments and arrangements to deal with internal conflicts where guerillas and terrorists feature.

Notes

1   The author is grateful to Andrew Tan of the Institute of Defence and Strategic Studies for his invitation to write, and to him and Kumar Ramakrishna for editing this paper.

2   The civil war in Lebanon (1975–1982)—between the Shiites, Sunnis, Maronites and the Druzes—led to the collapse of the state, creating the conditions for several terrorist groups to establish a presence. Foreign policy considerations forced Syria to control some of these groups. The JRA, PIRA, LTTE, ASALA, PKK, RAF, Turkish Left and Palestinian groups trained and operated from the Syrian-controlled Bekaa valley in Lebanon. Until Israeli intervention and the PLO withdrawal to Tunis, southern Lebanon remained a perfect training ground for several groups. With many Middle Eastern regimes ceasing their support for terrorism with the Oslo accords, the bulk of the terrorist groups shifted to Asia. Soviet intervention (1979–1989) had led to the collapse of the Afghan state and foreign policy considerations—notably Kashmir—led Pakistan to create and support the Taliban. The Taliban's brand of Islam provided an opportunity for several foreign terrorist groups to establish a presence in Afghanistan to wage multiple campaigns wherever Muslims appeared to be suppressed, as well as against the West.

3   Respectively, they performed the first acknowledged chemical, cyber-, and transcontinental mass-casualty terrorist attacks.

4   Dr Abdullah Azzam, "The founding charter of Al Qaeda Al Sulbah, Al Jihad [The principal journal of the Arab *mujahideen*]," Peshawar, March 1988.

5   While violent political conflicts involve under 100 deaths per conflict per year, low-intensity conflicts involve under 1,000 deaths per conflict per year. High-intensity conflicts involve over 1,000 deaths per conflict per year. The fatalities comprise combatants and non-combatants.

6   Albert Jongman, "World Conflict and Human Rights Map 2002," The Interdisciplinary Research Programme on Causes of Human Rights Violations (PIOOM), The Netherlands.

7   Remote-control bomb technology originating in the Middle East has been found in Latin America, Africa, Europe, and in Asia. Mike Dolamore, Defence Intelligence Staff, Ministry of Defence, U.K., personal communication, February 1999.

8   Michael Williams, *Population in Asia and the Pacific, The Far East and Australasia* (London: Europa Publications, 1996), p. 3.

9   For conflict data, see Alex Schmid and Albert Jongman, "World Conflict and Human Rights Map 1998," The Interdisciplinary Research Programme on Causes of Human Rights Violations (PIOOM), The Netherlands; Charles King, *Ending Civil Wars*, Adelphi Paper 308 (Oxford: Oxford University Press, 1997); Peter Wallensteen and Margareta Sollenberg, "The End of International War?

Armed Conflict 1989–1995," *Journal of Peace Research*, Vol. 33, No. 3 (1996), pp. 353–370; Ted Robert Gurr and Barbara Harff, *Ethnic Conflict in World Politics* (Boulder: Westview Press, 1994); and Peter Chalk, *Grey-Area Phenomena in Southeast Asia: Piracy, Drug Trafficking and Political Terrorism* (Canberra: Strategic and Defence Studies Centre, Australian National University, 1997).

10 Jongman, "World Conflict and Human Rights Map 2002."

11 Schmid and Jongman, "World Conflict and Human Rights Map 1998."

12 From 1979 to 1991, the CIA shipped to Afghanistan, via Pakistan, 400,000 AK-47s, 700 U.S.- manufactured Stingers, Italian-made anti-personnel mines, 40–50 Swiss-designed anti-aircraft guns, Egyptian mortars, British Blowpipe surface-to-air missiles, 100,000 Indian rifles, as well as 60,000 rifles and 8,000 light machine-guns from Egypt, and over 100 million rounds of ammunition. Chris Smith, "Light Weapons and Ethnic Conflict in South Asia," in Jeffrey Boutwell *et al.* (eds.), *Lethal Commerce* (Cambridge, MA: American Academy of Arts and Sciences, 1995), pp. 62–64; Marvin B. Schaffer, "The Missile Threat to Civil Aviation," *Terrorism and Political Violence*, Vol. 10, No. 3 (Autumn 1998), p. 72.

13 Since the end of the Cold War, the interstate armed confrontations have been limited to Iraq–Kuwait, Serbia–NATO, Spain–Morocco and a few border disputes including Ecuador–Peru, India–Pakistan, India–Bangladesh, Eritrea–Ethiopia, and the two Koreas. It is likely that most contemporary international conflicts will trigger a multinational military and/or political response.

14 Studies by Wallenstein and Gurr on the vulnerability of geographic regions confirm that South Asia and Sub-Saharan Africa are currently experiencing a high level of conflict and have peculiar features making them more prone to conflict than other regions.

15 In June 2002, the Interior Ministry of Pakistan revealed that there were 600,000 students, including 18,000 foreign students studying in 8,000 *madrasahs* (Islamic schools). Attempts to regulate the curricula, overseas students and flow of finances triggered protests by Ittehad-e-Tanzeemat, an alliance of the *madrasahs*. "Pakistan Clerics Threaten National Protest," Islamabad, AP, 9 July 2002.

16 *Annual Terrorism Report*, Washington D.C.: U.S. State Department, 1998. Aimal Khufia Action Committee was a previously unknown group.

17 Gilles Kepel, a leading scholar on the Islamists makes the point more poignantly than any other Western scholar. Gilles Kepel, *Jihad: The Trail of Political Islam* (Cambridge, MA: The Belknap Press, 2002).

18 *Annual Terrorism Report*, 1998. "Fuqra members have purchased isolated rural compounds in North America to live communally, practice their faith, and insulate themselves from Western culture...Fuqra members have attacked a variety of targets that they view as enemies of Islam, including Muslims they regard as heretics and Hindus. Attacks during the 1980s included assassinations and fire bombings across

the United States. Fuqra members in the United States have been convicted of criminal violations, including murder and fraud."

19 Interviews with Pradhan, Inspector General of Police, Kathmandu, May 1997; Amod Gurug, Head, Counter-Terrorism, Kathmandu, June 1998; and Tony Davis, Thailand, personal communication, April 2000.

20 They are: All Nepal Youth Association Chennai Committee Tamil Nadu, India; United Liberation Front of Assam (ULFA); Northern Bihar Liberation Front (NBLF); Baharatiya Communist Party (Maoist); Maoist Communist Centre (MCC); People's War Group (PWG); Revolutionary Organization of Radical Youth League; Bharat Ekta Samaj; LTTE; Shining Path; Revolutionary International Movement and the League of Philippine Students.

21 M. E. Ahrari and James Beal, *The New Great Game in Muslim Central Asia* (Washington: Institute for National Strategic Studies, National Defence University, 1996).

22 Dr John Anderson, Central Asian Expert, Oxford, April 2000. See also John Anderson, *International Politics of Central Asia* (Manchester: Manchester University Press, 1997).

23 Michael Leifer, *Dictionary of the Modern Politics of Southeast Asia* (London and New York: Routledge, 1995), p. 1.

24 For the background to guerilla conflicts, see Andrew Tan, *Armed Rebellion in the ASEAN States: Persistence and Implications*, Canberra Papers on Strategy and Defence, Australian National University, No. 135, 2000.

25 Chalk, *Grey-Area Phenomena in Southeast Asia*, pp. 60–61.

26 Chalk, *Grey-Area Phenomena in Southeast Asia*, p. 61.

27 Chalk, *Grey-Area Phenomena in Southeast Asia*.

28 Philippine intelligence identified Surendren Ponaiya alias Chunjen as a key member of the LTTE operating out of the Philippines.

29 Paul George, "Islamic Unrest in the Xinjiang Uighur Autonomous Region," Canadian Security Intelligence Service Publication, Commentary No. 73, Spring 1998.

30 In February 1997, Uighur separatists conducted a series of bus bombings in Urumqi that killed nine persons and wounded 74. Uighur rioting earlier in the month in the city of Yining caused as many as 200 deaths. Uighur exiles in Turkey claimed responsibility for a small pipe bomb that exploded on a bus in Beijing in March which killed three persons and injured eight. In August, Uighur separatists were blamed for killing five persons, including two policemen. The Chinese government executed several individuals involved in both the rioting and bombings. Beijing claims that support for the Uighurs is coming from neighbouring countries, an accusation these countries deny.

31 Also see Chien-peng Chung, "China's War on Terror," *Foreign Affairs*, Vol. 81. No. 4 (July/August 2002), pp. 8–12.

32 King, *Ending Civil Wars*, pp. 84–87. King lists 47 conflicts, which he defines as civil wars, unresolved internal disputes and areas of major unrest.

33 Innovative approaches to peace-making are rare in South Asia. An exception was when India's federal government sought help from the Roman Catholic Church to persuade tribal separatists in northeastern Tripura state to join peace talks in June 1998. Officials have also enlisted the church to help bring peace to Nagaland. Traditionally, the church has been reluctant to mediate between separatists and the government, fearing that this might attract charges that the church is close to extremists.

34 Denis Pluchinsky, "Ethnonational Terrorism—Themes and Variations," in Gunnar Jervas (ed.), *FOA Report on Terrorism* (Sweden, June 1998).

35 Hans Binnendijk, *1997 Strategic Assessment: Flash Point and Force Structures* (Washington: National Defence University, 1996).

RELIGION AND
TERRORISM

7

GLOBALIZATION, RESISTANCE AND THE DISCURSIVE POLITICS OF TERROR, POST-SEPTEMBER 11

Farish A. Noor

Understanding the Nature and Impact of Global Terrorism

The terrorist attacks on the United States of America on 11 September 2001[1] have shown us that terror is indeed universal. If it can strike at the heart of the most powerful country in the world today, then it can also strike anywhere, anytime and in any way.

But by focusing on the singular event of September 11, we are in danger of particularizing a phenomenon that is far more universal than we might care to admit. The fact is that terror and terrorism has been with us before September 11, and it remains with us till today. The question is one of how to understand it. While some Western countries like the United States remain bent on pursuing their agenda at whatever human cost, the rest of the world stands dumbfounded before the absurdities around us. Palestinian civilians are being killed on a daily basis; their homes, businesses, schools and places of worship are destroyed with impunity, yet the media continues to depict the Palestinians themselves as "terrorists." Israel, on the other hand, has been given a blank cheque to do whatever it wills in the occupied territories—and is portrayed as a state exercising its right to defend itself. Against what, one might ask. And who, indeed, are the so-called "terrorists" that we are supposed to guard against? To top it all, the nation that placed itself at the vanguard of the new "global war on terror"—the United States of

America—was itself the only country that has ever been accused of practising state terrorism by the World Court.[2]

Terrorism today happens to be an extremely complex and confounding phenomenon. It is both local and global, particular and universal. Its causes cannot—and should not—be traced back to any essentialist understandings of cultural specificity or identity. Nor would anyone attempt a micro-specific pathological approach to the question of why a particular individual would be driven to such a course of action. There is no blueprint, genetic code, recipe or secret ingredient to the phenomenon. Nor should we think in terms of physics and simple laws of causality.

Rather than thinking in terms of physical causality, we would propose a different approach instead. Ours is the view that terrorism is a phenomenon that comes into being if and when a number of conditions and variables— both internal and external—apply. For that, our focus will be two-fold. (We do not suggest that this approach is final or exhaustive.) For the sake of this paper, we will look at two important areas in particular: Firstly, the sphere of religio-political discourse and how it opens the way for the shift towards a more radicalized form of political contestation which may involve violence. And secondly, the socio-political terrain of societies that serves as the backdrop where such discourses and counter-discourses may emerge in the first place. For reasons that we hope will become clearer later, our argument is that these two spheres of socio-political life are intimately related and impact upon each other.

The Discursive Coordinates of Terrorism

> "Osama bin Laden has become the symbol of *jihad* all over the world."
>
> **Mufti of the *Markaz Da'wat wa'l Irshad*,**
> **Headquarters of the Pakistani *Laskar-e-Tayyeba* (Army of the Pure)**

As mentioned above, any discussion of the nature and causes of terror and terrorism has to avoid the pitfalls of cultural essentialism. There is always the temptation to find the reasons and causes of terror in the hearts and minds of the terrorists themselves. By doing so, "terrorism" is personalized to the point where it becomes a pathological problem of the individual, rather than the system he resides within. This is the best way to avoid getting to grips with the problem itself, and it serves as a convenient discursive strategy to turn our attention away from the underlying structural, institutional and political conditions that make terrorism come about in the first place.

This problem becomes even more acute when terrorism is expressed via the medium of religious discourse. If and when terror and its uses are justified and articulated via the discourse of religion, there will invariably be the (mistaken) tendency to equate terror and violence with that religion in particular. Here analyses often make the mistake of trying to find the causes of terror in the belief and value system of the terrorists themselves. In the 1980s and 1990s, there was much talk of the "revenge of God" in Western academic circles. The emergence of religiously-inclined political movements was seen as a return to a politics of primordialism, and religion was seen as somehow being antithetically opposed to modernity and progress.

Here it is important to note that the dichotomy between religion and modernity is a false one. Religions are far too complex to be so categorized, and it is impossible to claim that all religions are either "for" or "against" modernity. While there are still many millenarian and revivalist movements in the world, we often forget that religion has also been a force for positive change in many cases. The democratic popular uprisings against authoritarian governments in Indonesia, Philippines and Burma/Myanmar provide us with clear-cut examples of how the discourse of religion can and has been used to mobilize the masses for the sake of civil society and democracy. We would be making a serious mistake if we thought that all religions were fundamentally violent, reactionary and opposed to modernity. Yet these errors persist in the depiction of one religion in particular: Islam.

Now, more than ever, Islam and the culture of Muslims have been equated with terrorism and violence. A neat chain of equivalences has been drawn which equates Islam with "terror," "fanaticism," "extremism" and violence of all kinds. This chain of equivalences is neither essential nor natural, but rather man-made and deliberate.

The myth of the "Islamic threat" should not be taken seriously as an epistemic category but rather a discursive tool crafted for specific political and ideological reasons. As Edward Said has argued in his book, *Orientalism* (1978), such caricatured images of Islam and Muslims have been with us for centuries and, unfortunately, they remain with us still. Said's astute observation that such instrumental fictions work precisely because they are false remains true today, as it was when he first articulated it. Though few academics and intellectuals would take seriously the propositions of the likes of Huntington[3] (1993), who claimed that the Western world would soon be faced with two monolithic and homogenous civilizational adversaries—the Muslim world and the Asian world—such fictions continue to serve political, strategic and hegemonic interests nonetheless.

At the root of this misunderstanding is the failure to comprehend how and why religion and religious discourse have come to play such an important role in the political campaigns and activities of numerous liberation movements and militant organizations. Failure to understand the appeal and utility of religious discourse in turn hinders our own understanding of the problem, and thus prevents us from coming up with any answers ourselves.

The Internal Dynamics of Religio-Political Struggle

"The rise of Islamism was only possible when the availability of Islam could be articulated into a counter-hegemonic discourse."

Bobby Sayyid, *A Fundamental Fear: Eurocentrism and the Emergence of Islamism*.[4]

The ASEAN region has experienced a radical shift towards the religio-political register in no uncertain terms. While in the 1960s and 1970s, most of the opposition movements in the region were mainly secular and nationalist in flavour and character, the 1980s witnessed the slow disintegration of these opposition fronts and the emergence of a new group of actors: religious militant movements who based their activities on the discourse of religion rather than secular politics.

This was certainly the case with most of the opposition movements in Thailand, Philippines and Indonesia. In Thailand, the predominantly secular Patani United Liberation Organization (PULO, established 1968) soon found itself sidelined when the more Islamist-oriented Barisan Bersatu Mujahideen Patani (United Mujahideen Front of Patani) that was established in 1985. Likewise in the Philippines, the secular-oriented Moro National Liberation Front (established 1969) led by the academic-turned-activist Nur Misuari was in time sidelined by the more Islamist-oriented Moro Islamic Liberation Front of Salamat Hashim that was formed in 1984.

Indonesia in turn has witnessed the rise of a number of extremist radical movements, many of which have turned to religion as the primary discourse for political mobilization. With the help of rogue elements within the Indonesian Army and security forces, groups like the Front Pembela Islam and the Laskar Jihad under the leadership of Jaafar Umar Thalib have tried to force their way into the mainstream of Indonesian society and marginalize older, more established Islamist movements like the Nahdatul Ulama and Muhammadiyah.

In all these cases, a common pattern emerges: As the more established religio-political movements began to achieve political success and enter the political mainstream of their respective societies, new and more radical groups would emerge along the margins to question and critique their counterparts who have made it to the centre of the political arena.

One would have to ask the question why such groups have appeared and why they have resorted to the use of an increasingly militant and exclusionary religious discourse for their struggles. The answer lies in part with the factors we have highlighted earlier. The appeal of religious discourse lies in the fact that it is universal in its scope and meaning; that it provides a framework for a moral/ethical critique of power and that it foregrounds a religiocentric viewpoint from which society can be reconstructed. In most of these cases, the shift closer towards the religious register was occasioned by a growing scepticism and disillusionment with the conventional modes of political dialogue and negotiation. Frustration with ruling elites and centralized governments, coupled with the failure of the democratic political process, have simply led these groups to taking up the only means left available to them: the use of arms justified by the adroit deployment of religious discourse.

In the case of Indonesia and the Philippines in particular, the apparently endless rounds of behind-the-scenes double-dealings and sell-outs between the leaders of government and opposition movements undoubtedly played a part in the radicalization of those groups who felt that their interests were being sold out and compromised as well. The MILF, for instance, emerged partly as a result of frustration with Nur Misuari's inability to gain significant concessions from the central government in Manila. This was also the case in Indonesia, where the more established Islamist movements like the Nahdatul Ulama and Muhammadiyah had managed to learn the rules of democratic politics and were actively engaged in what Robert Hefner calls the process of "civil Islam" (i.e., using Islam as a discourse of democracy and civil liberties) but were then accused of "diluting" the cause of their struggle by other, previously marginal groups like the Front Pembela Islam and the Laskar Jihad.

The new groups that have emerged on the scene in ASEAN—the Front Pembela Islam and the Laskar Jihad in Indonesia, Abu Sayyaf and MORO in the Philippines, Barisan Mujahideen in Thailand and even their smaller (though no less radical) counterparts like the Jemiah Islamiah and the Kumpulan Mujahideen Malaysia in Singapore and Malaysia—all share one thing in common: the use of religious discourse as a means of gaining leverage over their co-religionist competitors and adversaries. By upping the ante in the "holier than thou" race against their competitors, such groups hope to gain an upper hand in the battle for support and the contest for new recruits and followers.

This attempt to constantly outbid one's opponents and competitors in the race of religio-political hegemony was most clearly demonstrated during the aftermath of September 11, and a close reading of the events that followed in the wake of the attack might give us some clues to help us understand the mechanics of religious and political extremism in general. Though a common pattern was seen all over the ASEAN region, the contest was particularly complex and the stakes particularly high for one country in particular: Malaysia.

Osama bin Laden's Popularity: How the Global Became Local, and Vice-Versa

"Any number of people can use (Islam) for their own objectives. The main thing for them is to gain power. We are going to be faced with this problem for a long time. We know that we in Malaysia are vulnerable to such forms of extremism, like every other country in the world. Every one of us is vulnerable."

**Prime Minister Dr Mahathir Mohamad,
17 November 2001**[5]

The rest of this paper sets out to examine the complex developments that took place in Malaysia in the wake of the September 11 terrorist attacks on New York and the Pentagon in the United States of America. In particular, it aims to study the ways and means through which the events in the U.S. were seen, understood and re-contextualized in the local Malaysian context by the two main Malay-Muslim parties in the country, the ruling United Malays Nationalist Organization (UMNO) party and the main Malay-Muslim opposition Pan-Malaysian Islamist party (PAS).

Our thesis is that the events of September 11—occurring as they did in a country that is a superpower and whose hegemonic grip on the rest of the globe is undeniable—had an indirect impact on other localities far away. The locality in question here is the discursive and political terrain of Malaysia, and the events of September 11 were interpreted and used by both UMNO and PAS as a trigger for further political mobilization on the local level. The success of these parties' tactics depended, however, on their reading of the event itself and how it was going to be interpreted by the local Malaysian public—which happens to be a highly complex and heterodox constituency divided along cleavages of race, ethnicity, religion and class.

The attacks on New York that took place on September 11 caught the Malaysian government by surprise. For the government of Dr Mahathir, it would be yet another unsolicited external variable that would have to be dealt with in the same way as the Iranian Revolution, the Soviet invasion of Afghanistan, the Salman Rushdie *"Satanic Verses"* controversy, the Gulf War, the Bosnian conflict and the war in Chechnya. The Afghan conflict of the 1980s, for instance, compelled the UMNO-led Malaysian government to commit itself to a pro-Islamic stand, thanks to pressure from the Islamist opposition parties and movements at home. But the Islamization race between UMNO and PAS that was being accelerated thanks to external variable factors such as these only contributed to the inflation of Islamist discourse in the country and the raising of the level of public expectations. During the Bosnian conflict, the Malaysian government played a leading role in voicing the concerns of the Muslim community worldwide. But by the time of the Chechen conflict, the government's vigorous defence of Muslims abroad was comparatively dampened thanks to the growing influence of Islamic radicalism in its own backyard.[6]

Even before the attacks on 11 September 2001, the Malaysian government was already taking the threat of growing Islamist militancy in Malaysia seriously. Political leaders, senior members of government and heads of the state's security services were openly discussing the problem of growing militancy among some sections of Malaysian society, particularly the younger generation of Malay-Muslims, students returning from abroad and the local Islamist parties and movements. By 1999–2000, the Malaysian political scene was abuzz with stories about *jihadi* and *mujahideen* cells operating all over the country: The spectacular arms heist at Gerik, Perak by the al-Maunah group[7] and the string of bank robberies, killings and kidnappings by the so-called "*jihad* gang" earlier the same year had been a cause of concern for Malaysians in general[8].

In August 2001, the government had detained ten Islamist activists— many of whom were members of PAS—on the grounds that they belonged to an underground militant group called the Kumpulan Mujahideen Malaysia (KMM, Malaysian Mujahideen Movement). The leader of the group was said to be Ustaz Nik Adli Nik Mat[9], the 34-year-old son of the *Murshid'ul Am* (Spiritual Leader) of PAS, Tuan Guru Nik Aziz Nik Mat. Though Nik Adli was only a teacher at a religious school in the state of Kelantan (of which his father was the Chief Minister), the authorities claimed that he had studied in the *madrasahs* of Pakistan and that he had spent time training and working with *mujahideen* militants in Afghanistan. Several of the other men arrested had also travelled to Pakistan for religious education and military training with the *mujahideen* operating along the Pak-Afghan border.[10]

PAS's official media organ *Harakah* described the arrests of the KMM members as part of the Mahathir administration's attempt "to woo the Americans."[11] The paper also claimed that PAS would intensify its efforts to show how UMNO was anti-Islam.[12] For the leaders of PAS, their ex-*mujahideen* members' position as role models for the rank and file of the party, and their commitment to the Islamist struggle was seen as exemplary forms of conduct to be emulated, not criminalized.

In the same month that PAS members were being rounded up, Malaysia's Foreign Minister, Syed Hamid Albar, stated that clandestine "Islamist militant" networks were operating in the cross-border regions between Malaysia, Indonesia, Thailand and the Philippines. The kidnapping of Western tourists off the coast of the East Malaysian state of Sabah by Abu Sayyaf guerillas operating from their base in Basilan was cited as a prime example of the new sort of asymmetrical security threat faced by the governments in the region.

In an effort to seize the initiative on the issue, Kuala Lumpur played host to the leaders of Indonesia, Thailand and the Philippines—Presidents Megawati Sukarnoputri, Thaksin Shinawatra and Gloria Arroyo—who had visited the country to discuss matters of bilateral concern, one of which was the problem of Islamist militant networks operating in the region. Soon after, the governments of Malaysia, Indonesia and Philippines issued a series of statements to the effect that they would henceforth be increasing the level of cooperation among their intelligence and security services to deal with the problem of religious militancy in Southeast Asia. The gravity of the situation was made more apparent when the 26-year-old Malaysian youth, Taufik Abdul Halim, was blown up in a shopping mall in Jakarta by an explosive device that he was carrying himself. His intention was to detonate the device in the shopping centre at a time when it would be full of customers.[13]

Thus matters had already come to a head in Malaysia and in the other countries of the ASEAN region long before the two hijacked American Airlines jetliners crashed into the twin towers of the World Trade Centre. The attacks on New York and the global media campaign that followed in its wake merely accelerated the deterioration of relations between the government of Malaysia and the Islamic opposition in the country. Here was a case of a global event having a multiplier effect on what was a local and domestic political struggle.

PAS's Response to the American Bombing of Afghanistan and After

On 7 October 2001, after nearly four weeks of tension and nervous anticipation, the United States finally struck. In a series of late-night sorties, American guided cruise missiles rained down upon a number of military targets in Afghanistan, including Taliban training camps near Kabul, Kunduz, Mazar-e Sharif and Kandahar. American and British jets soon broke down the defences of the country, leaving ordinary Afghan civilians at the mercy of their new-found enemies. The response from the Islamist movements worldwide came as fast as the news of the attacks were spread via the Internet.

The following day, Malaysia's Prime Minister Dr Mahathir openly stated his dissatisfaction with the American-led attack. In a press conference held in Parliament, the Prime Minister said that "war against these countries will not be effective in fighting terrorism."[14] Although he was also careful to state that the attack on Afghanistan should not be regarded by anyone as an attack on Islam and the Muslim world, Dr Mahathir did question the wisdom behind the action and pointed out the negative consequences that were sure to follow.[15] Domestic political concerns were also not far from the mind of the Prime Minister. In a thinly-veiled warning to the Malaysian Islamist parties and groups that might think of extending their support to Osama or the Taliban, he pointed out that "we will not tolerate anyone who supports violence and will act against these irresponsible people or anyone who backs terrorism."[16] The situation, however, was clearly out of hand by then. While the Prime Minister was trying to calm the fears of foreign investors, Western embassies and tourists in the country, the local police and security forces were put on alert and the American embassy (which was closed as it was Columbus day in the United States) was placed under guard.

On the same day (8 October), the leaders of PAS came out with their strongest statement against the Americans yet. For the *Murshid'ul Am* (Spiritual Leader) of PAS, Tuan Guru Nik Aziz Nik Mat, the attack on Afghanistan was clearly an attack on Islam and Muslims in general. Speaking out in defence of the Taliban government, he claimed that:

> "The U.S. hates the Taliban because the latter is firmly committed to upholding Islamic values. Osama bin Laden is just an excuse for the U.S., which has time and again shown its hostility towards Islam, to wage war against the religion."[17]

PAS's president Ustaz Fadzil Noor also stated that the attacks were not only against Afghanistan's Taliban regime, but that they constituted a direct assault on Muslims the world over. Speaking to local and foreign journalists in a press conference of his own, Fadzil Noor said that "America has attacked a small and defenceless country like Afghanistan without showing the world strong reason or proof, (and) they are war criminals."[18] He then added, "If the Americans are really waging a war against terrorism, why don't they attack Israel, who are terrorists against the Palestinians?"[19] The president of PAS ended the interview with a clarion call to arms when he stated that "all Muslims must oppose these criminals—this time, there is no denying a call for *jihad*."[20]

The logic of PAS's campaign was couched in terms of an oppositional dialectic that pit the West against the Muslim world. Having drawn a chain of equivalences between the United States, Western Europe, Israel and the so-called "Zionist conspiracy" to overthrow and dominate the Muslim world, PAS also drew a second chain of equivalences which linked together Islam, the Taliban, Osama bin Laden and themselves as the defenders of Islam and the Muslim *ummah*. What eventually emerged was a zero-sum logic of confrontation which—like George Bush's now-infamous "you are with us or against us" statement—left no middle ground for waverers and neutral parties.

Things finally came to a climax on 10 October when PAS declared a *jihad* against the United States and its Coalition partners and gave the go-ahead for its members to openly join and support the Taliban. The party's Secretary-General Nashruddin Mat Isa stated that:

> "If there are any PAS members who would like to go for *jihad,* we cannot stop them because *jihad* is a religious duty. They don't need to seek party approval if they wish to take up the fight in Afghanistan."[21]

Soon after PAS leaders like Fadzil Noor, Mohamad Sabu and Mahfuz Omar were calling for a total boycott of all American goods and services, and even for the Malaysian government to send troops to Afghanistan to help resist the American-led attacks.[22]

Immediately after Friday *Juma'ah* prayers on 12 October, PAS leaders called for a massive gathering outside the American embassy in the diplomatic quarter of Ampang, Kuala Lumpur. The gathering was meant to serve as a show of support for PAS leaders who intended to deliver a memorandum to the U.S. ambassador (who had just been posted to the capital) and to demonstrate PAS's endorsement of Osama bin Laden and the Taliban. By 2:00 p.m., about three and a half thousand PAS supporters showed up to demonstrate in front of the embassy. Most of them had come directly from the mosques located at the KLCC and *Tabung Haji* complex nearby, and many more came from the mosques in Kampung Baru and Kampung Datuk Keramat. This was certainly the biggest demonstration that had been organized in Kuala Lumpur after the *reformasi* demonstrations of 1998. But this time round, the mood and tenor of the gathering had an altogether different edge to it. Many of the younger members of the party were wearing T-shirts, banners and arm-bands with slogans like "*Allahuakbar*," "*Lailla ha illallah*" and "*Jihad*" on them. Placards and banners were hoisted with slogans like "*Stop the War*," "*We love Jihad*," "*Crush America*" and "*Taliban/ Afghans are our brothers*" written on them.

The mood turned sour when the police ordered the crowd to disperse. Just as the PAS supporters began to line up to perform their prayers (*solat hajat*) before the entrance of the embassy, the armoured police truck let loose a blast from its water cannon and doused the crowd with chemical-laced water. PAS's noisy and emotional demonstration had shown just how far the party was prepared to go to get its point across. But what the leaders of the party did not account for was the reaction that was to follow.

PAS's Reversal of Fortunes in the Wake of the Afghan Bombing Crisis

The reaction to PAS's demonstration of force came from two important quarters: Firstly, the non-Malay and non-Muslim communities in the country—already shocked by PAS's declaration of *jihad* and show of support for the Taliban—were appalled by the rhetoric and tenor of the Friday demonstration. The local non-Malay press gave significant coverage to the event, with photos of PAS supporters marching in the streets and quotes from the PAS leaders themselves. PAS's call for a *jihad* against the "enemies of Islam" clearly had a negative impact on the perception of PAS by the non-Muslims in the country. Overnight, fears of renewed religious militancy were rekindled thanks to the fiery rhetoric of the PAS leaders and followers themselves. These fears were intensified even further as a number of churches were attacked and burnt in different parts of the country. The Christian Federation of Malaysia later issued a statement claiming that those responsible for the arson attacks were motivated by anti-Christian sentiments aroused in the wake of September 11, though they did not single out PAS as the main culprit.[23]

Soon after, the non-Malay parties in the Barisan Nasional began to lend their weight as well. The Women's Wing of the MCA (Wanita MCA) organized a number of public forums to discuss the problem of religious militancy and the controversial issue of the Islamic state in Malaysia. The vice-president of the Gerakan party, Dr S. Vijayaratnam, argued that the governments of the West (and the United States in particular) should "review whatever positive perceptions" they may have had of PAS in the light of recent developments within the party itself and the stand that it chose to take over the Afghan issue.[24]

The other constituency to be affected by PAS's sudden reversion to radical politics was the international diplomatic and business community. Already worried about the political instability in the region as a whole, the latest developments in Malaysia did not go down well with foreign investors who were already worried about the safety of their investments in the country.

Unaware (or oblivious to) the negative image that it would create for itself at home and abroad, PAS's decision to support the Taliban and declare a *jihad* against the West was the biggest own-goal scored by the party against itself over the past few years. By publicly voicing its stand in favour of Osama and the Taliban, the party had alienated itself from vast sections of the local and international community, and pushed itself back to the margins of the local political scene. For many local and foreign observers, it was as if the veil had finally fallen, and PAS had revealed its true self at last. Despite the fact that the more urbane and polished technocrats within the party had been speaking the language of democracy and human rights for the past few years, it was now clear where the sympathies and loyalties of the *Ulama* leadership really lay. The image of the young PAS supporter with clenched fist in the air, wearing an Osama bin Laden T-shirt and shouting "destroy the American *kafirs* and Jews" dealt a major blow to the image of the party in the same way that the image of the ex-DPM Anwar Ibrahim with a black eye dealt a major blow to the credibility of the state's security and judicial institutions three years earlier.

The situation was exploited to the full by the Mahathir administration, which saw it as the best justification for its own policies *vis-a-vis* the local Islamist opposition. Henceforth, the Malaysian government's crackdown on Islamist cells and networks—both real and imagined—would receive less criticism from foreign and local observers. (The same was true of the crackdown on the Islamist opposition in other Muslim countries like Indonesia and Pakistan.[25]) By presenting itself as the face of moderate and progressive Islam at work, the Mahathir government had managed to out-flank the Islamist opposition and reposition itself successfully.

This fact was made all the more clearer when the American Trade Representative Robert B. Zoellick (who was on a visit to Malaysia and the other countries in the region) publicly stated that President Bush "was pleased with the support given by Malaysia."[26] The United States then extended its thanks to the Mahathir administration for the support it had shown to the U.S. despite the difficulties it had to face from the local opposition (meaning PAS). The American Trade Representative was also careful to mention all the key words that were necessary for the upward shift in bilateral relations to register: Zoellick stated that Washington viewed Malaysia as an Islamic country which could "serve the others as a role model for leadership and economic development" not only for the region but for the rest of the Muslim world as well. As an Islamic country, Malaysia was described as "modern," "progressive," "liberal" and "tolerant"—precisely the terms that were required to form a positive chain of equivalences that the Mahathir administration was looking for.

This new understanding would later be cemented when the leaders of Malaysia and the United States finally met for the first time (on 20 October) at the APEC conference held in Shanghai a few weeks later. After the meeting between Dr Mahathir and George Bush, both men agreed to seek ways and means to combat the threat of international terrorism and to increase the level of cooperation in both trade and security matters. The cherry on the cake came in the form of George Bush's observation that the Malaysian Prime Minister was a man he "could deal with" and who also had "a good sense of humour." For the dour-faced *Ulama* of PAS, this was no laughing matter.

Lessons from September 11—The Impact of External Variable Factors on the Domestic Politics of ASEAN

This paper began by trying to highlight the obviously political nature and content of terms like "terror," "terrorism" and "terrorist." We have tried to show that the deployment of such ideologically-loaded terms has always been political by nature, and it is a truism to say that a "terrorist" one day can easily be labelled a "peacemaker" the next—depending on the variable political factors at work.

In the wake of September 11, the Western media, in particular, has been guilty of painting a distorted picture of the ASEAN region as a whole as a hotbed of religious extremism and radicalism. The confounding behaviour of some marginal Islamist movements obviously helped to reinforce that view, and the sight of thousands of angry young Muslims marching in the streets of Kuala Lumpur and Jakarta did little to improve the image of ASEAN as a region of peace and political stability.

But as we have tried to show, the decision to "adopt" Osama bin Laden and the Taliban as part of their cause was certainly not an accident on the part of these radical movements themselves. When groups like the Abu Sayyaf, Laskar Jihad, Front Pembela Islam and even established political parties like PAS in Malaysia took up the cause of the Afghan *jihad* against the West, they were, in fact, engaged in a war of position against their local adversaries on the domestic political scene.

The fact that Osama and the Taliban had been "glorified" thanks to the extensive media coverage given to them by the American media also meant that they had been transformed into universal empty signifiers that were devoid of meaning and content. In time, Osama and the Taliban simply came to mean anything and everything that was anti-American. It is for this reason that the plastic image of Osama managed to gain such a broad appreciative audience all over the world, from Latin America to China. [27]

It would therefore be an error to read the events of post-September 11 in ASEAN on the surface level only. Wearing Osama or Taliban T-shirts does not make one a *jihadi* terrorist any more than wearing a pair of Nike shoes makes one a committed American capitalist. While it is true that politics in the predominantly Muslim countries of ASEAN have indeed shifted closer towards the Islamic register, we would still have to look beneath and beyond the surface phenomena of political rhetoric and slogans to understand the underlying dynamics of local political contestation and adversarial politics at work. The entry of Osama into the space of local ASEAN politics marked the entry of the universal/global into the particular/local—but this simply means that political contestation in ASEAN today is being fought on a number of registers and spheres. The postmodern global village has arrived in no uncertain terms, and what was once a local political process is today part of a global current instead (and vice-versa).

Faced with these realities, the victors in such conflicts will be those who are able to understand and anticipate the consequences of their actions in relation to other developments taking place simultaneously all over the world. The success of the Mahathir administration was due partly to its correct reading of the reaction to the September 11 event. The UMNO-led BN government correctly estimated the sense of shock, horror and apprehension that was bound to emerge in specific sections of the Malaysian community—the urban middle-classes, the non-Malay and non-Muslim minorities and the foreign business/diplomatic community. Sensing the growing sense of alarm among those who felt that Malaysia was in danger of being drawn into the web of international "Islamic terror," the leaders of UMNO were quick to address the issue and to placate the fears of the general public. Nothing was spared in the effort to ensure the Malaysian (and international) community that the Malaysian state would remain on its secular, moderate and capitalist course. UMNO leaders were careful to insist, time and again, that theirs was a brand of "modern," "progressive," "liberal" and "tolerant" Islam that would not allow itself to be hijacked by "militant" and "extremist" elements. Here was a case of a local political elite correctly interpreting the mood swings and shifts in perception that were bound to be brought about by the events that took place thousands of miles away in New York.

PAS, on the other hand, was held captive by its own local constituency. Failing to recognize the swing in public opinion, the leaders of PAS mistakenly brought the party to the brink of ruin by declaring that they would support the *jihad* called for by Osama bin Laden and the Taliban. Seemingly unaware of the catastrophic results that were bound to follow, the PAS leadership pressed on regardless down a path that would only lead to its marginalization and isolation in the country. Here was an example of a political party that totally failed to understand the magnitude and depth of the mood swing in Malaysia, both among the Malays and non-Malays.

What the future holds for ASEAN and the political movements and parties within its borders is, as always, an open question. Globalization has contributed to the collapse of traditional borders as well as the dimensions of time and space. Localities co-exist in the same historical/temporal moment along with global currents. Neither time nor space can be mapped out as they once were. Faced with these ever-shifting variables, the countries of the ASEAN region will undoubtedly remain exposed to external variable factors such as the rise of extremism and violence abroad. Major world events and catastrophes will have an immediate impact on their own societies as well. Likewise, the subtle shifts in discourse and political language will also help to shape the content and meaning of local discursive economies.

In the midst of all this, talk of "terror" and "terrorism" can only make sense if one has a snapshot view of the world. Groups like Laskar Jihad, Front Pembela Islam, Abu Sayyaf and even PAS in Malaysia may appear as radical, extremist, even terrorist by today's standards, but these standards are bound to shift and change in the days and months to come. Any talk of "terror" and "terrorism" in the heart of ASEAN will therefore have to take into account the shifting political realities of this uneven and unequal world. The fine line between the politician and the terrorist is often marked by contingency and variability, and even the most unlikely of characters may end up being an accidental terrorist if the political environment of the day defines him so. The universal terrorist is a symptom of the age we live in.

Notes

1 The attacks on the United States of America on September 11 began during the early hours of the day and followed each other in rapid succession. At around 8:45 a.m., September 11, a hijacked American Airlines jet—Flight 11—flying out of Boston, Massachusetts, crashed into the north tower of the World Trade Centre. Soon after, at around 9:03 a.m., a second hijacked airliner, United Airlines Flight 175 from Boston, crashed into the south tower of the World Trade Centre and exploded. It was only by 9:17 a.m. that the Federal Aviation Administration shut down all New York City area airports. One hour after the first attack, President George Bush, while speaking in Sarasota, Florida, stated that the country had suffered an "apparent terrorist attack." Minutes after the statement (at around 9:45 a.m.), another American Airlines airliner—Flight 77—crashed into the Pentagon. At 10:05 a.m., the south tower of the World Trade Centre collapsed. Soon after the second tower followed suit. Finally at 10:10 a.m., the fourth United Airlines airliner—Flight 93—crashed in Somerset County, Pennsylvania, southeast of Pittsburgh. The speed of the attacks made it extremely difficult for emergency measures to be taken effectively. What complicated matters further for the ground-level emergency staff was the fact that the two towers that were hit were extremely unstable. When the towers finally collapsed, hundreds of New York firemen and rescue workers were also trapped and killed by the falling debris.

2 In his book *9-11*, the American academic Noam Chomsky began by questioning the terminology of the new "global war against terror" itself. As he puts it: "To call this a 'war against terrorism' however, is simply propaganda, unless the 'war' really does target terrorism. But that is plainly not contemplated, because the Western powers could never abide by their own definition of the term, as in the US Code or army manuals. To do so would reveal at once that the US is a terrorist state, as are its clients." (p.16) In other parts of the book, he explains how and why the U.S. itself should be considered a terrorist state along with its clients: "It is worth remembering—particularly since it has been uniformly suppressed—that the US is the only country that has been condemned for international terrorism by the World Court and that rejected a Security Council resolution calling on states to observe international law." (p. 44) Noam Chomsky, *9-11* (New York: Seven Stories Press, 2001).

3 Samuel Huntington, "The Clash of Civilisations," *Foreign Affairs*, Vol. 72, No. 3 (Summer 1993).

4 Bobby Sayyid, *A Fundamental Fear: Eurocentrism and the Emergence of Islamism* (London: Zed Books, 1997), p. 73.

5 Prime Minister Dr Mahathir Mohamad's keynote speech delivered at the Conference on Terrorism organized by the Institute for Strategic and International Studies (ISIS-Malaysia), Kuala Lumpur, 17 November 2001.

6   The official stand taken by the Malaysian government during the Chechen conflict was that it was an "internal security problem" that was entirely within the purview of the Russian government. At no point did the Malaysian government express support or sympathy for the Chechen resistance movement—though it did voice its concerns about the flagrant abuse of rights and numerous acts of terror committed by the Russian troops against the population of Chechnya.

7   In June 2000, the Malaysian public was stunned by the sudden revelation that a major arms heist had taken place in the town of Gerik in Perak. The heist was carried out by a group of fifteen men who were dressed in Army uniforms, driving Pajero jeeps painted green to look like Malaysian Army vehicles. After infiltrating the two Army camps, they managed to get away with more than one hundred pieces of military hardware including hand-held rocket launchers, machine-guns and automatic rifles. The group was finally tracked down to their hideout in Sauk, where they were encircled by government security forces and the Army. After a brief siege and shoot-out, the members of the group were forced to surrender— but not before they had killed two of their (non-Muslim) hostages. In the trial and investigation that followed, it was revealed that those responsible for the arms heist were members of a local Malay *silat* (martial arts) group called al-Maunah which was led by an ex-Army corporal named Mohammad Amin Razali. They were accused of trying to topple the Malaysian government and to overthrow the King in order to bring about an Islamic state by force of arms. The al-Maunah group was put under surveillance and ten of its leaders were sentenced to ten years imprisonment each. The Islamic party PAS claimed that the entire episode was a government-orchestrated *sandiwara* (play-acting) that was meant to tarnish the name of Islam and Islamist movements in general. The government accused PAS of having sympathy with such movements, but to its embarrassment it was soon revealed that some of the al-Maunah members also belonged to the ruling UMNO party.

8   In the same month that the al-Maunah group was arrested and put on trial, a second Islamist "militant" group was identified in the country. This was the so-called "*jihad* gang" that was alleged to be responsible for a number of bank robberies, kidnappings and murders in the country. The group was also accused of several attacks on non-Muslim places of worship, attacks on business premises they regarded as *haram* (unlawful) in Islam and the murder of an Indian member of Parliament (MP Joe Fernandez of the MIC). After a failed robbery attempt on a bank, two members of the gang were wounded and taken into custody. Once under police custody, the wounded members of the gang were made to confess and, during their interrogation, they revealed the identities of themselves and their fellow gang members. The group was finally rounded up by 7 June. The Malaysian authorities then revealed that most of the members of the gang had participated in numerous *jihad* campaigns in Afghanistan and Ambon, Indonesia.

Many of them were also graduates from foreign Islamic universities and *madrasahs* in Pakistan, Egypt and the Arab states.

9   Ustaz Nik Adli Nik Aziz was one of the sons of Tuan Guru Nik Aziz Nik Mat, the *Murshid'ul Am* (Spiritual Leader) of PAS and Chief Minister of Kelantan. In his youth, he had been educated at both government and religious schools in his home state of Kelantan. He then travelled to Pakistan to study at the *Jami'ah Dirasah Islamiah Madrasah* in Karachi. After that, he moved to Peshawar where he studied at the *Ma'ahad Salman*, which was known to have close connections to the Deoband seminary and *madrasah* networks. It was in Peshawar that Nik Adli was first introduced to Afghan fighters and members of the *mujahideen*. He then travelled to Afghanistan and took part in the *mujahideen* campaign against the Russians. Little is known about Nik Adli's *mujahideen* connections, save that he took part in numerous campaigns and left for Malaysia when the conflict subsided. Back in Malaysia, he taught at the religious school in Kampung Melaka (which happened to be his father's constituency) and lived an ordinary life. He was never involved in local PAS politics. In 1999, he was said to have taken over the leadership of the Kumpulan Mujahideen Malaysia (KMM), a clandestine group that was formed by an ex-*mujahideen* and PAS activist, Zainon Ismail, on 12 October 1995. (Nik Adli's younger brother, Nik Abduh, was also educated in the Indian sub-continent. He studied at the *Darul Ulum Deobandi* seminary in Deoband, North India.)

10   Those who were arrested included Zainon Ismail (who was said to be the original founder of the KMM), Mohamad Lutfi Arrifin (member of the PAS Youth Wing of Kedah), Nor Ashid Sakip (Head of PAS Youth at Sungai Benut), Ahmad Tajudin Abu Bakar (Head of PAS Youth at Larut), Salehan Abdul Ghafar, Abu Bakar Che Doi, Alias Ghah, Ahmad Fauzi Daraman and Asfawani Abdullah. Most of them were active members of PAS and religious school teachers by profession.

11   "Tangkapan KMM di bawah ISA: Usaha PM Ambil Hati Amerika," *Harakah*, 16–31 August 2001.

12   *Ibid.*, p. 32.

13   The youth in question was a 26-year-old Malay from Johor by the name of Taufik Abdul Halim. He was carrying the bomb in his bag to the shopping centre in Jakarta when it blew up prematurely, causing serious injuries which finally led to the loss of an arm. While in hospital, he was placed under police custody and subsequently questioned by members of the Malaysian and Indonesian security forces about his involvement with a group of Islamist militants who were thought to be responsible for the bombing of several churches in Java as well. Indonesian security services claimed that a number of young Malays from the peninsula were thought to be active in these Islamist militant cells operating in Java.

14   "We do not support war against any Muslim nation: PM," available at http:// www.Malaysiakini.com, 8 October 2001.

15 A senior aide to the Prime Minister, speaking on condition of anonymity, said, "Malaysia's stand is that if the attacks target specifically Osama bin Laden then they are acceptable, but not a widespread strike that will cause civilian casualties." See "We do not support war against any Muslim nation: PM," available at http://www.Malaysiakini.com, 8 October 2001.

16 *Ibid.*

17 Mohd Irfan Isa, "Osama an excuse to wage war against Islam: Nik Aziz," available at http://www.Malaysiakini.com, 10 October 2001.

18 "US embassy under guard, PAS labels Americans 'war criminals'," available at http://www.Malaysiakini.com, 8 October 2001.

19 *Ibid.*

20 *Ibid.*

21 See Nur Abdul Rahman, "Serangan Amerika langkah permusuhan ke atas umat Islam," *Harakah*, 11 October 2001; and "PAS declares 'jihad' over attacks in Afghanistan," available at http://www.Malaysiakini.com, 10 October 2001. Nashruddin was also quick to add that PAS's definition of *jihad* covered a "wide spectrum including calling for peace, calling for justice and not just taking up arms." He also noted that "we (PAS) are not saying that we are going to create a troop to do that. PAS is also not going to sponsor anyone."

22 Tong Yee Siong, "Mahfuz wants Gov't to provide military aid to Taliban," available at http://www.Malaysiakini.com, 11 October 2001. In a press statement delivered at a press conference, the leader of the Youth Wing of PAS, Mahfuz Omar declared that the Malaysian government should mobilize the member states of the Organization of Islamic Countries (OIC) to fight against the U.S., "in any manner required." Mahfuz also stated that the "OIC should declare the US as a terrorist state and the number one enemy of Islam." He then called on the Malaysian government to temporarily severe all diplomatic and economic ties with the U.S.— Malaysia's largest foreign investor and export market.

23 See Tong Yee Siong, "Church body believes arson attacks linked to extremists," available at http://www.Malaysiakini.com, 6 November 2001. Between September to October, four churches were attacked by unknown arsonists in various states: Johor, Kedah and Selangor. The Christian Federation of Malaysia, the umbrella body to local churches, felt that there was a possible link between religious extremism and the arson attacks on the four churches. The CFM's principal secretary, Wong Kim Kong, stated that the CFM was not convinced that the attacks were carried out by an organized group. "The acts of violence and sabotage were related to religious extremism but they were most probably done by members of the local community," he said.

24 Tong Yee Siong, "Review 'positive' perception of PAS, Gerakan tells US," available at http://www.Malaysiakini.com, 14 October 2001. The vice-president of Gerakan said that previously the U.S. was sympathetic to PAS's cause of struggle in domestic

politics. However, he then added that the U.S. should now "know its friends" following the demonstration at its embassy on Friday. In a statement issued to the press, he stated, "Please look at who burns the American flag now, and who has been moderate and supportive of the US, even to the extent of volunteering cooperation to assist in the apprehension of terrorists responsible for the September 11 calamity."

25 As the crisis developed, the governments of many Muslim states were forced to take action against Islamist opposition parties and movements in their own countries. On 17 October, the Pakistani government of Pervez Musharraf charged the leader of the Jamia'tul Ulema-e Islam (JUI), Maulana Fazlur Rehman, with treason after he had made the claim that President Musharraf had "sold the country to the Americans." Apart from Fazlur Rehman, two other senior JUI leaders were also charged with treason—Ataur Rehman and Abdul Qayyum. In response to the arrests, JUI spokesman Hafiz Riaz Durrani said that they rejected the sedition charges and warned that the JUI party will launch a countrywide campaign against the government's action.

26 Tong Yee Siong, "US thanks Mahathir for support, understands Malaysia's dilemma," available at http://www.Malaysiakini.com, 15 October 2001. At a special press conference held in Kuala Lumpur, the U.S. Trade Representative Zoellick stated that the U.S. "respects Malaysia for all the internal challenges and tensions it has to deal with, which makes its support more meaningful." He also denied that the Mahathir government's objection to the U.S. air strikes on Afghanistan could jeopardize the countries' bilateral trade: "Our trade ties are based on close economic relationship. The support we received in many areas will only strengthen the nature of our relationship." He added that "I don't see any negative variety [of views] in there. The difference of views is understandable."

27 While on a field trip to Hanoi in December 2001, the author encountered scores of Vietnamese teenagers who were proudly showing off their Osama bin Laden T-shirts and badges. This was, we would argue, an expression of residual anti-Americanism going back to the Vietnam war rather than a conscious conversion to Osama's *jihad*.

8

INDONESIA'S ISLAMS AND SEPTEMBER 11: REACTIONS AND PROSPECTS

Rizal Sukma

"Let's take up arms for a jihad *against the U.S."*
(Noer Bahri Noor, an obscure cleric, Makassar,
28 September 2001)

*"Muhammadiyah would not get involved in such a
radical move."*
(Ahmad Syafii Maarif, chairman of the second largest Islamic
organization with 28 million members, Muhammadiyah, 28 September
2001)

*"We are not like Muslims in other countries. Islam in Indonesia is tolerant
and moderate."*
(Ahmad Syafii Maarif, 8 November 2001)

Introduction

The horrific terrorist attacks on September 11 in the U.S. clearly reinforced
the notion of a borderless world. The impacts of the attacks were
immediately, and still are, felt across the globe. This was clearly
demonstrated in various domestic reactions in many parts of the world,
especially within the Muslim world. Indonesia was no exception, and soon

faced a formidable challenge to handle the impacts of the event on its domestic political scene. Indeed, the event posed a serious challenge to the Megawati government, especially its ability to handle domestic political issues with an identifiable Islamic dimension. The event also demonstrated the importance of Islam as a political force capable of influencing the political process in post-Suharto Indonesia.

This paper examines and explains the reactions of the Muslim community in Indonesia to the September 11 terrorist attacks on the United States, and the subsequent American retaliation against Afghanistan. The paper is divided into three sections. The first section explores the general reactions and the content of the debate within the Muslim community. The second section discusses the pressure exerted by radical Islamic voices against Indonesia's government. The third section examines the voices of moderate Islam during the anti-U.S. saga and explains why it appeared to have gone "missing."

The Domestic Reactions: Differences Within A Pluralistic *Ummah*

The general reactions from Indonesia's Islamic community to the September 11 terrorist attacks in the U.S., like in most other countries, have been that of surprise, followed by standard condemnation. On 12 September, for example, Indonesia's government issued a standard statement condemning the attacks. Condemnations were also voiced by several Muslim leaders who generally deplored the attacks and described them as barbaric acts committed by evil people. However, the sympathy quickly turned into a mixture of resentment and antipathy when the U.S. pointed to Osama bin Laden as the mastermind behind the attacks. An intense debate soon ensued in which much of the debate focused on why it happened, who did it, and how Indonesia and the Muslims should respond to the American attack on Afghanistan and the subsequent American-led war on global terrorism.

The Debate on the Causes and Perpetrators of the Attacks

Regarding the question of why it happened, the most common response among Indonesian Muslims, and indeed among ordinary Indonesians in general, has been to describe the attacks as a result of American policy towards the Middle East, especially towards the Israeli-Palestinian conflict. Many believed that the U.S. had pursued a double-standard policy towards the region in general, and towards Palestinian-Israeli conflict in particular. Many pointed out that the double-standard policy was manifested in three areas. First, while preaching the norms of democracy in other parts of the world, the U.S. continued to support many non-democratic regimes in the Middle East.[1] The ambivalent attitude of the U.S. towards the Algerian regime was often cited as an example.[2] Second, while presenting itself as a champion of human rights, the U.S. continued to support the violation of human rights by Israel against Palestinians.[3] Third, the U.S. is largely indifferent whenever the victims of oppression and human rights violations are Muslims.

Such ambiguity in U.S. policy is believed to have been caused by its unfavourable perceptions of Islam. It is common among Indonesia's Muslims to see the U.S. as a power that harbours suspicion towards Islam, especially since the end of the Cold War. In that context, the U.S. is seen as an arrogant power that often disregards and ignores the interests and feeling of others in the pursuit of its own interests. For example, Din Syamsuddin, the Secretary General of the semi-official Council of Indonesia's Ulama (MUI), called on the U.S. "to undergo introspection on its own policy" and "no longer be arrogant."[4] The U.S. support of authoritarian regimes across the Muslim world, including Suharto's Indonesia, is "regarded as collusion in the oppression of the average Muslim."[5]

Despite the common reference to the U.S. policy in the Middle East as the main reason behind the attacks, many doubted and resented the explanation given by the U.S. regarding who was responsible for the attacks. By accusing Osama bin Laden and Al Qaeda of the attacks, the U.S. was seen to have intentionally discredited both Islam and the Muslim community worldwide. On this issue, for example, Din Syamsudin argued that "it is likely that the preliminary evidence was a result of fabrication. We are not convinced that the attacks on the WTC were carried out by Middle Eastern Muslim groups which do not have such a high professionalism."[6] Some even believed that the attacks on WTC were carried out by the Central Intelligence Agency (CIA). Suripto, a former official at Indonesia's National Intelligence Coordination Agency (BAKIN), maintained that "I am convinced that they (CIA) did it, even though this is only my guess."[7] There were also references to the possibility that the attacks were orchestrated by Israel in order to corner the Muslims.

Regarding the position that Indonesia should take, the Indonesian Muslim community was in fact divided into three groups. The first group, the radical Islamic groups, called for *jihad*, urged Indonesia to severe diplomatic ties with the U.S., and warned the government not to prevent those who wanted to go to Afghanistan to wage *jihad* from going. The second view, held by mainstream Islamic organizations such as Muhammadiyah and NU, rejected both *jihad* and the severance of diplomatic ties with the U.S.[8] The proponents of this view, while they opposed the U.S. air strikes, were also quick in saying that reactions by radical groups were only hurting the country by scaring off investors and tourists. The third view maintained that Indonesia should play an active role in urging the United Nations (UN) to stop the bombings of Afghanistan and then take a prominent role in solving the problem of international terrorism through means other than war.

Reactions to American Retaliation

While the views of Indonesians differed regarding the questions of who was responsible and how Indonesia should respond, Indonesians of all streams, from traditionalist Islam to secular nationalists, were almost unanimous in expressing their displeasure at the American use of military force. In this regard, two distinct views can be discerned.

The first view, expressed mainly by militant Islamic groups, maintained that the U.S. military campaign in Afghanistan was no more than a war against Islam.[9] These groups argued that Afghanistan was only a beginning of a wider American war against the Islamic world. For example, Muhammad Kalono, commander of Laskar Jundullah, clearly stated that the American attack against Afghanistan would be considered an attack against Islam. He also threatened that "if one bomb is dropped on Afghanistan, we will attack all American assets in Indonesia."[10] Debates in the U.S. on the possibility of extending war on terrorism to, for example Iraq and Iran, were seen as the evidence for what they believed as American intention to eliminate Islam. In short, the American attacks against Afghanistan should be opposed strongly regardless of whatever cost it might entail for Indonesia.

The second view, while not subscribing to the view that the U.S. campaign in Afghanistan was a war against Islam, was critical of the use of military force against Afghanistan in particular and in combating international terrorism in general. Their objections to the military campaign carried out by the U.S. in Afghanistan were two-fold. First, the attacks were unjust because the U.S. had not provided solid evidence regarding the involvement of the Taliban and Al Qaeda in the September 11 attacks. Second, the military action was seen as ineffective in combating terrorism. Amien Rais, for example, expressed the hope that in dealing with the terrorists, the U.S. would use the law, and not resort to force, or by bombing other countries accused of harbouring them.[11] Imam Prasodjo, a leading political scientist from the University of Indonesia, also doubted the efficacy of the use of force in overcoming terrorism and urged the U.S. "to alleviate the problem of (world's) poverty so that radicalism directed against the U.S. and other rich countries could be reduced."[12] Second, it was also argued that the attacks on Afghanistan contravened human rights, and would make ordinary Afghan civilians the victims.[13] The attacks were seen to have ignored three principles of international law: namely, proportionality, the absence of armed conflict between the attackers and the defenders, and the principle of the presumption of innocence until proven guilty.[14]

In short, it is important to note that the opposition against the U.S. military campaign in Afghanistan was not necessarily a manifestation of their support for Osama bin Laden or the Taliban, but more as a reflection of two general perceptions. First, it was believed that ordinary Muslims were, once again, the victims of U.S. policy.[15] Second, the military attacks on Afghanistan were seen as counter-productive and in breach of the principles of humanity.

Where Has the Moderate Gone? The Radical Takes Charge

When strong and intimidating reactions from radical Islamic groups began to dominate much of the domestic and international media coverage, the tolerant image of Indonesia's Islam was soon put under serious test. That tolerant image seemed to have been overshadowed by voices of anger expressed on the streets of Jakarta, especially in front of the American embassy, by angry Muslims equating American attacks on Afghanistan with attacks on Islam. The image deteriorated further when leaders of radical Islamic groups threatened to expel foreigners and that a *jihad* would be waged against the U.S. Some Islamic organizations even began to recruit volunteers to be sent to Afghanistan to fight alongside the Taliban. The situation worsened when the police seemed reluctant to take action against such threats. Worried about the threats, the U.S. embassy authorized a voluntary evacuation of American citizens, an act that added further pressure on Indonesia's already shaken international reputation. When the voice of mainstream groups within the Islamic community was not heard, worries grew both in Indonesia and abroad that Islam in Indonesia had been successfully hijacked by radical minority groups.

In fact, the radicals that took to the streets constitute a minority group within the highly pluralistic Islamic community in Indonesia. Three groups were particularly active in these anti-American protests. The first was the Islamic Defenders Front (FPI), an organization that became infamous after having attacked and closed down a number of bars and entertainment places in Jakarta since 1999. The FPI, led by a number of Indonesians of Arab descent, quickly established itself as a militant Islamic group with more than 20,000 members, mainly in Jakarta and Solo. The second group, the Islamic Youth Movement (GPI), is also a small Islamic group comprising mainly militant youths. While the GPI has several branches across Indonesia, only those in Jakarta and a few other smaller cities have been actively involved in street protests against the U.S. This group also claimed that it had sent around 300 hundred members to fight against the U.S. in Afghanistan. The third group was Laskar Jundullah, a minor Islamic group based in Yogyakarta with several hundred followers in Jakarta.

The scope of the protests became alarming when several hard-line Islamic groups, such as the Islamic Defenders Front (FPI) and the Laskar Jihad (Jihad Troops) began to warn Americans to leave Indonesia immediately.[16] They also threatened to use their paramilitaries to "sweep" hotels and other places in search of American visitors. Some even went to the extent of threatening to attack American facilities and interests in Indonesia should the U.S. carry out its plan to attack Afghanistan. Concerned about the growing magnitude of anti-American protests and threats to American interests and citizens, the U.S. ambassador to Indonesia, Robert Gelbard, requested a security guarantee from the Indonesian police.[17] When he felt that the police would not be able to extend such a guarantee, the U.S. embassy was forced to close for two weeks.[18]

The most serious development, however, occurred on 25 September when Indonesia's Council of Ulamas (MUI), stated its position. The Council, a semi-official body of Indonesian clerics, issued a declaration calling "on Muslims in the world for *jihad fii sabilillah* ("fight in the path of Allah") should the aggression by the U.S. and its allies against Afghanistan and the

Islamic world occur."[19] The MUI's Secretary General Din Syamsuddin, arguing that the aggression towards Afghanistan could be seen as an act of hostility and hatred against Islam and Muslims, and as an act of injustice, terrorism and a form of imperialism, called on "the U.S. government to reflect on the injustices it has been responsible for and the double standards it has adopted, especially the violations against human rights that have affected the Muslim community."[20] Two other important points included in the Council's statement—the condemnation of the September 11 terrorist attacks and its opposition to the planned "sweeping" against American citizens—were understandably overshadowed by the call for *jihad*. In effect, the MUI's declaration of *jihad* was seen as "one of the harshest statements of support for the Taliban heard from any state-sponsored religious body in the Muslim world."[21]

The pressure intensified when the U.S. finally went ahead with its plan to attack Afghanistan and the Taliban. As anti-U.S. protests now began to pose a challenge to the Megawati presidency, the government was forced to release, on 8 October, a six-point statement on the issue.[22] The statement noted, firstly, that the government expressed a deep concern that a military act was finally carried out. Second, Indonesia noted the statement by the American government that the operation was only launched against terrorist training camps and military installations, and that the operation was not meant as an act of hostility against Islam. Third, the government of Indonesia hoped that the operation would be strictly limited in terms of targets and duration so that it would minimize civilian casualties. Fourth, Indonesia called on the United Nations to undertake a collective response to restore the situation. Fifth, the government warned that reactions and sympathy from Indonesian society should not be expressed in ways contrary to the law. Finally, Indonesia would provide humanitarian assistance to ease the suffering of the people of Afghanistan.

Such a position, however, angered radical groups in Indonesia, especially due to the fact that the government failed to condemn U.S. military action against Afghanistan. The statement, which stopped short of criticizing the U.S. military campaign, was also seen as a statement of support for the U.S. Consequently, anti-American protests intensified. Radical groups began to burn American flags and effigies of President Bush. Threats to expel American citizens intensified. In Makassar, South Sulawesi, the Japanese flag at the consulate there was hauled down by a group of radical students.[23] Several Islamic organizations began to launch a campaign to boycott American goods and products. Some even began to register volunteers to be sent to join the Taliban in Afghanistan in their fight against the U.S. The MUI condemned the U.S. military campaign as "a manifestation of arrogance and oppression," renewed its call for *jihad*, and urged the Indonesian government to temporarily freeze its diplomatic relations with the U.S. and its allies.[24] Din Syamsuddin even declared that "the MUI will not bar the Muslims [in Indonesia] from taking up arms to wage *jihad*. That is part of human rights."[25] The call by the MUI for Indonesia to break its diplomatic ties with the U.S. was increasingly echoed by other radical Islamic groups.

Such a turn of events clearly put the Megawati government on the defensive. Megawati finally bowed to the pressure when, on 14 October at the Istiqlal Grand Mosque in Jakarta, she issued a sharp criticism of the U.S. military campaign in Afghanistan. She declared that "it is unacceptable that someone, a group or even a government—arguing that they are hunting down perpetrators of the terror—attack people or another country for whatever reason." She also maintained that "there are rules that need to be observed. Without observing those rules, the action initially meant to combat violence at the end would itself become a new act of terror and violence" and that "blood cannot be cleansed with blood."[26] The speech, especially the criticisms against the U.S., was widely seen in Indonesia and abroad as a significant departure from Indonesia's previous stance on the issue. As mentioned earlier, in its statement on 8 October, the Megawati government refrained from criticizing the American attack, expressing instead the hope that "the operation is strictly limited in terms of targets and duration so that it would minimize civilian casualties."[27]

The next day, however, the police dispersed a major anti-American protest by the Islamic Defenders Front (FPI) in front of the parliament building in Jakarta. There was violence on both sides, and more than a dozen people were injured when the police broke up the demonstration. It seemed that the message was clear. The government would not tolerate further threats to social order and its international reputation. Vice-President Hamzah Haz, who had been critical of American policy after September 11, was, by mid-October, toning down his rhetoric and downplaying differences between his own and Megawati's positions.[28] Within days, the sight of anti-American protesters calling for *jihad* quickly disappeared from the streets of Jakarta and other major cities. Habied Raziq, leader of FPI and the most vocal opponent of the American campaign in Afghanistan, began to tone down his rhetoric and now filed a law suit against the police, claiming that the police had violated their human rights. He also publicly stated that FPI members had not searched for foreigners and would not do so in the future, maintaining that "the issue is only talks."[29]

Strong criticisms by President Megawati of American attacks on Afghanistan, however, did improve the domestic situation. The MUI leaders, for example, began to clarify its earlier call for *jihad*, arguing that such a *jihad* could be undertaken in many forms other than war. It was at this time that key Muslim leaders from the mainstream Islamic organizations, such as the Nahdlatul Ulama (NU) and Muhammadiyah, began to fill in the public discourse with more rational and moderate views. The chairman of Muhammadiyah, Ahmad Syafii Maarif, for example, strongly denounced the threats against foreigners and Americans as "uncivilized and barbaric" and argued that Indonesia would not survive its economic crisis without American help.[30] He also disapproved the plan by some Islamic organizations to send volunteers to fight alongside the Taliban in Afghanistan. Others, such as NU chairman Hasyim Muzadi and the president of the State Institute of Islamic Studies (IAIN), Azyumardi Azra, called on Indonesian Muslims to focus more on Indonesia's national problems. Demands that Indonesia break its diplomatic relations with the U.S. were also dismissed as unrealistic and irrational.

Regardless of how the event had turned after Megawati's speech, however, the main question frequently asked, especially by outsiders, is "What happened to the moderates in Indonesia?" or, "Could Indonesia's tolerant brand of Islam give way to radical fundamentalism following September 11?"[31]

The "Invisible" Moderate and the Future of Indonesia's Islam

As mentioned earlier, the radical voices expressed on the streets of Jakarta only represented a minority within the majority of Islamic community in Indonesia. Nevertheless, as attention was disproportionably given to them, their views were presented as if they were the dominant views of Indonesia's Muslims. Indeed, the media did play a crucial role in creating such an impression. It failed to capture a broader and more comprehensive picture of the debate within Indonesia's Muslim community. In reality, moderate voices—especially from the moderate and mainstream Islamic organizations such as the Nahdlatul Ulama (with approximately 38 million members) and Muhammadiyah (with approximately 28 million members)—had also made their voices clear. However, as the media was often drawn into making anti-American euphoria on the streets as headlines, those moderate voices were often lost.

For example, the chairman of Muhammadiyah, Ahmad Syafii Maarif, had rejected the call for a worldwide *jihad* issued by Taliban rulers on 17 October should the U.S. attack a Muslim country, warning Indonesian Muslims not "to show emotional ties to the Taliban."[32] He also reacted strongly to the call for *jihad* by MUI, saying that it "would only raise people's emotions and provoke radicalism. I don't think it's wise to use *jihad* in that way."[33] He also condemned the "sweeping" against foreigners as "barbaric and uncivilized" and appealed to those demanding the suspension of diplomatic ties with the U.S. "to use their common sense."[34]

Moderate views were also expressed by Amien Rais, chairman of the People's Consultative Assembly (MPR) and also former chairman of Muhammadiyah, who, in the past, was often seen as "a not-so-moderate" Islamic leader. Responding to the MUI's call for *jihad*, for example, Rais warned Indonesian Muslims "not to resort to *jihad* so hastily and easily." He also stated that "I personally do not want to join the bandwagon and call for *jihad*, unless the U.S. launched indiscriminate attacks on Afghanistan without distinguishing civilians and military targets, and extend the war to other Muslim countries *in the name of religion*."[35] On the "sweeping" threats, it seemed that Rais' opinion was even stronger than other Muslim leaders when he stated that, from the Islamic point of view, such acts are *haram* (strictly forbidden).[36] Responding to the demands that Indonesia break its ties with the U.S., he warned that "despite our condemnation of American attacks on Afghanistan, we should not sacrifice the larger national interests of our country."[37]

As mentioned earlier, strong criticisms by President Megawati of American attacks on Afghanistan did improve the domestic situation.

By late November, mainstream Islamic forces seemed to have been successful in their attempts to counter the views of the radicals. Even though the U.S. continued its military campaign in Afghanistan well into Ramadhan (the Islamic holy month started on 17 November), there were no major anti-American protests carried out by radical Islamic groups. The return of the mainstream moderate voices was further consolidated when top leaders of NU and Muhammadiyah, Ahmad Syafii Maarif and Hasyim Muzadi, met on 2 January 2002. The meeting was meant to forge a common platform between the two Islamic groups in addressing serious challenges facing the Muslim community in particular and Indonesia in general. During the meeting, both leaders expressed their concerns of growing Islamic radicalism in Indonesia. They also stressed that the NU and Muhammadiyah, as the two largest Islamic organizations in Indonesia, should ensure that a moderate and tolerant face of Islam would continue to be the mainstream in the country. In doing so, both organizations agreed to pay more attention to radical Islamic groups, and explain to them what a true face of Islam should be.[38]

Despite the fact that moderate voices within Indonesia's Islam have now returned to the main stage, the problem of religious radicalization, however, remains one of the most intriguing issues in the country. As correctly noted by Hefner, "rather than reflecting broad public sentiment, however, extremist statements like those calling for *jihad* against the U.S. have more to do with a bitter struggle now unfolding between moderates and hard-liners for the hearts and minds of the Muslim community."[39] Even though that struggle is far from over, there are reasons to believe that Indonesia would remain a force that represents a moderate face of Islam in the years to come. That, however, would depend on the ability of the Indonesians to carry out the current democratic reform, and pay more attention to addressing the problems of rule of law and law enforcement. These two prerequisites for democratic reform would ensure that differences in religious interpretations could only be settled in a peaceful manner. These is also the precondition to create a feeling of justice in society which, in turn, would undermine the grounds for grievances and prevent them from turning into support for radicalism.

Notes

1   See Musthafa Abd Rahman, "Hegemoni AS dan Reaksi Islam Politik," *Kompas*, 18 November 2001.
2   See, for example, Musthafa Abd Rahman, "Amerika Serikat dan Gerakan Islam Politik," *Kompas*, 21 October 2001.
3   See various comments along this line in *The Jakarta Post*, 13 September 2001; and *Republika*, 24 September 2001. Former President Abdurrahman Wahid also made a remark along this line. See *Republika*, 17 September 2001.
4   *Media Indonesia*, 13 September 2001; and also in *Kompas*, 16 September 2001.
5   Kirsten Schulze, "Militants and Moderates," *The World Today*, January 2002, p. 12.
6   *Republika*, 17 September 2001.
7   *Republika*, 22 October 2001.

8   *The Jakarta Post*, 29 September 2001. A polling conducted by *Tempo* newspaper also revealed that 81.5 percent of respondents rejected the call for breaking diplomatic ties with the U.S. See *Koran Tempo*, 22 October 2001.

9   See various statements in *Republika*, 17 October 2001.

10   *Suara Karya*, 20 September 2001.

11   *Suara Karya*, 17 September 2001.

12   *Media Indonesia*, 22 September 2001.

13   See, for example, the press release by The Indonesian Association for Legal Aid and Human Rights (PBHI), *Republika*, 13 October 2001. A similar view was also expressed by The Association of Indonesian Churches (PGI), *Republika, ibid.*

14   *Republika*, 20 October 2001.

15   See statements by leaders of various Islamic organizations in *Kompas*, 20 September 2001 and *Republika*, 21 September 2001.

16   *The Jakarta Post*, 22 September 2001.

17   *Koran Tempo*, 22 September 2001.

18   *Kompas*, 28 September 2001.

19   *The Jakarta Post*, 26 September 2001.

20   *Ibid.*

21   Robert W. Hefner, "Muslim Politics in Indonesia After September 11," testimony, available at http://www.house.gov/international_relations/hefn1212.htm.

22   Statement of the Government of Indonesia on Military Action in Afghanistan, 8 October 2001.

23   *The Jakarta Post*, 10 October 2001.

24   See *Pernyataan Sikap Majelis Ulama Indonesia dan Organisasi/Lembaga Islam di Indonesia* [Statement by Indonesia's Council of Ulama and Indonesia's Islamic Organizations and Institutions], issued in Jakarta, 8 October 2001.

25   "Afghanistan Pun Membara [Afghanistan is on Fire]," *Panji Masyarakat*, 17 October 2001.

26   "Unacceptable: Looking for Terrorists by Attacking Other Countries," *Tempo Interaktif*, available at http://www.tempointeraktif.com/news/2001/10/14/1,1,18,id.html, accessed on 24 February 2002 at 13:34 p.m. (Indonesian time). The complete text of the speech is available at http://www.indonesianembassy.org.uk.

27   Statement of the Government of Indonesia on Military Action in Afghanistan, 8 October 2001.

28   "Mega Akhirnya Kecam Amerika [Mega Finally Condemns America]," *Suara Merdeka*, 16 October 2001.

29   Bill Guerin, "Will Indonesia's Leader Please Step Forward," *Asia Times On-Line*, available at http://www.atimes.com, 20 October 2001.

30   *Satunet.com*, 17 September 2001.

31 Lyall Breckon, "Solid in Support of the U.S. ...So Far," *Comparative Connections*, 3rd Quarter 2001 (July–September 2001).

32 *The Jakarta Post*, 18 September 2001.

33 *The Jakarta Post*, 29 September 2001.

34 This comment was reported at http://www.mandiri.com on 11 October 2001.

35 *Kompas*, 28 September 2001. Italics added.

36 *Ibid.*

37 Amien Rais, "Kita Memang Lemah [We Are Seriously Weak]," *Adil*, available at http://www.detik.com, 8 November 2001.

38 The author participated in the meeting as a member of Muhammadiyah's Central Executive Board. He has also been assigned by Syafii Maarif to represent Muhammadiyah in the Muhammadiyah-NU Joint Task-Force charged with the task of formulating a Plan of Action for the program.

39 Hefner, "Muslim Politics in Indonesia After September 11."

COUNTERING THE
NEW TERRORISM

CHAPTER 9

COUNTERING NBC TERRORISM

Ely Karmon

From the methodological point of view two remarks should be made: The first one concerns the problem of definition. Today, many authors and specialists, mainly Americans, use a variety of terms: mega-terrorism, super-terrorism, terrorism of weapons of mass destruction (WMD), and one of the latest—catastrophic terrorism.[1] We prefer to use the more classical term, non-conventional terrorism, referring thus to the use or the threat to use chemical, biological, nuclear and radiological agents or weapons.

The second remark is more substantial. It concerns the effect of non-conventional terrorist attacks. Most researchers consider the weapons used in such attacks as WMD.

We distinguish between limited—or mass destruction—non-conventional terrorist attacks and extreme—or mass annihilation—ones. The difference lies in the number of potential victims from such an attack. Only extreme non-conventional terrorist attacks could produce the destruction of a whole big city with many thousands of victims and contaminate a large area for a long period of time. The limited ones can cause hundreds, perhaps even more victims, but only on a limited scale (for instance in a stadium, an embassy, a mall, etc., and without contaminating the place for a long period of time).

Conclusions Based on ICT Research[2]

In order to decide on an approach for countering NBC terrorism, we should first evaluate the real threat represented by terrorist organizations in the short and medium term. The present analysis is based on a research project carried out by the author at ICT in 1998–99 and whose conclusions are briefly presented here.[3]

We collected publicly-available reports of incidents and built a database, not a complete or exhaustive one, but which surely included most of the known and significant incidents.

The incidents were classified by the period of occurrence (divided into three decades), the continent and country of occurrence, and by their degree of severity. It must be stressed that we tried to identify only incidents of terrorism, i.e., those violent acts with a political background, a difficult task in itself.

Categories and Period of Occurrence (see Annex I)

The incidents of nuclear terrorism sharply declined over the past three decades, from 120 incidents during the 1970s to only 15 in the 1990s. In contrast, the incidents of chemical and biological terrorism showed a gradual but stable rise. In the 1970s, there were 14 incidents of chemical terrorism and 10 incidents of biological terrorism; in the 1980s, there were 34 incidents of chemical terrorism and 13 incidents of biological terrorism; whereas in the 1990s there were 36 reported incidents of chemical terrorism and 18 incidents of biological terrorism.

Severity (see Annex II)

The incidents were divided into seven categories according to their degree of severity. This permitted a more refined analysis of the data.

The threats represented 55 percent of the incidents: 20 percent were threats to use WMD in terrorist attacks. In this category, the threats to use chemical agents represented the majority of incidents (55 percent), the threats to use biological weapons, 25 percent, and the nuclear terrorism threats, 20 percent. Threats against facilities represented 34 percent of the incidents, all of which were threats against nuclear reactors and installations.

Of the total number of incidents, 25 percent were related to an actual terrorist attack. A total of 13 percent of the incidents represented action against facilities of weapons of mass destruction, the majority against nuclear facilities, but always when nuclear material was absent from the facility and thus did not present a real physical danger to the environment.

A further 12 percent of the incidents represented actual use of non-conventional agents. In this category were included incidents that resulted in casualties but also incidents in which the perpetrators succeeded in placing the materials at their destination without causing any injuries. Of the actual use of agents of mass destruction, 88 percent of the incidents were incidents of chemical terrorism.

Location (see Annex III)

Almost 53 percent of the incidents occurred in the United States. Nearly 28 percent of the incidents occurred in Europe.

The incidents that took place in the Middle East represented only 4 percent of the total. Of those, 10 out of 12 were incidents of chemical terrorism and two were of a biological nature. However, it should be noted that Middle Eastern countries (Egypt, Iraq, Iran and possibly Sudan) made relatively massive use of chemical weapons in warfare, implying that these countries and their proxies had less moral qualms about using such weapons.

A total of 10 percent of the incidents occurred in Asia, mainly Japan (majority were incidents of chemical terrorism) and less than 2 percent occurred in South America and Africa.

Conclusions of our Original Research

From the existing data, it was shown that the developed, industrial world (U.S., Europe and Japan) was the main target of non-conventional terrorism, the United States leading the targeted countries.

This could mean that an industrial-technological infrastructure is necessary for the development of a non-conventional capability by a terrorist organization. The WMD facilities targeted (nuclear or chemical plants, military weapons, etc.), are also usually found in these countries.

The fact that very few incidents were registered in the Middle East and South America could imply that this kind of terrorism was less used in areas where conventional terrorism was widespread and successful.

The only real, successful chemical terrorist incidents in the past have been the Aum Shinrikyo's sarin gas attack in Matsumoto in order to kill three judges in 1994 and the Tokyo subway attack on March 15, 1995, which killed 12 people and injured some 5,000. The Matsumoto attack is not only the first real chemical terrorist attack, but also the most sophisticated one, because it used a more advanced dissemination method than the one in Tokyo.[4] According to Bruce Hoffman, it was not Aum but the Liberation Tigers of Tamil Eelam (LTTE) who were the first insurgent guerilla or terrorist organization to stage a chemical weapons attack.[5] In June 1990, the group used chlorine gas in its assault on a besieged Sri Lankan armed forces camp. The attack—like Aum's five years later—was relatively crude, thus again suggesting the impediments to mounting more sophisticated operations employing CBRN weapons.

The only serious radiological incident, which turned out to be a mock or hoax attack, has been the deposit in a Moscow park on November 23, 1995 of "a radioactive container," in fact, a barrel containing radioactive elements, by Chechen terrorists. The quantity of the material in the container and its radioactivity (cesium-137 used in X-ray equipment and some industrial processes) did not represent a serious threat of contamination of the area, leading to possible damage to people's health.[6]

The research conclusion has been that the known terrorist organizations do not have the capability to produce or acquire real non-conventional weapons. Even in cases where they may succeed in producing and using simple, low-level non-conventional weapons, the number of victims would be limited to several dozen or hundreds, as in the case of the sarin gas attack by the Japanese Aum Shinrikyo in March 1995 in the Tokyo subway (12 people dead and several thousands wounded, the majority lightly), in spite of the highly technological character of the organization. Therefore, for the near future, we predicted the more deadly use of conventional weapons and the preparation of low-grade non-conventional attacks to be used in cases of extreme strategic developments (for instance, the use of chemical or biological agents by radical Islamists after the destruction of a Muslim holy shrine).

As noted, it was concluded that the existing terrorist organizations and groups have the potential to perpetrate only limited attacks. But it must be stressed that the political and psychological consequences of such limited attacks would be enormous for any country involved. The anthrax letters of September to October 2001 in the U.S. have demonstrated the significant psychological, social, economic and political damage of a campaign that produced "only" five dead and some 25 injured.

The Implications of the September 11 Attacks and the Anthrax Campaign

The use of hijacked planes as WMD was anticipated by our research, although not on such a huge scale and with such relatively easy success in the heart of the U.S. It must be stressed that Israel was prepared since the 1970s for such a scenario and its air force downed a suspect Libyan civilian plane over the Sinai desert in the 1970s. A small Lebanese civilian plane was shot down near Tel-Aviv by helicopters in May 2001 because it was feared to be a Hezbollah suicide operation.

In the short history of bio-terrorism, only a few terrorist groups have attempted to acquire biological agents, and even fewer have actually attempted to use the agents. The number of known victims from bio-terrorist incidents is also very limited and there have been almost no known fatalities. Some attacks have specifically targeted individuals, while others have focused on the contamination of food and water. Most terrorist groups have used dissemination techniques unlikely to cause mass casualties.

The Japanese terrorist cult, Aum Shinrikyo, is the only group known to have shown an interest in developing aerosol dissemination capability.[7] Aum Shinrikyo's biological program was primitive, although they had a team of some 10 very well-prepared physicists.

Only the Rajneeshee cult incident in 1984 resulted in a relatively high number of victims (751 people became sick), though there were no deaths. The cult's members contaminated salad bars in local restaurants in The Dalles, Oregon with salmonella typhi (typhoid) in order to influence the outcome of a local election. The only known fatal cases reported in the literature were those of bio-crimes (nine cases from 1900 till today) and accidents (in 1979, a release of anthrax spores from a Soviet biological weapons facility in Sverdlovsk killed at least 66 people).

In 1998 and 1999, there was a campaign of threats (33 in 1998 and 46 in 1999) in the United States to perpetrate attacks using anthrax, but no anthrax was used. Some of these threats were contained in letters, most of them addressed to abortion clinics between October 1998 and January 2000. All of these turned out to be hoaxes.[8] Therefore, the anthrax attacks after September 11 can be considered as the first successful bio-terrorism attacks.[9]

The *modus operandi* used during the October 2001 campaign of anthrax letters was not a mass-destructive attack but rather a series of symbolic attacks against individuals representing the media and American power centres. It has even been speculated that all of the cases of anthrax exposure in the

Washington area were the result of the one letter sent to Senator Tom Daschle. It is still not clear whether this is true. According to one specialist, the available open-source evidence strongly suggests that the attacker had access to specific weaponization technology, anthrax culture of the Ames type, and probably immunization against anthrax. The one place where all three of these factors would occur together is a weapons-related research facility. Lately, it was reported that the FBI's search for the person who mailed the anthrax-laced letters that killed five persons had focused on a former U.S. scientist who worked at a government laboratory where he learned how to make a weapons-grade strain of the deadly bacteria.[10] According to a CNN report of 27 March 2002, almost six months after the anthrax letters began turning up in the mail, the mystery of who sent those deadly missives and why persists.

The low level of technology employed, while using a relatively virulent strain of the bacteria, could imply that the perpetrators did not have the sophisticated means to disseminate the anthrax as an aerosol.

The anthrax campaign using simple letters mailed through the federal postal system also showed the lack of preparedness of the authorities concerned, considering that the country had invested a large amount of money and technological effort in preparing itself for WMD attacks since the mid-1990s.

Prognosis For the Future

From all the data published concerning the findings in Al Qaeda bases in Afghanistan, it seems that there was no real production or purchase of non-conventional agents or weapons, although there was a clear interest to acquire or perhaps develop such a capacity.

There is, however, in the near future, the danger of limited, low-level chemical, biological or radiological attacks. The most serious danger is the threat of attacks against existing civilian chemical or nuclear facilities in the developed countries.

Countering the Threat

The countering of NBC terrorism must include several parallel measures: securing the intelligence; the denial of chemical, biological, radiological and nuclear agents, specific hardware and know-how to terrorist and rogue elements; the preparation of specialized teams to deal with NBC attacks in the field; investment in the research and development of detection, protection, decontamination, and treatment equipment and supplies; and finally international coordination in law enforcement, sharing of operational intelligence and police cooperation in the monitoring and tracking of suspected NBC terrorists.

The Intelligence Level

The threat of large-scale acts of terror and the potential for non-conventional terrorism will only intensify the need to prevent terrorist schemes and give warnings before such acts happen. The utmost importance of an early warning appeared clearly after the September 11 attacks in the U.S.: the U.S. Air Force was not at all prepared to deal with the scenario of the use of hijacked civilian planes for suicide attacks inside the country. In the case of surprise chemical or nuclear terrorist attacks, even the first-echelon emergency response teams could be destroyed before they have acted. In the case of biological threats, on the other hand, an early warning could at least permit the immunization of the endangered population. Therefore, it is important to develop a list of alert indicators to warn of the imminent use of chemical, biological or radiological/nuclear agents.

The existence of small groups and cells of highly-motivated religious extremists, right-wing fanatics, unpredictable esoteric or millenarian cults, which in many ways act anarchically, means that the work of penetration and infiltration of these groups will be highly difficult. Thus, the use of human sources, HUMINT, should be expanded and perfected; the counter-terrorism expertise, the cultural knowledge and the language aptitudes of HUMINT officers should be improved.

It is important that intelligence services also cover the so-called gray zones and do not permit the formation of "blind spots" in the overall intelligence picture, such as in Afghanistan recently, Somalia, some other areas in Africa, the jungles of the Philippines or Indonesia, etc. Such "holes" in intelligence coverage would permit terrorist groups to find safe havens in such places, turning them into bases from which to develop and proliferate.

This means that government investment in intelligence capabilities, both human and technological, must be enhanced on a very large scale.

Denial of Know-How, NBC Agents and Production Facilities to Terrorists

With regard to the proliferation of non-conventional agents and weapons, particularly to the extent that it may be used in terrorism and affect the security of entire countries, the next decade will certainly present the most formidable task. The challenge in this case is two-fold: On the one hand, there is the necessity of penetrating and monitoring the activities of the various groups and organizations in their attempts to acquire or use these weapons. On the other hand, there is the need to identify, monitor and neutralize the providers of raw materials, technology and know-how used in the preparation of such weapons. This mission is linked to the overall task of preventing the proliferation of WMD by rogue states, but it is more intricate in many ways.

This means that the interaction and the cooperation between security and military establishments, the scientific community and industry must be strengthened and developed in a manner that can help identify at the earliest possible stage the interest shown by rogue elements in non-conventional capabilities.

Special attention should also be given to the poor security at chemical and nuclear facilities in the former Soviet Union states, mainly Russia, and the potential for former or active scientists and technicians in these sensitive facilities to assist terrorist organizations in achieving a non-conventional capability.

In the industrialized countries (but also in many poorer countries which have become the receptacles of such waste for economic reasons), chemical and nuclear waste facilities, as well as transportation routes for such wastes, should also be considered as potential sources of raw material for terrorist organizations—or targets for attack by these same organizations. Therefore, strict security measures must be adopted for these facilities, deposit sites and transportation means.

Particularly noteworthy is the case of the two Pakistani nuclear scientists who probably advised bin Laden in his effort to develop some kind of nuclear or radiological capability, although it is not yet clear how much they knew about the practical steps in this enterprise and how much information they provided to Al Qaeda.[11] Recently, it has been suggested that hundreds of small radioactive power generators scattered across the Soviet Union decades ago—and largely forgotten—could fall in the hands of terrorists.[12]

On the other hand, it should be noted that Russia has created a special elite force to defend its nuclear facilities and bases, and it seems that the security at these installations has greatly improved.

Another area of concern is the interest that organized criminal elements show in the "lucrative" activity of nuclear theft, although it must be stressed that, until today, most of the known cases of smuggling of radiological/nuclear materials have been either "scam" operations by swindlers or sting operations mounted by the police and security services. The great difficulty facing the police and security services is that the connections between organized crime and terrorist organizations are difficult to monitor.

The funding of such illicit transactions, which involve great sums of money, implies the need for strict monitoring of the flow of funds and money-laundering. The measures taken in this area by the U.S., Europe and other countries as a consequence of the 9-11 attacks illustrate the importance of this aspect of terrorist activity. For instance, it was discovered that a large Muslim charity based in Illinois—intimately connected to Osama bin Laden for years—had had contacts with terror operatives trying to obtain weapons of mass destruction for Al Qaeda.[13]

In some cases, these counter-terrorist measures might imply restrictions on civil rights and liberties as well as the right of the public to obtain information. These developments could be manifested in several ways:

- There might be a need to monitor the personal background of students and researchers involved in, as well as the curriculum development of, projects that could generate knowledge exploitable for the purpose of illicit or violent activities (in this respect the investigation of the anthrax letters affair in the U.S. is suggestive);
- There is already a trend to limit and censor the amount of open scientific and security information accessible on the Internet (the U.S. has decided to limit the data published on governmental sites concerning military and defence issues, data on WMD, civilian oil, gas, chemical and nuclear facilities, etc.; at ICT, we have deliberately limited, from the very beginning of our activity, the amount of data on the Internet and even the links to sites connected to CBRN know-how);
- Countries producing dual-use chemical, biological or radiological materials may have to enact strict laws concerning the

commercialization of these products and find the most efficient ways to monitor and insure their implementation.

Finally, the physical security and limitations of access to sensitive civilian chemical, biological and nuclear facilities, plants and laboratories should be greatly improved. Lately, the U.S. and some European states have even taken military steps in order to defend such facilities, mainly nuclear power plants, in light of the growing amount of information indicating the interest of, or plans by, Islamist groups to attack them.

The Creation of Specialized Intervention Teams and Emergency Tools

The U.S. has been the most advanced country in the preparation of the necessary emergency infrastructure to cope with the aftermath of a chemical/ biological/nuclear terrorist attack. *The Defence Against Weapons of Mass Destruction Act* has permitted the training in CBRN preparedness for 120 major cities across the U.S., a number that has recently increased to 157. This includes training of emergency responders and medical personnel, chemical and biological exercises in cities across the United States, and improvements in the planning and coordination of federal, state, and local agencies dealing with WMD terrorism.

The U.S. has also developed training publications, technical reports, and planning guides, as well as established a Chemical Biological–Rapid Response Team (CB–RRT), including its emergency communications system. The U.S. had already created NEST (Nuclear Emergency Search Team) in the 1970s, which, from 1975 to 1993, intervened some 30 times in nuclear-related incidents.

Unfortunately, few other countries can invest similar levels of financial, scientific and technological resources in the defence against the non-conventional terrorist threat. Therefore, there is a need for the U.S. to help and support other countries to prepare themselves in this field. In this connection, the Office of the Coordinator for Counter-Terrorism of the State Department (S/CT) already trains nations hosting American diplomatic and military facilities in a CBRN preparedness program and first-responder awareness training. The S/CT also manages the inter-agency Foreign Emergency Support Team (FEST), designed to provide support to the victimized host nation in the event of an attack on a U.S. installation. This kind of assistance must be expanded to permit threatened countries to better prepare themselves for attacks not necessarily connected to American interests.

The International Cooperation in the Fight Against CBRN Terrorism

It is axiomatic today that cooperation on the bilateral, regional and international levels is essential in preventing and neutralizing the international terrorist threat. Without sincere and close cooperation between the various countries in the intelligence field, each country, as past experience has shown, will at some point become a victim of terrorism.

A very interesting and important development has been the creation of the Terrorism Prevention Branch (TPB) of the United Nations, within the wider framework of the Centre for International Crime Prevention. The TPB intends, through research, to develop a set of practical pointers for UN member states to cope with the WMD terrorist threat. There have also been initiatives on the part of countries like France and Russia to improve international legislation at the United Nations level concerning the financing of terrorism or the prevention of nuclear terrorism.

The advanced industrial countries—not only the G-8 countries but also Singapore, China, India, South Korea, Brazil, and others—should invest and participate in a coordinated international effort to develop technical prevention tools because in the long run, every country could be a target for an NBC attack or blackmail.[14]

Traditional international arms control measures are less effective in monitoring and controlling proliferation efforts by small terrorist groups, and might not detect the development of a biological or chemical weapons capability using only commercial supplies and equipment. Rather than non-state actors, traditional arms control measures might be effective in influencing the behaviour of state sponsors of terrorism. It is important to build an international consensus against CBRN weapons proliferators as well as isolate states that develop such weapons. It is therefore necessary to develop at the UN, and elsewhere in the international arena, new agreements and legal tools of arms control to cope with the threat.

Annex I
Table of Incidents by Categories and Period of Occurrence

Period	No. of incidents			
	Nuclear	Chemical	Biological	Total
1970–1979	120	14	10	144
1980–1989	32	34	13	79
1990–1998	15	36	18	69
Total	167	84	41	292

Annex II
Table of Incidents by Degree of Severity

Severity	No. of Incidents			
	Nuclear	Chemical	Biological	Total
Threats to Use WMD	10	28	13	51
Threats Against WMD Facilities	98	-	-	98
Attempts to Acquire WMD	11	6	7	24
Possession of WMD	1	8	6	15
Attempted Use of WMD	2	4	10	16
Action Against Facilities of WMD	43	3	-	46
Actual Use of WMD	2	35	5	42
Total	167	84	41	292

Annex III
Diagram of Incidents by their Location

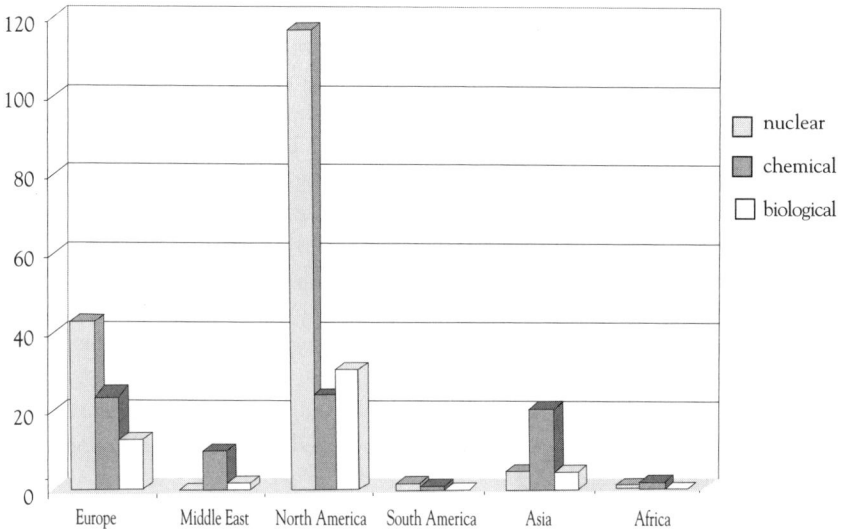

120
100
80
60
40
20
0

nuclear
chemical
biological

Europe Middle East North America South America Asia Africa

Notes

1   See, for instance, Ashton Carter, John Deutch and Philip M. Zelikow, "Catastrophic Terrorism," *Foreign Affairs*, Vol. 80, No. 1 (November 1998).

2   See "Weapons of Mass Destruction—The Threat from Terrorist Organizations," several articles on the subject, in the framework of an international research project in the years 1998–99, by The International Policy Institute for Counter-Terrorism (ICT) at The Interdisciplinary Centre Herzliya, The Interdisciplinary Centre for Technological Analysis and Forecasting at Tel-Aviv University, and the Fondation de la Recherche Strategique in Paris, unpublished.

3   See Ely Karmon, "Trends in Contemporary International Terrorism," in *Countering Suicide Terrorism—An International Conference* (ICT, Herzliya: 2001), pp. 47–60.

4   On June 27, 1994, an Aum Shinrikyo team used a truck, a fan, and a computer system, which opened a valve that released a slow drip of liquid sarin onto a heater, spraying it for 20 minutes; seven innocent people died.

5   See Bruce Hoffman, "New and Continuing Forms of Terrorism and the Debate Over Future Terrorist Use of CBRN Weapons," in B. Roberts (ed.), *Hype of Reality: The "New Terrorism" and Mass Casualty Attacks* (Alexandria, Virginia: CBACI, 2000), pp. 207–224.

6   See Vladimir Orlov, "Preventing Threat of Nuclear Terrorism: The Case of Russia," *Disarmament Diplomacy* (November 1997).

7   In 1990, Aum Shinrikyo used a large truck fitted with a compressor system and six hidden vents, in order to spread botulinum strain, unsuccessfully, at Tokyo's international airport and the U.S. naval bases in Yokohama and Yokosuka. In 1993, Aum tried, over four days, to spread anthrax from a high building with a steam generator, sprayer and fans—again without result.

8   On bio-terrorism, see the comprehensive updated work by W. Seth Carus, *Bioterrorism and Biocrimes: The Illicit Use of Biological Agents Since 1900* (Washington, D.C.: Centre for Counterproliferation Research Working Paper, National Defence University, August 1998, revised February 2001).

9   See Ely Karmon, "The Anthrax Campaign: An Interim Analysis," available at http://www.ict.org.il/articles/articledet. cfm?articleid=401, October 2001.

10   On this subject, see Barbara Hatch Rosenberg's article, "Analysis of the Anthrax Attacks," available at http://www.fas.org/bwc/news/anthraxreport.htm.

11   See *The New York Times*, 3 November 2001.

12   In Georgia, on the Black Sea, a search is underway for at least two of the devices, called radiothermal generators, or RTGs, believed to have been abandoned and then stolen after the closing of a Soviet military base. See *The Washington Post*, 18 March 2002.

13   See "Muslim Group, Leader Charged: Ill.-Based Charity Linked to Bin Laden, Accused of Perjury," *The Washington Post*, 1 May 2002.

14   The Czech Republic, for instance, is very advanced in chemical and biological defence technology.

CHAPTER 10

COUNTERING THE NEW TERRORISM OF AL QAEDA WITHOUT GENERATING CIVILIZATIONAL CONFLICT: THE NEED FOR AN INDIRECT STRATEGY

Kumar Ramakrishna

Several months after the horrific terrorist attacks by Osama bin Laden's Al Qaeda network against the World Trade Centre in New York and the Pentagon in Washington, and following the defeat of the radical Islamic Taliban regime that had been harbouring Al Qaeda in Afghanistan, the goals of the "second stage of the war on terror" being waged by the American-led Coalition are becoming clearer. There appear to be two broad policy imperatives: First, during President George W. Bush's State of the Union address on 29 January, he characterized Iraq, Iran and North Korea as an "axis of evil" primarily because of their weapons of mass destruction (WMD) programmes, and declared his intention to prevent such so-called rogue states from succeeding in developing operational WMD capabilities. Second, on 11 March, Bush declared that America intends to provide training and military aid to enable friendly governments to neutralize terrorist organizations operating within their borders. In this regard, Bush mentioned the military assistance being extended to the Philippines, Yemen and Georgia in their fight against Al Qaeda-linked terrorist organizations.[1] What is clear is that America has expanded Coalition war aims. From the original focus on disrupting Al Qaeda cells worldwide, Washington now seeks to forestall the "danger of the terrorists' teaming up with a small group of nations seeking to develop nuclear and biological weapons."[2] As Bush explained on 11

March, "Terrorist groups are hungry for these weapons, and would use them without a hint of conscience."[3] So adamant is Bush in eliminating the WMD potential of rogue states that it appears that America is making preparations for an armed attack against Iraq. Accordingly, Vice-President Richard Cheney embarked on a tour of the Middle East to marshal the Arab diplomatic backing for this projected operation.[4] Then, in late May, President Bush himself made his way to Europe to, among other things, secure the support of the European allies for a projected military operation against Saddam Hussein.[5] Moreover, as Cheney was making his way to the Middle East, a Pentagon nuclear posture study was leaked which called for the development of a new generation of nuclear weapons capable of ensuring "unilateral assured destruction" of states striking at America with WMD assets. Significantly, the study identified *inter alia*, Syria, Libya, Iran and Iraq—all Muslim states—as potential targets for nuclear strikes.[6]

This paper warns that there are grave dangers inherent in the Bush administration's strategy for the second phase of the war on terror. The apparent American propensity to emphasize military-coercive solutions to the problems of radical Islamic terrorism and WMD proliferation amongst rogue states—many of which as noted happen to be Muslim regimes—is highly counter-productive. Against the wider backdrop of the bloody and seemingly intractable Israeli-Palestinian conflict, as well as the continuing dearth of good political and socio-economic governance of Muslim populations from Egypt to the Philippines, Coalition strategy is gradually generating civilizational enmity between the West and Islam. Moreover, the supreme irony is that such enmity would only ensure that Al Qaeda would always be able to draw on a continually self-replenishing worldwide pool of disaffected young Muslims in order to remain an existential threat to American security. It is argued that to eradicate the so-called "new terrorism" of Osama bin Laden, without accelerating the dangerous drift toward civilizational enmity, requires a proper strategic mix of policy instruments that carefully circumscribes the use of military force. The war against terrorism must be re-conceptualized as an ideological and political war for the hearts and minds of the borderless, transnational Muslim nation, or *ummah*. Hence, instead of pursuing a predominantly military-coercive approach to wiping out radical Islamic terrorist networks worldwide, and indeed expanding the war by attacking sovereign Muslim states whose links to the September 11 tragedy—the single *casus belli* for this war on terror — is highly dubious, the U.S.-led Coalition must carefully control the use of force and greatly expand efforts within the ideological and political realms. Following Andre Beaufre, the great French strategist, we may say that the Coalition will have to employ an *indirect strategy* against Al Qaeda if it wants to defeat it without sparking a wider civilizational conflict between the West and Islam, thereby rendering the war against Osama bin Laden unwinnable.

Deconstructing the "New Terrorism"

As is now known, Al Qaeda's political objective is to set up Islamic states committed to the unequivocal observance of *shariah* law in Muslim lands from the Middle East to Southeast Asia. It intends to do so by first deposing moderate Muslim governments, and this in turn requires eliminating the American support that helps sustain such regimes. It is against this wider political background that we must examine more carefully the so-called "new terrorism" and discern what is indeed "new" and what isn't. In this respect, it must be noted that in military-strategic terms, Al Qaeda is waging a guerilla war against the West and, in particular, the United States. This guerilla war has a transnational character and is not confined to any particular state because the constituency which bin Laden seeks to win the support of is not a specific Muslim population but rather the 1.2 billion-strong Muslim *ummah* or nation, which transcends state and ethnic boundaries. However, it must be emphasized that while this transnational guerilla war may be quite unlike a conventional, geographically delimited guerilla conflict as theorized by Mao and Giap, it nevertheless remains in essence a guerilla war: Like Vo Nguyen Giap before him, Osama bin Laden knows that he cannot engage American forces directly as he does not have the military strength to do so. Hence, like Giap, he intends to defeat America by targeting not its military might but rather what he perceives to be its critical vulnerability or soft underbelly: the American public.[7] However, while bin Laden and Giap may share similar views about what Clausewitz called the "centre of gravity" of the United States, there is a critical difference between the *operational* strategies both used to target this weak spot. Giap sought to achieve his political goal of Vietnamese reunification by undermining public support within America, but he never tried to break the resolve of the American people by sponsoring mass terror attacks within the American "theatre of operations." Rather, Giap sought to gradually erode American popular will by stubbornly remaining undefeated within Vietnam. Technically speaking, therefore, Giap adopted an indirect approach against America in two ways:

at the strategic level by bypassing the armed forces and targeting public will, and within the American theatre by not striking physically at Americans, but rather seeking to produce a debilitating psychological effect on them by indefinitely prolonging the Vietnam War. On the other hand, while bin Laden, like Giap, seeks to bypass the armed forces of the U.S. and strike at the will of the American public, unlike Giap, he is willing to strike *physically* at Americans, as the September 11 attacks clearly proved. Osama bin Laden is thus fighting indirectly at the strategic level, but directly at the operational, theatre level, against American civilians.

While the essence of the Al Qaeda grand strategy of avoiding strength and attacking weakness is familiar enough, there are nonetheless precisely three features of the terrorism it employs which can be considered as novel: the enhanced capacity of the terrorists to plan and carry out attacks; the increased vulnerability of modern societies to terrorist strikes; and the religious-messianic motivation of the terrorists, which appears to predispose them to mass-casualty strikes. The first two characteristics of the new terrorism are a direct consequence of globalization—what Anthony McGrew calls the "multiplicity of linkages and interconnections between the states and societies which make up the modern world system."[8] Globalization has augmented terrorist capabilities in several ways. First, the rapid proliferation and decreasing cost of communications technology such as satellite telephones, e-mail and faxes have enabled terrorist organizations to control and coordinate their operational activities more efficiently than before: The information revolution has enabled groups like Al Qaeda to form *networks* of widely dispersed, operationally self-reliant and thus from an official perspective, elusive cells, that are nevertheless held together coherently by a shared ideology and doctrine.[9] Second, satellite television channels such as CNN and Al-Jazeera in Qatar not merely enable terrorist groups to evaluate the political and economic impact of their violent acts, they also help terrorists closely monitor the government policies and strategies formulated in response, thereby providing them with the opportunity to keep one step ahead of the authorities. For example, because reports of the plans of American law enforcement agencies to adopt racial profiling of terrorists circulated quickly round the globe, it would seem that Al Qaeda may simply resort to using non-Arabs for future strikes on American soil and at American targets.[10] Third, globalization processes also enable terrorist groups to secure the funds needed to sustain their operations. For instance, the Internet enables terrorist organizations to arrange funds transfers around the world far more efficiently than before, while also expediting the traditional clan-based *hawala* system of moving money between countries, a practice still found in Middle Eastern and Asian societies. The illicit sale on global markets of drugs and diamonds is similarly facilitated. In fact, Michael T. Klare has observed that modern terrorist organizations, in opening offshore banking accounts, establishing foreign offices, transmitting instructions via fax and satellite phones, and wiring monies across borders, resemble conventional multinational firms.[11] Fourth, globalization processes have also enhanced access to weaponry and technical expertise. Using state-of-the-art encryption technology, terrorists can make secure online purchases of explosives as well as small arms such as rifles, machine-guns, land mines, man-portable anti-tank weapons, light mortars, and rocket-propelled grenades (RPGs). In addition, through accessing the voluminous information available on the World Wide Web, terrorists can plan effective operations involving "kidnapping, bomb-making and assassination."[12]

This ability to tap the vast information resources of the World Wide Web, enables terrorist organizations to "adapt their structure and strategy, including their use of violence, to their environment and to the degree and kind of pressure that governments can bring to bear against them."[13] This suggests that the well-educated new terrorists, many of whom seem to possess backgrounds in science and engineering,[14] can think up creative ways of inflicting mass casualties quite apart from simple reliance on WMD. In other words, modern societies must also be alert not merely to the threat of WMD use by terrorists, but also to various "modalities of mass destruction (MMD)." Thomas Homer-Dixon points out in this regard that:[15]

> ...modern societies are filled with supercharged devices packed with energy, combustibles, and poisons, giving terrorists ample opportunities to destructive ends. To cause horrendous damage, all terrorists must do is figure out how to release this power and let it run wild or, as they did on September 11, take control of this power and retarget it.

Homer-Dixon identifies, for instance, large gas pipelines running through urban areas, the radioactive waste pools of nuclear reactors, and chemical plants as providing "countless opportunities for turning supposedly benign technology to destructive ends."[16]

Not only has globalization significantly increased the capacity of terrorists to wreak havoc, it has also enhanced the vulnerability of modern societies to the new terrorism in two ways. First, states have increasingly porous borders. People movements in and out of countries in recent decades have been greatly facilitated by the increasing convenience and affordability of air travel, and this has had direct implications for the current conflict with Al Qaeda: On the one hand, Muslim diaspora communities incorporating small but significant minorities of radical elements have sprung up in America and European countries. Moreover, in the case of the Middle East and Southeast Asia, the movement of thousands of Muslims between these regions and the centres of radical Islamic teaching in South Asia both during and after the Afghan *jihad* against the Soviet Union, has resulted in the exposure of scores of moderate Muslims, from Morocco to the Philippines, to radical Islamic ideas. Furthermore, it should not be forgotten that the Internet also contributes to the ideological permeability of modern societies, as the tenets of radical Islamic thinking can be disseminated effortlessly across national boundaries via cyberspace. Apart from what James Rosenau once called the "penetrated" nature of the modern state, moreover, globalization processes have rendered modern societies extremely vulnerable to the new terrorism in another critical way. As Homer-Dixon has argued, a modern state represents not merely an extremely complex and densely-packed network of cities, highways, railways, airports and power grids, but more importantly, a "tightly-coupled, very unstable, and highly nonlinear psychological network." This network is wired together tightly by "Internet connections, satellite signals, fiber-optic cables, talk radio, and 24-hour television news." These tight interconnections greatly expedited the rapid outward spread of the shock of the September 11 attacks. Consequently, Al Qaeda's strikes had their "biggest impact" on the "collective psychology" of Americans and their "subjective feelings of safety and security." In other words, the complex psychic network that makes up modern societies "acts like a huge megaphone, vastly amplifying the emotional impact of terrorism."[17] Because Al Qaeda, as we have seen, seeks to physically target the American public, this novel feature of modern globalized societies significantly enhances its potential impact.

Added to the enhanced capacity of latter-day terrorist organizations to wreak havoc, and the increased vulnerability of modern societies to such attacks, a third novel characteristic of the new terrorism is its *religious-messianic content*. As David Rapoport argues, we are witnessing the "fourth wave" of terrorism. While terrorist groups in the first wave, which lasted from the 1880s to the 1920s, sought political and civil reforms within authoritarian political systems like Czarist Russia, the second wave which encompassed the 1920s to the 1960s was characterized by terrorist organizations like the Irish Republican Army and Irgun in Palestine, seeking national self-determination and freedom from colonial domination. Like the first and second waves which overlapped, the latter wave also intersected to a degree with the third wave of terrorism in the 1970s, which was defined by left-wing revolutionary organizations such as the Red Brigades and the Japanese Red Army faction, which saw themselves as vanguards for the Third World masses. Following the Iranian revolution of 1979 and the Soviet defeat in Afghanistan ten years later, however, it appeared that "religion now provided more hope than the prevailing revolutionary ethos did."[18] In this context, what Steven Simon and Daniel Benjamin call "religiously motivated terrorism," appears to characterize the latest wave of terror.[19]

Moreover, the religious-messianic motivation of the new terrorists appears to encourage the perpetration of mass casualties and indiscriminating terror. Previous terrorist organizations, whether motivated by political, nationalist anti-colonial, or revolutionary goals, were careful to refrain from indiscriminate attacks on civilians, precisely because they recognized that ultimately, "wanton violence could be counter-productive," and they needed popular support to attain their political aims.[20] Al Qaeda, on the other hand, because it is ideologically predisposed to see all Americans, civilian and combatant alike, as infidels, seems to have little compunction in targeting non-combatants. Moreover, the messianic orientation of the Al Qaeda leadership appears to explain their lack of discrete, negotiable political demands apart from the stated intent to eliminate Western and American influence from Muslim lands as a prelude to setting up truly Islamic governments. Hence, as Simon and Benjamin argue, the worrying new characteristic of the new terrorism is "the absence of a plausible political agenda" which is correlated with the "increased lethality of attacks" due to the "absence of constraints on violence."[21] This lack of concern for mass civilian casualties is certainly one key reason why the horrific September 11 strikes were mounted. Nevertheless, despite a primordial hatred of infidels that justifies the use of virtually unlimited force against them, bin Laden remains an utterly rational man: After all, he remains an experienced commander who possesses considerable operational experience from the Afghan *jihad* against the Soviets.[22] In this context, bin Laden, shrewdly judging the American public to be unwilling to bear major sacrifice—an assessment which he appears to have developed as a consequence of President Clinton's decision to withdraw U.S. forces from Somalia in 1993 following the combat deaths of 18 servicemen—as noted, deliberately seeks to generate very high levels of fear and anxiety amongst the American public. He probably holds that at some point in the campaign—probably after another series of spectacular mass-casualty strikes—the people will compel the American government to disengage from the Muslim world. The desire to directly target and destroy the will of the American people by employing extra-normal means of destruction against them is also precisely why Al Qaeda has sought to acquire WMD capabilities, and may be plotting other MMD strikes.

The Real Challenge: Killing a "Hydra" by "Draining the Swamp" it Draws Sustenance From

In sum, while the essence of the Al Qaeda grand strategy of avoiding American strength and hitting American weakness is, in fact, familiar to us, the enhanced capacity of terrorists to rain death and destruction on societies, the increasingly pronounced vulnerability of such societies to such attacks, and the religious-messianic predisposition of these terrorists to mass-casualty terrorism, are what makes this phenomenon quite distinct from previous terror waves. It would seem that while a great deal of action can and should be taken to blunt the offensive potential of Al Qaeda, as well as improve homeland security, these measures in and of themselves are unlikely to eliminate the existential Al Qaeda threat. Even if the Coalition succeeds in disrupting Al Qaeda cells across the world, even if the transnational terrorist funding flows are interdicted, and even if radical Muslims are somehow denied capabilities to produce and deliver weapons of mass destruction, the threat would not necessarily be eradicated. Globalization has expedited what Thomas Friedman calls the "democratization" of finance, technology, and information. Consequently a fanatically-determined radical Islamic core that is scattered throughout the world—but leveraging on communications technology to coordinate activities and manpower movement—can, over time, generate new cells, reconstruct disrupted logistics and funding networks while clandestinely restoring access to WMD capabilities.

The basic problem is that as long as sizable pockets of disgruntled, anti-American young Muslims remain in countries from Nigeria to the

Philippines, there will always be a radical Islamic movement posing an existential threat to Western and especially U.S. interests. For this reason, Robert A. Levine is absolutely correct in characterizing Al Qaeda as a "living organism that generates new cells as old ones die,"[23] while Duncan Campbell rightly compares the network to a "many-headed hydra."[24] It should not be forgotten that while most Muslim governments supported the Coalition's air campaign against the Taliban, which began on October 7, 2001, considerable disquiet was still palpable among Muslims worldwide. In Southeast Asia for instance, the Islamic fundamentalist political party PAS called on Malaysian Muslims to wage a *jihad* against the U.S.,[25] while Jakarta was hit by waves of anti-American demonstrations.[26] Hence, post-Afghanistan military campaigns undertaken against other Muslim states not directly connected to the September 11 attacks, and more civilian deaths, however collateral and unintended, would provoke significant Muslim unrest throughout the world. Thousands of angry Muslim youths would rally to Osama bin Laden's cause. Hence Deputy Secretary of Defence Paul Wolfowitz's comment soon after September 11 retains its prescience: Victory over the radical Islamic threat will ultimately require the West to "drain the swamp" of disgruntled, anti-Western Muslims. The West needs to *kill the radical Islamic hydra*, not interminably snip at its many heads.

If we accept that the real key to this war against the new terrorism requires killing the radical Islamic hydra, it follows that questions of reducing homeland vulnerability, improving Coalition intelligence-sharing, tightening immigration controls, interdicting terrorist money flows, assisting friendly states to combat terrorist groups within their borders, and maintaining the multinational diplomatic momentum against terror, while important, should be re-conceptualized as short-term, *second-order* issues. The first-order questions should relate to what longer-term strategies are needed to drain the swamp of recruits for Al Qaeda and its affiliated terrorist organizations in the Middle East, South Asia and Southeast Asia. One school of thought in this respect argues that governments in the Middle East and Southeast Asia ought to improve the delivery of social welfare and economic opportunities, so as to prevent their growing young male populations from falling prey to radical Islamic propaganda excoriating decrepit governmental performance.[27] In this connection, it should be noted that radical organizations such as Hamas, Hezbollah and even Al Qaeda have won support in poorer Muslim countries through their social welfare activities. It should also be conceded that another powerful attraction of such radical groups is that they meet not just the material needs of young people but also through Islam, they make a deliberate attempt to satisfy the spiritual quest of restless young men for a sense of meaning, personal dignity, and a powerful sense of group identity.[28]

The search for meaning brings us to the second school of thought concerning how exactly to drain the swamp of disgruntled young Muslims willing to rally to the messianic Al Qaeda cause. Scholars like Daniel Pipes feel that it is far too simplistic to suggest that radical Islamic terrorists are the products of economically downtrodden backgrounds. He cites Egyptian research that suggests that radical Islamists, in fact, tend to be "young (early twenties), of rural or small-town background, from the middle or lower middle class, with high achievement and motivation, upwardly mobile, with science or engineering education, and from a normally cohesive family." He adds pointedly that rather than being "the children of poverty or despair," they actually seem like "ideal or model young Egyptians."[29] This suggests that Adrian Karatnycky may have a point when he argues that like "the leaders of America's Weather Underground, Germany's Baader-Meinhof Gang, Italy's Red Brigades, and Japan's Red Army Faction, the Islamic terrorists were university-educated converts," who have "grown contemptuous of 'soft' and corrupt elites and are drawn to the romance of revolutionary guerilla movements."[30] In Martin Kramer's view, these leadership elements of the radical Islamic terrorist organizations tend to be potential "counter-elites" who for some reason, despite their wealth, "cannot translate their socio-economic assets into political clout."[31] Hence, as Shibley Telhami points out, they deeply resent "their inferior position in society because they 'know better,' and because they are also more aware of their capacity to affect change."[32] This suggests that more than mere socio-economic reform, what is more crucial is political reform aimed at opening up the political space to enhance participation and democratic accountability, and eliminating official corruption. Often an "Islamic ideology" also provides these counter-elites "with a critique of society and an agenda for radical social change,"[33] while serving as a powerful tool to "recruit a following among the poor, who make valuable foot-soldiers."[34]

Now if all Islamic fundamentalists want is greater socio-economic and political reform so as to move closer to actualizing the ideal of a good Islamic government under God, this would not necessarily be a bad thing, as at least there would be a basis for accommodating these demands. As Mark Huband notes, while Islamic fundamentalists seek to Islamize Muslim society, they are quite willing to accept a variety of methodologies for doing so. Thus "variations exist as to whether the political power they are seeking should be held by authoritarian theocrats, influential imams making firm but diplomatic suggestions to open-minded secularists, or Muslim democrats relying on a parliamentary system to Islamize society."[35] The problem only arises when certain Islamic factions consider it spiritual anathema to even dialogue with secular Muslim political leaders and seek therefore to Islamize society at the point of a gun. This virulent, exclusionist ideological strain is what Al Qaeda represents. Thus, while democratic and socio-economic reforms do help to alleviate the pool of Muslim discontent that might be exploited by Al Qaeda, it is hard to escape the conclusion that the deepest root of the new terrorism is ideological. This implies that ideological counter-programming, or in short, education, is required. Moreover, it seems that a *liberal arts* form of education which encourages critical, analytical, multidimensional thinking may prove particularly crucial: Two of the leading scholars on religious fundamentalism, Scott Appleby and Martin Marty, argue that it is no accident that "fundamentalist movements' middle management and rank and file frequently have educational and professional backgrounds in applied sciences, technical and bureaucratic fields."[36] Pipes similarly notes that a "disproportionate number of terrorists and suicide bombers have higher education, often in engineering and the sciences."[37] Appleby and Marty suggest that this is why Islamic fundamentalists "read scriptures like engineers read blueprints—as a prosaic set of instructions and specifications," and hence "the complex, multivocal, ambiguous treasury of mysteries is reduced to a storehouse of raw materials to be ransacked as needed for building a political program." They add wryly that few "poets or cosmologists find their way into fundamentalist cadres."[38]

The Ideological Component of an "Indirect Strategy" Against Al Qaeda

Because the real root cause of radical Islamic terrorism cannot be solved by short-term air strikes but rather by patient, longer-term ideological counter-programming, to kill the radical Islamic hydra requires what is called an "indirect strategy." According to the great French strategic theorist Andre Beaufre, while a direct strategy involves the application of military force as the primary means of imposing one's will on an enemy, with diplomatic, economic and propaganda instruments orchestrated in support of the main military thrust, in indirect strategy, military force is carefully calibrated to support and not scupper the primarily non-military means to impose one's will on the enemy.[39] In the 1991 Gulf War, the centre of gravity was the Iraqi armed forces in Kuwait, and all instruments of policy were orchestrated to support the central military thrust against Saddam's forces. This was thus an illustration of direct strategy. In the current war against Al Qaeda, on the other hand, because bin Laden cannot wage his war without willing terrorists, the centre of gravity remains the hearts and minds of the transnational Muslim *ummah*. This implies that what is required is an overall approach elevating primarily ideological and, as we shall see, political measures. Diplomatic and military-coercive measures, while important, must play a strong supporting role within this indirect strategy framework.

What should be the content of the ideological component of a Coalition indirect strategy? Basically, Muslims the world over must be persuaded that Islam *can* co-exist with modernity, and it is possible and desirable to be both a good Muslim and still be thoroughly engaged with a modern capitalist world system. The fundamentalist Islamic clerics, particularly of the Saudi Wahhabi and northern Indian Deobandi schools which are amongst the ideological progenitors of both Al Qaeda and the Taliban, basically argue that the reason why Islamic societies have fallen behind the West in all spheres of endeavour has been because they have been seduced by the amoral and material accoutrements of Westernization and have thus deviated from the original pristine teachings of the Prophet. Hence, the fundamentalists want to reform Islam—in the case of radical fundamentalists like the Taliban and Al Qaeda, by force, if necessary—and re-institute the laws, traditions and practices of seventh-century Arabian Islam. In other words, the Islamic fundamentalists—like the Egyptian Muslim Brotherhood—want to re-create a *Dar al-Islam*, the realm of Islam, separating it from the *Dar al-Kufr*, the realm of unbelief. The *Dar al-Kufr* has also been called the *Dar al-Harb*, or realm of war. The quintessential fundamentalist act of *hijra*, or emigration from the *Dar al-Kufr* to the purist *Dar al-Islam*, can take several forms. It may signify, for each believer, a personal spiritual retreat from worldly values and practices. In other cases, it might even imply a conscious physical extraction out of the *Dar al-Kufr* community to remote localities where a commune-like *Dar al-Islam* may be created. Then there is the radical interpretation of *hijra* that goes even further, calling for not merely spiritual and physical separation but active *jihad* against the realm of unbelievers. We may thus say that radical Islamic fundamentalists possess an extremely literal interpretation of the *Dar al-Harb*, or realm of war.[40] What the West should be doing in this respect is to discreetly back the moderate Islamic clerics who call for the right of all Muslims to exercise *ijtihad*, or independent reasoning, which would enable them to adopt lifestyles according to conscientious individual interpretations of Islam, rather than slavishly adhere to the authoritarian *fatwas* of small coteries of radical Islamic clerics who pursue political goals under the guise of religion. As the leading moderate Malaysian Islamic scholar Farish Noor puts it, Islam "is simply too important to be left in the hands of the Ulama [religious clerics]."[41]

To expedite *ijtihad* amongst Muslims everywhere requires the modernization of education across the Muslim world. Certainly, the study of Islamic history and the memorization of the *shariah* law is the entitlement of Muslims everywhere. However, as the former Thai Foreign Minister Surin Pitsuwan, a devout Muslim, laments, the original spirit of inquiry—which led Arab Muslim intellectuals of the past to attain great heights of achievement in science, philosophy, and the arts—has long been absent from Islamic education in general. Rather, the general principle in too many religious schools appears to be "memorization, stop thinking, stop rationalizing."[42] The end-result has been the production of generations of young people predisposed to see the world as irrevocably divided between the *Dar al-Islam* and *Dar al-Kufr*—or even worse, in the case of those with a radical Islamic education from the Saudi-financed Wahhabi schools in Pakistan and Afghanistan—as the *Dar al-Harb*. In the latter case, young men emerge utterly steeped in the skewed Al Qaeda world-view. As Mohamed Charfi argues, therefore, to prevent the development of a dangerous tunnel vision amongst young Muslims everywhere, traditional religious education must simply be supplemented by exposure to works by Islamic scholars like Averroes and Avicenna that examine how Islam can engage with a real-world environment in which "sexual equality, human rights and the development of democracy" are burning issues of the day.[43] Similarly, contemporary works by scholars such as Indonesia's Nurcholish Majid and Iran's Abdul Saroush could also be studied at university level as they are "trying to extract the prophetic truths from the Koran to show the inherent compatibility of modern-day concerns with the sacred texts."[44] The issue of undergraduate education is especially pertinent, because of the so-called "youth bulge" affecting many Muslim countries. Roy Mottahedeh argues in this respect that such education should be in the vernacular, so as to "reach the underprivileged, create the textbooks and even the language of discourse, and allow a discourse that draws on the cultures of these countries." Moreover, Mottahedeh argues strongly for a liberal arts emphasis that encourages critical thinking and writing "about both the human and scientific spheres." He adds that the "graduates of such an expanded liberal arts education system would be forces for economic development."[45]

In sum, the ideological component of a Coalition indirect strategy to disembowel Al Qaeda requires that ways and means be found to promote what Graham Fuller calls a "Muslim Reformation and the eventual emergence of a politics at once authentically Islamist yet also authentically liberal and democratic."[46] Similarly, Mottahedeh calls for an ambitious new "Fulbright Plan" to establish "well-funded liberal arts institutions" teaching in vernacular languages and offering bachelor's degrees in "Cairo, Karachi and kindred places" throughout the Muslim world.[47] Over the long term, the graduates of these institutions, grounded in the Islamic faith yet, through the discipline of *ijtihad*, able to confront and dialogue meaningfully with other civilizations, will be able to speak out and "reclaim centre stage"[48] from the radical Islamic exclusionists.

The Political Component

A Coalition indirect strategy must also seek to immediately and aggressively combat the virulent anti-Americanism that unfortunately characterizes the majority of Muslims everywhere. Merely seeking to encourage the reform of Islamic education, while important, is not enough; it is quite possible to be a moderate Muslim ideologically and still be anti-American politically. This is because of a widespread perception that the *Dar al-Islam* "has fallen behind in economic development, education, science and democratization" because of a worldwide Jewish-American conspiracy to keep Muslims downtrodden.[49] This attitude is further exacerbated not just by incessant radical Islamic propaganda, but by American public relations gaffes, rapidly transmitted throughout the wired-up Muslim world. As Philip Taylor points out, a "photograph of an American cruise missile bound for Baghdad during Operation Desert Fox with the words 'Happy Ramadan' chalked on the side is still widely remembered" throughout the realm of Islam.[50] This deeply-ingrained anti-Americanism has resulted in a strong tendency to doubt Washington's good intentions as well as its pronouncements. This explains the stubborn belief amongst many street-level Muslims that the September 11 attacks were actually the work of the Mossad, and that videotapes of bin Laden all but admitting culpability for the strikes were, in fact, doctored by American intelligence services.[51] No matter how daunting the task, however, there remains an urgent need to aggressively push the message that the West in general, and America in particular, is a friend of Islam. Hence, considerably more publicity must be given to, *inter alia*, the historical efforts of American Presidents to seek solutions to the Israeli-Palestinian conflict, the Western contribution to the liberation of Kuwait from Iraqi aggression, as well as the humanitarian interventions in Somalia, Bosnia and Kosovo in which the aim was to save thousands of Muslims from genocidal slaughter.[52] In fact, the images of joyful Afghans celebrating the demise of the Taliban in the company of American forces and continuing Western efforts in the political and economic rehabilitation of Afghanistan offers much positive grist for the Western strategic information mill, and have to be exploited.

In this connection, the Bush White House was right in deciding to make permanent the Coalition Information Centre that was established soon after the air campaign in Afghanistan commenced. The Centre, in seeking to counter "what the White House sees as a rising tide of anti-Americanism,"[53] seeks to project a "unified message" from the White House, Pentagon, State Department and other Coalition partners. In addition, it is fortunate that earlier plans within the Defence Department to start up an Office of Strategic Influence, which among other things, would have sought to "plant disinformation with overseas journalists," were shelved.[54] Given the serious credibility problem America has throughout the Muslim world, to be seen to be telling the truth and nothing but the truth is the pressing necessity. More generally, to mount an effective campaign to counter Muslim anti-Americanism requires a much-needed augmenting of American public diplomacy capacity. This should involve a reversal of the short-sighted 1999 decision to collapse the old United States Information Agency into the State Department. This move alienated many able public diplomacy officers, who felt constrained by bureaucratic red tape and a general perception that they were "second-class citizens."[55] In addition, Anthony J. Blinken argues, *inter alia*, for a "rapid response program to correct or clarify distortions of U.S. policy," that American diplomatic staff posted to Muslim countries should actively engage the local mass media more often, and that the Muslim programming of both the Voice of America and Worldnet need further enhancement.[56] On the other hand, Washington should also put pressure on countries such as Saudi Arabia, Egypt and Iraq to rein in their controlled, anti-Western mass media, and instead "adopt laws and policies that promote greater media freedom." As David Hoffman points out, while a free media may not necessarily be pro-West, "it does at least open new space for moderate voices that can combat anti-Western propaganda." Hoffman also notes that in the Middle East, national radio and television, and not transnational satellite television, are the most important media. On the one hand, the relatively high cost of satellite dishes reduces the potential audience for Arabic channels like Al-Jazeera, while international satellite stations like CNN and BBC do not offer local and national news. Moreover, the relatively low literacy rates hamstring the effectiveness of print media.[57]

The Diplomatic Component

Philip Taylor has correctly argued that "to be effective, propaganda requires image and reality to go hand in hand, and hence Western 'reality' has to prevail not just in the short term but also over the longer haul."[58] In other words, in order for the key ideological and political instruments of a Western indirect strategy against Al Qaeda to have real bite, they need to be strongly supported by concrete diplomatic activity geared toward addressing the "sources of the intense anti-Americanism that now roils the Arab and Islamic world and forms the backdrop for Al Qaeda attacks."[59] The relationship between anti-Americanism and terror is "complicated and indirect," and somewhat similar to "that between oxygen and fire. Oxygen does not cause fires—the sparks must come from somewhere else—but fire requires oxygen to rage."[60] Hence, the myriad sources of Muslim disgruntlement at the West in general and America especially, spontaneously generate "political oxygen" which can be ruthlessly exploited by radical Islamic elements to fan the flames of anti-Americanism and engender the civilizational enmity which helps Al Qaeda recruit its troops. Hence, it is of the utmost importance to harness Coalition diplomatic energies to address the sources of Muslim discontent, thereby buttressing the main ideological and political thrust of Western indirect strategy worldwide.

In this respect, the Coalition must remain deeply engaged in the reconstruction and rehabilitation of Afghanistan. While the Americans should be lauded for rapidly defeating the much-vaunted Taliban forces and their Al Qaeda allies in the field, it is increasingly apparent that a significant number of Afghan civilian casualties were generated. Coupled with the widespread perception amongst Muslims that Afghanistan was "abandoned" by America in the early 1990s after the Soviet withdrawal, if Washington fails to remain engaged this time, the political fallout in the Muslim world will be considerable. Thus, the United States and its Coalition allies must work together to assist the Karzai government to provide internal and external security as well as generate much-needed economic development. To this end, Coalition governments should work together to encourage foreign investment in Afghanistan as a way to expedite postwar reconstruction. Second, the Coalition should focus more diplomatic energies on resolving the status of Jerusalem and Palestine. As former Thai foreign minister Surin Pitsuwan argued recently, a strong sense of "primordial" resentment exists among "all Muslims around the world," that their sentiments about Jerusalem, which, after Mecca and Medina, is the third holiest site in Islam, have never been seriously accommodated.[61] As Pitsuwan argues, the failure of the international community to seek a just solution to the problem has resulted in "frustration, inadequacy, the sense of being left out, the sense of being done injustice," sentiments that have been "overwhelming to the point of desperation."[62] On 13 March, the UN Security Council endorsed, for the first time, the concept of an independent Palestinian state. This should be followed up by strong pressure on both Israelis and Palestinians to end the vicious cycle of violence they have been locked in since October 2000.[63]

Coalition diplomatic activity should also be geared towards improving the socio-economic performance and political accountability of Muslim governments and states with significant Muslim populations.[64] The socio-economic dislocations resulting from a decrepit Indonesian economy, for instance, generate political oxygen that has been exploited by radical Islamic groups such as Laskar Jihad, which has been linked with Al Qaeda, to boost recruitment. The appeal of Laskar is not confined to the ideological level; like its counterparts in the Middle East such as Hamas and Hezbollah, Laskar not only advocates armed struggle but also, and quite importantly, promotes social welfare. Thus, the Coalition has a strong incentive to enhance trade, aid and investment links with Jakarta so as to strengthen its capacity to help its population enjoy decent living standards—and thereby diminish the appeal of radical Islamic teaching. In this respect, it is heartening that the World Bank in mid-March pledged US$35 million for a social fund set up by Manila to promote development within the Mindanao region of the southern Philippines—where Al Qaeda-linked terrorist organizations are currently operating.[65] More generally, foreign aid should be boosted. It is inconceivable that the United States currently provides the least foreign aid amongst all the industrialized countries—"barely one-seventh of 1 per cent of gross domestic product."[66] Instead of the US$750 million Washington has proposed for "international assistance" in 2003, analysts argue that what is needed is "at least $4 billion to $5 billion annually to finance programs that promote modernization and economic opportunity in the Islamic countries of the Middle East and Central and South Asia."[67] On 15 March, Bush in fact announced a "US$5 billion increase, spread over three years, in foreign aid to poor nations that support human rights, adhere to strong systems of law and have open markets." However, Democrats and development experts argued that the increase, which would not take effect until 2004, "was too little, too late," and frankly "paled beside Bush's proposed US$48 billion increase in military spending."[68]

It has to be said that former British Prime Minister Margaret Thatcher's "advice" to the American "superpower" that it should focus on military action rather than "social work" is singularly unhelpful.[69] A mini Marshall Plan for Indonesia, the largest Islamic country in the world, for instance, would greatly assist it in making a successful democratic transition. Not only would this buttress both the stability of the country and regional security, a stable, democratic and Islamic Indonesia would, more than anything, project the utterly critical ideological message that Islam can co-exist with democratic modernity. The significance of this was not lost on Paul Wolfowitz, a former U.S. ambassador to Indonesia, who observed that Indonesia "stands for a country that practices religious tolerance and democracy, treats women properly, and believes Islam is a religion of peace."[70] Therefore, the world's largest Muslim country "ought to be a model to the rest of the world [of] what Islam can be."[71]

The Military-Coercive Component

The final component of an effective indirect strategy to disembowel the Al Qaeda hydra is also the one fraught with the most dangers. To be sure, there will be times in the war on terror that military force must be used, as it was in Afghanistan, to destroy Al Qaeda terrorist training camps and possibly even facilities for conducting research into WMD development. In addition, there will be a need to use military power to eliminate Al Qaeda-linked radical Islamic fighters in combat. Moreover, throughout the world, it will be necessary to disrupt radical Islamic terrorist networks through detentions of individual Muslims suspected of complicity in terror plots. However, because of the intrinsic ideological-political character of this war on terror, the pressing need is to persuade Muslims that the West is a friend of Islam, through both words and deeds. Thus, any necessary military action and coercive measures employed against Al Qaeda-linked terrorist organizations in the Philippines, Yemen and elsewhere must be *carefully calibrated and controlled.* The collateral civilian deaths arising from American air strikes gone horribly wrong,[72] improper behaviour on the part of American soldiers towards captured Muslim combatants, as in the case of 27 pro-Karzai government fighters captured at Oruzgan in late January and "brutally beaten by U.S. soldiers" before being released,[73] and the continuing half-hearted application of the Geneva Convention to captured Taliban and Al Qaeda detainees at Camp X-Ray in Cuba,[74] all constitute political oxygen which radical Islamic propagandists—aided and abetted by sympathetic television networks like Al-Jazeera—can rapidly exploit to persuade Muslims that, despite its friendly rhetoric, the West is indeed at war with the Islamic nation.

For these same reasons, Washington planners must seriously reconsider taking military action against Muslim states implicated in WMD programmes, especially Iraq. Even America's European allies find great difficulty in finding the precise link between Iraq and the September 11 tragedy, let alone America's Muslim allies and the wider Muslim *ummah.* Furthermore, Washington appears to be giving insufficient weight to the objections of key Muslim allies like Jordan and Turkey to military operations against Iraq. Amman is worried that a military strike against Saddam would incite its Palestinian majority to unrest, thus destabilizing the kingdom, while at the same time severing the Iraqi oil pipeline on which the Jordanian economy depends.[75] One of Ankara's worries is that an American attack on Saddam would destabilize the already-parlous Turkish economy, and scare off much-needed foreign investment.[76] Washington must not be seen to be less interested in working to end Israeli-Palestinian violence than in bringing the Arab states on board for a strike against Saddam. Otherwise, it would be sending the politically disastrous message that it tacitly supports Israeli military force in the Occupied Territories against one part of the Muslim "family," while preparing to strike another part of the Muslim "family" with more military force.[77] Arab-Muslim membership of the Coalition would be endangered.

Nicholas Kristof has noted that within some Washington circles and elsewhere, there is a feeling that the best way to avoid another September 11 is to forget about winning Muslim hearts and minds and just concentrate on being feared. In this respect, he cites Cicero's dictum: *Oderint, dum metuant*—let them hate, as long as they fear.[78] The great danger is that this seemingly stubborn American fixation with military-coercive measures in the war on terror will inadvertently transmute it into a wider civilizational war between the West and Islam. The threat of civilizational enmity should not be confused with Samuel Huntington's classic "clash of civilizations" thesis, which has rightly been criticized as virtually ossifying the ideational boundaries between the West and Islam. Certainly, as scholars like John Esposito have pointed out, considerable cultural, scientific and philosophical exchanges took place between both civilizations down the centuries.[79] The concept of civilizational enmity put forth here is more contingent, depending for its activation on situational stimuli. David Brown, in developing a paradigm for examining the relations between the state and ethnicity in Southeast Asia, observes that while ethnicity as a sociological category—in comparison to class—seems to "offer a more all-embracing and emotionally satisfying way of defining an individual's identity," he cautions against over-reliance on a rigid, "primordialist" interpretation of ethnic self-definition, and suggests that a more balanced analysis must take cognizance of "situationalist" factors:[80]

> In sociology and anthropology, ethnic attachment has frequently been explained as a response to situational threats from dominating others, so that individuals react by forming appropriate defensive groups. The perception of the "them" is mirrored by the sense of "us."

Likewise, while the average moderate Muslim—like his Christian and Hindu counterparts—can, to some extent, be expected to identify himself "primordially" as belonging to a distinct civilization, his sense of civilizational consciousness need not necessarily represent the predominant element of his overall identity set, utterly eclipsing other simultaneously-held identities such as being a doctor or lawyer, a *Star Trek* fan, or a Malaysian or Egyptian citizen. However, should Muslims in different states perceive that their civilization is being victimized by the Western "other," and this perception is played up by radical Islamic "civilizational entrepreneurs," so to speak, moderate Muslims may well become radicalized, "rally around the flag," and deliberately and more consciously identify themselves as part of a wider Muslim "us" versus the infidel Western-American "them." For example, in his travels through the shanty towns of Turkey in 1994, Robert Kaplan noted the emergence of civilizational enmity amongst Turks who, in response to media reports, were gradually "revising their group identity, increasingly seeing themselves as Muslims being deserted by a West that does little to help besieged Muslims in Bosnia and that attacks Turkish Muslims in the streets of Germany."[81] In similar fashion, the American air campaign against the Taliban regime in Afghanistan, which began on 7 October 2001, generated a discernible closing of Muslim ranks. In a recent article, for example, Samuel Huntington noted that while in most Muslim countries, many people "condemned" the September 11 attacks, "huge numbers denounced the American response." Implicitly endorsing the contingent civilizational enmity perspective, he added that the "longer and the more intensely the United States and its allies use military force against their opponents [in Afghanistan], the more widespread and intense will be the Muslim reaction." Ultimately, "a prolonged [American] response to September 11 could produce Muslim unity."[82] His comments are applicable not just to the Afghan theatre, but more generally to the war on terror. In the current context, therefore, an American invasion of Iraq without concomitant progress in ending Israeli-Palestinian violence would generate additional political oxygen which—in a supreme irony—would not only create the civilizational enmity America seeks to avoid, but also ensure a steady supply of fresh recruits into Al Qaeda's ranks.

Conclusion

The central argument of this paper is that to counter the "new terrorism" of Al Qaeda requires first and foremost an effort to re-conceptualize the conflict. The war on terror should not be seen as a primarily military-coercive one, but rather as essentially ideological-political in character. That is, while uncovering and disrupting the financing, logistical and operational plans of Al Qaeda and physically eliminating its terrorist foot-soldiers are important, these are in fact less crucial than drying up the pool of disaffected Muslims that may become willing Osama recruits. It is argued that to kill the radical Islamic hydra requires an indirect strategy. This means orchestrating diplomatic and military activity so that these support rather than undermine the two main thrusts: longer-term ideological measures emphasizing educational reform designed to promote a Muslim reformation, as well as more immediate political measures aimed at gradually neutralizing the virulent anti-Americanism that renders young Muslims highly susceptible to radical Islamic appeals. If the American-led Coalition opts to prosecute this war on terror through primarily military-coercive means, paying scant attention to the political effects of its military mistakes in particular, the potential for generating a dangerous civilizational enmity between the West and Islam cannot be ruled out. Not only would this destabilize friendly Muslim governments as well as allied states with significant Muslim populations, a steady supply of anti-American, radicalized young men would continually replenish Al Qaeda ranks. Hence, if, in the short term, the U.S. decides to override the objections of allied Muslim governments and invades Iraq, while neglecting to take stronger measures to try to bring about a durable Israeli-Palestinian peace, a dangerous drift towards what Charles Krauthammer once called the "global intifida" would gather momentum. The need for an indirect strategy is thus greater than ever.

Notes

1   Elizabeth Bumiller, "Bush Vows to Aid Other Countries in War on Terror," *The New York Times on the Web*, available at http://www.nytimes.com/2002/03/12/international/12PREX.html, 12 March 2002.

2   David E. Sanger, "Eye on Iraq, Bush to Set Out War's Next Phase," *The IHT Online*, available at http://www.iht.com/articles/50761.html, 11 March 2002.

3   Bumiller, "Bush Vows to Aid Other Countries in War on Terror."

4   Howard Schneider, "Arabs Want Cheney's Focus on Mideast Crisis," *The IHT Online*, available at http://www.iht.com/articles/50763.html, 11 March 2002.

5   William Pfaff, "Not About to Change their Minds," *The IHT Online*, available at http://www.iht.com/articles/59010.html, 27 May 2002.

6   John H. Cushman, "Pentagon Nuclear Goal Likely to Worry Allies," *The IHT Online*, available at http://www.iht.com/articles/50752.html, 11 March 2002.

7   John Mackinlay comes to a similar conclusion when he argues that bin Laden's "tactical concept follows a classical insurgent approach." John Mackinlay, "NATO and Bin Laden," *RUSI Journal*, Vol. 146, No. 6 (December 2001), p. 37.

8   Anthony G. McGrew, "Conceptualizing Global Politics," in Anthony G. McGrew and Paul G. Lewis (eds.), *Global Politics: Globalization and the Nation-State* (Cambridge: Polity Press, 1992), p. 23.

9   John Arquilla and David Ronfeldt, "Osama bin Laden and the Advent of Netwar," *New Perspectives Quarterly*, Vol. 18, No. 4 (Fall 2001), pp. 23–33.

10 Eric Pianin and Bob Woodward, "Terror Concerns of US Extend to Asia," *The Washington Post*, 18 January 2002, p. A18.

11 Michael T. Klare, "Waging Post-Industrial Warfare on the Global Battlefield," *Current History*, Vol. 100, No. 650 (December 2001), p. 435.

12 Thomas Homer-Dixon, "The Rise of Complex Terrorism," *Foreign Policy* (January/ February 2002), pp. 54–55.

13 David Tucker, "What is New about the New Terrorism and How Dangerous is It?" *Terrorism and Political Violence*, Vol. 13, No. 3 (Autumn 2001), p. 13.

14 See below.

15 Homer-Dixon, "Rise of Complex Terrorism," p. 55.

16 Homer-Dixon, "Rise of Complex Terrorism," p. 60.

17 Homer-Dixon, "Rise of Complex Terrorism," pp. 57–58.

18 David C. Rapoport, "The Fourth Wave: September 11 in the History of Terrorism," *Current History*, Vol. 100, No. 650 (December 2001), pp. 419–424.

19 Steven Simon and Daniel Benjamin, "The Terror," *Survival*, Vol. 43, No. 4 (Winter 2001–2002), p. 5.

20 Peter L. Bergen, "Picking Up the Pieces: What We Can Learn From—and About— 9/11," *Foreign Affairs*, Vol. 81, No. 2 (March/April 2002), p. 172.

21 Simon and Benjamin, "The Terror," pp. 5–6.

22 The curious characteristic of the well-educated Al Qaeda terrorists is their seeming ability to combine the rational and the irrational in their thinking. A pilot acquaintance pointed this out in explaining that he personally could not understand how the "911" hijackers who piloted the aircraft into their targets were able to maintain the rational thought processes needed to fly the planes while knowing all the while that they were deliberately going to commit not just mass murder but mass suicide.

23 Robert A. Levine, "A Pair of Sober Questions About the Slog After Early Victories," *The IHT Online*, available at http://www.iht.com/articles/41118.html, 7 December 2001.

24 Duncan Campbell, "Futile Campaign against the Head of a Hydra," *The Guardian (U.K.) Online*, available at http://www.guardian.co.uk/Print/ 0,3858,4303748,00.html, 21 November 2001.

25 Michael Richardson, "Mahathir Boosted by Terrorism Stance," *CNN.com*, available at http://www.cnn.com/2001/WORLD/asiapcf/southeast/10/31/ malaysia.mahathir/index.html, 31 October 2001.

26 Atika Shubert, "Indonesia Braces for Friday Protests," *CNN.com*, available at http://www.cnn.com/2001/WORLD/asiapcf/southeast/10/11/ret.indon.protests/ index.html, 11 October 2001.

27 For instance, Susan Sachs, "The Despair Beneath the Arab World's Growing Rage," *The New York Times*, 14 October 2001, Late edn., Final, Section 1B, p. 10. See also Sir Michael Alexander, "A Global Civil War," *RUSI Journal*, Vol. 146, No. 6 (December 2001), p. 12.

28 John L. Esposito, *The Islamic Threat: Myth or Reality?* (New York and Oxford: Oxford University Press, 1999), p. 147.

29 Daniel Pipes, "God and Mammon: Does Poverty Cause Militant Islam?" *The National Interest* (Winter 2001/2002), p. 16.

30 Adrian Karatnycky, "Under Our Very Noses: The Terrorist Next Door," *National Review*, available at http://www.freedomhouse.org/media/0501nr.htm, 5 November 2001.

31 Cited in Pipes, "God and Mammon," p. 17.

32 Shibley Telhami, "It's Not About Faith: A Battle for the Soul of the Middle East," *Current History*, Vol. 100, No. 650 (December 2001), p. 415.

33 Esposito, *The Islamic Threat*, p. 147.

34 Martin Kramer, cited in Pipes, "God and Mammon," p. 17.

35 Mark Huband, *Warriors of the Prophet: The Struggle for Islam* (Boulder: Westview Press, 1999), p. 90.

36 R. Scott Appleby and Martin E. Marty, "Fundamentalism," *Foreign Policy* (January/February 2002), p. 20.

37 Pipes, "God and Mammon," p. 16.

38 Appleby and Marty, "Fundamentalism," p. 20.

39 Andre Beaufre, *Strategy of Action* (London: Faber and Faber, 1967).

40 Daniel Easterman, *New Jerusalems: Reflections on Islam, Fundamentalism and the Rushdie Affair* (London: Grafton, 1992), pp. 34–36.

41 Farish A. Noor, "Who Will Guard the 'Guardians of the Faith'?" transmitted to author via e-mail, 1 February 2002.

42 Surin Pitsuwan, "Strategic Challenges Facing Islam in Southeast Asia," lecture delivered at a forum organized by the Institute of Defence and Strategic Studies and the Centre for Contemporary Islamic Studies, Singapore, 5 November 2001.

43 Mohamed Charfi, "Reaching the Next Muslim Generation," *The New York Times on the Web*, available at http://www.nytimes.com/2002/03/12/opinion/12CHAR.html, 12 March 2002.

44 Karim Raslan, "Now a Historic Chance to Welcome Muslims into the System," *The IHT Online*, available at http://www.iht.com/articles/40072.html, 27 November 2001.

45 Roy Mottahedeh, "Help Get Education Running Again," *The IHT Online*, available at http://www.iht.com/articles/47879.html, 13 February 2002.

46 Graham E. Fuller, "The Future of Political Islam," *Foreign Affairs*, Vol. 81, No. 2 (March/April 2002), p. 59.

47 Mottahedeh, "Help Get Education Running Again."

48 Raslan, "Now a Historic Chance to Welcome Muslims."

49 Thomas L. Friedman, "Blunt Question, Blunt Answer," *The New York Times on the Web*, 10 February 2002.

50 Philip Taylor, "Spin Laden," *The World Today*, December 2001, p. 7.

51 Bergen, "Picking Up the Pieces," p. 174.

52 Bergen, "Picking Up the Pieces," p. 172.

53 Elizabeth Becker and James Dao, "Bush will keep Wartime Office Promoting U.S.," *The New York Times*, 20 February 2002, Late edn., Final, Section A, p. 11.

54 Mike Allen, "White House Angered at Plan for Pentagon Disinformation," *The Washington Post*, 25 February 2002, p. A17; Thomas E. Ricks, "Rumsfeld Kills Pentagon Propaganda Unit," *The Washington Post*, 27 February 2002, p. A21.

55 Kurt Campbell and Michelle A. Flournoy, *To Prevail: An American Strategy For the Campaign Against Terrorism* (Washington, D.C.: The CSIS Press, 2001), p. 143.

56 Anthony J. Blinken, "Winning the War of Ideas," *The Washington Quarterly*, Vol. 25, No. 2 (Spring 2002), pp. 101–114.

57 David Hoffman, "Beyond Public Diplomacy," *Foreign Affairs*, Vol. 81, No. 2 (March/April 2002), pp. 85–87.

58 Taylor, "Spin Laden," p. 7.

59 Ivo H. Daalder and James M. Lindsay, "Nasty, Brutish, and Long: America's War on Terrorism," *Current History*, Vol. 100, No. 2 (December 2001), p. 407.

60 Daalder and Lindsay, "Nasty, Brutish and Long," p. 407.

61 Pitsuwan lecture.

62 Pitsuwan lecture.

63 Sarah Left and agencies, "UN Security Council Backs Palestinian State," *Guardian Unlimited*, available at http://www.guardian.co.uk/israel/Story/0,2763,666617,00.html, 13 March 2002.

64 See Barry Desker and Kumar Ramakrishna,"Forging an Indirect Strategy in Southeast Asia," *The Washington Quarterly*, Vol. 25, No. 2 (Spring 2002), pp. 161–176.

65 Des Ferriols and Ding Cervantes, "Foreign Donors Pledge $2.8-B in Development Assist," *Philstar.com*, available at http://www.philstar.com/philstar/print.asp?article=70797, 13 March 2002.

66 Richard Sokolsky and Joseph McMillan, "Foreign Aid in Our Own Defense," *The New York Times*, 12 February 2002, Late edn., Final, Section A, p. 23.

67 Sokolsky and McMillan, "Foreign Aid in Our Own Defense."

68 Elisabeth Bumiller, "Bush calls for 15% Increase in Foreign Aid," *The International Herald Tribune*, 16–17 March 2002, p. 1.

69 Margaret Thatcher, "Advice to a Superpower," *The New York Times*, 11 February 2002, Late edn., Final, Section A, p. 27.

70 Cited in Michael Richardson, "Seeking Allies in Terror War, US Woos Southeast Asia," *The IHT Online*, available at http://www.iht.com/articles/40338.html, 29 November 2001.

71 Richardson, "Seeking Allies in Terror War."

72 Marc Herrold, a University of New Hampshire economist, estimates that 3,767 civilians were casualties between the beginning of the American air campaign on 7 October and 6 December. Carl Conetta, co-director of the Project on Defence

Alternatives, estimates 1,000–1,300 civilian deaths. Barry Bearak, "Uncertain Toll in the Fog of War: Civilian Deaths in Afghanistan," *The New York Times*, 10 February 2002, Late edn., Final, Section 1, p. 1.

73 "The Wrong Afghans," *The IHT Online*, available at http://www.iht.com/articles/47994.html, 14 February 2002.

74 See, for instance, "Halfway to Geneva," *The IHT Online*, available at http://www.ihtcom/articles/47640.html, 11 February 2002.

75 Michael R. Gordon, "Cheney Opens Toughest Part of Trip," *The IHT Online*, available at http://www.iht.com/articles/51031.html, 13 March 2002.

76 Howard Schneider, "U.S. Warned by Turkey and Jordan on Iraq War," *The IHT Online*, available at http://www.iht.com/articles/50786.html, 11 March 2002.

77 Schneider, "Arabs Want Cheney's Focus on Mideast Crisis."

78 Nicholas D. Kristof, "Cicero was Wrong," *The New York Times on the Web*, available at http://www.nytimes.com/2002/03/12/opinion/12KRIS.html, 12 March 2002.

79 Esposito, *The Islamic Threat*, p. 232.

80 David Brown, *The State and Ethnic Politics in Southeast Asia* (London and New York: Routledge, 1994), pp. xvi–xviii.

81 Robert D. Kaplan, *The Coming Anarchy: Shattering the Dreams of the Post-Cold War* (New York: Vintage, 2000), p. 29.

82 Samuel P. Huntington, "The Age of Muslim Wars," *Newsweek (Special Edition)*, December 2001–February 2002, p. 13.

CHAPTER 11

THE NEW TERRORISM: IMPLICATIONS AND STRATEGIES

Andrew Tan*

*The author acknowledges with thanks Rohan Gunaratna who vetted this article, as well as the contributions of Bruce Hoffman, David Wright-Neville, Ely Karmon, Rohan Gunaratna, Kevin O'Brien, Jusuf Wanandi, Kumar Ramakrishna, B. Raman, Don Porter, P. Saravanamuttu, Peter Chalk, Shaul Shay and Barry Desker to this conclusion, which draws on some of their ideas and comments expressed during the concluding session of the Workshop on the New Dimensions of Terrorism held in Singapore in March 2002. Needless to say, all errors are the author's alone.

Significance of September 11

The terrorist attacks on the World Trade Centre in New York, and the Pentagon in Washington, on 11 September 2001, shocked not just the United States but the entire world. The attacks are a watershed, with far-reaching implications for future security. With casualties topping three thousand, it is the first true mass-casualty terrorist act in modern times.[1] Prior to this attack, the worst terrorist attack was the one on an Abadan movie theatre in Iran in 1979 that killed between 400–500 people.[2]

It might appear to some that September 11 was no different from other terrorist attacks, particularly those that occur so frequently in the Third World, and that the reason why it received much attention was due to the fact that it occurred in the U.S.A. However, September 11 is not merely another major terrorist attack. Its significance lies in the fact that it marks the emergence of the "new" terrorism. In fact, the success of the September 11 attacks in causing a large number of casualties and the huge psychological and economic impacts it engendered, appear to validate the assertions of terrorist experts who have for years argued that something fundamental has changed to result in the emergence of a new, much more deadly form of terrorism, one which would be characterized by spectacular terrorist acts potentially involving mass casualties.

The prevailing image of "traditional" terrorism has been based on groups which emerged during the Cold War era, such as the ultra-leftist Japanese Red Army, and nationalist-type groups such as the IRA and the PLO. Such groups are characterized by their tight organization and hierarchical structure, and at times operated under the behest of a foreign government. These groups also usually had a clear set of political objectives and often issued communiqués taking credit for and explaining their actions.[3]

In recent years, there have emerged new terrorist groups which have joined these more traditional types. These groups have less comprehensible nationalistic or ideological motivations, embracing much more amorphous religious and millenarian aims. They are also less cohesive in their organization, with a more diffuse structure and membership. More significantly, these groups are potentially far more lethal than traditional terrorist groups given their attempts at mass-casualty terrorist acts, that is, acts calculated to kill very large numbers of people, using both conventional explosives or WMD, such as the sarin gas attack on the Tokyo subway attempted by the Aum Supreme Truth in 1995. Increasingly, such groups do not bother to explain or justify their attacks, as the 1995 Oklahoma bombing demonstrated. The implication of this is that such groups see violence as an end in itself, not just a means to an end.[4]

Besides, the dramatic developments in telecommunications, information and travel that have been the hallmark of increasing globalization have provided new channels for transnational terrorism. The internationalization of terrorism has become more pronounced as terrorist groups today operate in various countries, taking advantage of porous borders in a rapidly globalizing world economy. These transnational terrorist groups are thus much more difficult to track. In addition, they have also been able to exploit the new information economy and the Internet to reach a much wider base of support than was possible in the past.

They are also much less dependent on the support of states in their terrorist cause since they have become much more mobile and flexible, and no longer depend on fixed base areas to operate from.[5] The ethnic conflicts and disintegration of states in the post-Cold War era in various places such as Afghanistan, Yugoslavia and the former Soviet Union, have afforded them sanctuary in weak or failed states.

Following the dramatic events of September 11, there is now consensus among terrorism experts that Al Qaeda is the epitome of the new terrorism. Osama bin Laden's genius has been his ability to turn his organization into a global non-state multinational organization able to attract the support and dedication of many nationalities, with the ability to operate globally with little regard to borders. He, and his lieutenants in Al Qaeda, have thus been at the forefront of formulating the new terrorist paradigm—spectacular mass-casualty terrorist acts, multiracial memberships scattered all over the world, exploiting the advantages of the open, global interlinked economy, mastering of new technology in IT and communications, and even the (perhaps unintended) imitation of the latest organizational concepts. Its flat, non-hierarchical, decentralized and cell-like structure facilitates innovation and the taking of initiative. Although Al Qaeda does not yet have effective weapons of mass destruction, it is actively considering its use and is actively attempting to procure them.

September 11 also breached a number of thresholds. Compared to previous terrorist acts, it breached a moral threshold, making it acceptable to kill many thousands of people in one spectacular terrorist act. It demonstrated that it is possible to cause, through a single, spectacular mass-casualty terrorist act, huge political, economic and psychological impacts. It also demonstrates the utility and feasibility of asymmetric warfare—demonstrating the possibility of taking on a much more powerful state through either mass-casualty terrorist acts aimed at the civilian population, or attacks on carefully selected symbols or critical nodes of communications or finance, which the World Trade Centre represented. Indeed, the efficacy of the new terrorism will galvanize current and future forms of terrorism. Al Qaeda has provided a model for other radical terrorist groups to emulate and improve upon. As a result, the new terrorism will evolve to become more innovative in its strategies, display greater guile and stealth in its operations, and achieve much greater lethality in its effects. As a creature of globalization, the new terrorism, with its global scope of operations, could become even more menacing, thus posing a continuing threat to international security. The emergence of the new terrorism is, therefore, a pressing international security problem, and is not merely a security problem for the United States and its Western allies alone.

Clearly, those combating the new terrorism will need to understand the nature and *modus operandi* of the new terrorism. Different thinking is also required to devise appropriate and effective counter-measures to this emerging long-term threat to both human and state security.

Within Southeast Asia, the problem of radical Islam will not go away quickly, since in an age of globalization, the region cannot be sealed off from political and cultural developments in the world at large, particularly developments in the Middle East and within the wider Muslim *ummah* or community. What is happening in the Middle East is of particular significance, as the spread of radical Islamic ideology and the new terrorism are partly driven by developments in that region, where there remains widespread dissatisfaction with secular governments seen as apostate, oppressive, corrupt, immoral and non-responsive to grassroots issues.

One major issue has been the Israeli-Palestinian issue, which resonates strongly in Islamic communities in the world at large. The 2002 images of Jenin and of Yasser Arafat under siege from overwhelming Israeli military force, have galvanized even more anti-Western, anti-American feelings, and deepened the sense of anger and humiliation in the Muslim world, including Muslim communities in Southeast Asia.

In addition, the anti-West rhetoric that characterized the politics of many countries in the Middle East and Asia, which has been deployed for domestic reasons, has in effect also created an environment in which it is feeding the general suspicion of the West. This has also had the effect of facilitating radical Islamists in establishing themselves locally, and Al Qaeda in building a worldwide network.

Dealing effectively with the new terrorism is, therefore, a significant challenge, requiring strategies at three levels: domestic, regional and global.

The Domestic Level

While it seems that countries at risk from the new terrorism are the United States and its allies, those that are most at risk are, in fact, Muslim states. Al Qaeda and other Islamists despise their ruling elites as corrupt, effete and apostate. Saudi Arabia, in particular, is a country very much at risk as Osama bin Laden's initial dissatisfaction stems from conditions within Saudi Arabia itself, with an oppressive regime which he considers to be apostate. The presence of American forces in the Arabian peninsula is also a source of anger as it is said to constitute a source of defilement. The U.S. is seen as the source of evil, given its support of what bin Laden sees as a corrupt Middle Eastern order. Significantly, there is much support in Afghanistan and Saudi Arabia for Al Qaeda, with many Saudis involved in its operations, including the September 11 attacks.

Another country clearly at grave risk is Pakistan, which is important in the context of the new Islamic resurgence. In contrast to some other Muslim countries, Pakistan has huge Muslim mass movements, with radical Islam spread through thousands of unregistered *madrasahs* or religious schools. The spread of radicalism has also been fanned by widespread dissatisfaction with the dire economic situation. Because Pakistan is the only Muslim country that has a functioning nuclear capability, a radical Pakistan would have severe repercussions for world security.

There has also been rising concern about Southeast Asia, now described as a second front in the war against international terrorism. The country most at risk here is Indonesia. With thousands of heavily-jungled islands spread over a vast archipelago populated by the world's largest Muslim community, and in the context of a crisis of governance, deep economic difficulties and political instability, Indonesia is an especially attractive place for remnants of Al Qaeda to regroup. In addition, these same factors have also contributed to the alarming spread of radicalism in a country once better known for its eclectic Javanese mysticism.

Countries at risk, such as Saudi Arabia, Pakistan and Indonesia, are the ones at the forefront of the war against the new terrorism. Clearly, these countries need to get their own domestic houses in order.[6] The reform list is daunting—building institutions, putting into place systems of governance emphasizing transparency and accountability, rooting out endemic corruption, building epistemic communities and an effective civil society, and ensuring that minority voices are able to legitimately express and resolve their grievances. These would lay the fundamentals for a state's capacity to deliver economic goods and resolve domestic conflict. Conversely, failure to deal with these issues would result in a weak state, and eventually a failed one. Weak or failed states, as we have seen in Afghanistan and Somalia, tend to become fertile breeding grounds for militancy, and good hiding places for terrorists. Without political stability and socio-economic development, terrorism would have a free hand.

Regional Cooperation

September 11 has elicited quite an active public response from governments in Southeast Asia. There have been public pronouncements of support for the global war against terrorism, as expressed by the UN Security Council Resolutions 1368 and 1373. The ASEAN states also issued an ASEAN Declaration on Joint Action to Counter Terrorism. Multilateral cooperation in intelligence sharing, establishing uniform laws and counter-terrorism was stepped up under an Action Plan adopted in May 2002.[7]

Some states in the region, especially Singapore, Malaysia and Philippines, have provided invaluable assistance and intelligence to the U.S. These three countries also took tough measures against militants, arresting all known members of the militant group, the Jemiah Islamiah, which had planned to attack U.S. and Western targets in Singapore, a plot uncovered with the recovery, amidst Singaporean investigations, of a surveillance videotape in an Al Qaeda compound in Afghanistan in December 2001.

The Philippines subsequently took advantage of the situation to step up its war, with U.S. assistance, against Muslim insurgents in the southern provinces, given the well-documented links between these insurgents and Al Qaeda.

However, regional cooperation in countering terrorism has not been well-coordinated, due to the constraints of conflicting national interests and mutual suspicions. Whilst Singapore, Malaysia and the Philippines have been actively pushing for a regional mechanism to deal with the new terrorism, there has been palpable reluctance on the part of Indonesia. This reluctance to crack down on radical groups has to do with domestic political considerations, given the dependence of President Megawati for coalition support from Muslim parties, and the efforts by Muslim parties themselves in using Islam to bolster their positions. Tough action, such as the preventive detentions carried out by Malaysia and Singapore, would imperil the Megawati government given the probable strong domestic political repercussions of appearing to be responding to pressure from neighbours such as Singapore, and foreign powers such as the U.S. In addition, the presence of tensions between member ASEAN states has stymied deeper security cooperation, at both bilateral and multilateral levels.[8]

Yet, the central problem remains: How should regional states deal with the challenge of the new terrorism, given that it is clear that the new terrorism, namely Al Qaeda, has established a presence in Southeast Asia?

Given that the region is demonstrably not immune to the threat of the new transnational terrorism, there is, therefore, a clear need to make greater efforts at regional and international cooperation in intelligence sharing and in establishing a comprehensive regional terrorism database, and coordinated counter-terrorism strategies, in order to better deal with this emerging security menace. Recognizing this, the ASEAN states agreed to a number of practical measures in May 2002, including establishing principal contact points in each member country to facilitate the exchange of intelligence, and training in anti-terror intelligence gathering, psychological warfare, bomb detection and airport security.[9] Such avowed good intentions are laudable but the test is in the actual implementation of such measures, something for which political will is required.

International Cooperation and U.S. Leadership

Despite the widespread publicity given to terrorist attacks in the developed West, in reality, the overwhelming majority of terrorist attacks have occurred in Asia, the Middle East, Africa and Latin America. The salience of significant insurgencies and terrorism in the South demonstrate the failure of their governments to contain them due to a variety of reasons. This has had a spill-over effect, affecting the West today. Militant Islamic groups, for instance, have been forced to operate outside of the Middle East and have turned their attention to U.S. and Western targets due to their failure to make any major impact in countries such as Eygpt and Saudi Arabia.

Islamists also blame the West, particularly the U.S., for supporting the oppressive, corrupt and elitist regimes in those countries. Paradoxically, these same militants have taken advantage of the liberal democratic environment of the U.S., Canada, Australia and Western Europe to establish robust support networks that carry out propaganda, fund-raising, recruitment, as well as the procurement and transshipment of weapons. Yet, until the momentous events of September 11, Western governments had been reluctant to take action against terrorist groups operating openly in their countries on grounds of democratic freedom, since many of these groups did not directly target the West.

September 11 has changed that. Legislation has now been enacted, or is being debated, in many Western countries which would result in preventive detention of terrorists, the freezing or seizure of terrorist funds, the banning of designated terrorist organizations, and even the dismantling of front or support organizations such as innocuous-sounding charities, and legitimate businesses. This convergence in security perspectives will pave the way for greater international cooperation between the developed North and the developing South in addressing the problem of international terrorism.

Indeed, much can be done given that the developed North has much greater resources to counter the new terrorism. But U.S. leadership, at the international level, is crucial. Without U.S. global leadership, no progress can be made in the war against the new terrorism. The global reach of the new terrorism can only be effectively countered by the global reach, and military and economic resources, of the only true superpower today, namely, the United States. It is, therefore, important that the United States gets its counter-terrorist strategy at the global level right, as it has enormous implications for regional and domestic efforts by its allies. Indeed, strategic failure at the global level will have dire security consequences for global, regional and domestic security.

Winning Hearts and Minds

Getting the grand strategy right is important because the war against the new terrorism is a political one. Recalling Clausewitz, it is the political objectives that require sharp focus. The war against terrorism does not consist of a series of tactical military victories or a mounting body-count of militants exterminated or captured. Failure to devise a comprehensive political strategy to achieve a long-term political victory, and failure to address fundamental issues and causes, will mean a recurring hydra.[10]

Fundamentally, the conflict can be seen at two levels. At one level, it is a struggle to win over the hearts and minds of the Muslim world by convincing the overwhelming majority of the justness of the Western cause, thereby isolating the militants. At another level, it is a struggle between moderate and militant Islam, one which predates September 11 and Al Qaeda.

This follows that a broad, comprehensive political strategy emphasizing military, political, economic and social measures is necessary to achieve the political goal of defeating the new terrorism. Whilst vigorous military measures and passive WMD defence measures are necessary, the centre of gravity does not lie on battlefields but in the hearts and minds, indeed, the very soul, of the Muslim *ummah*. In this battle, the West and its allies are not alone. There is a moderate Islamic community which needs to gain the upper hand in this battle for the Muslim soul.

The international reach of Al Qaeda cannot be ignored. Indeed, in terms of organization, methods and ideology, it represents the cutting-edge of the new terrorism. Yet, it is important to note that the roots of Muslim rage and alienation lie fundamentally in local political, economic and social issues and conflicts, whether in Kashmir, Chechnya, Aceh, Patani or Mindanao, or indeed, even in Western Europe. In Southeast Asia, for instance, all three armed Muslim separatist rebellions, in Aceh, Patani and Mindanao, predated September 11 and Al Qaeda, and have been driven by the presence of local grievances.

In Aceh, there is much poverty and unemployment amidst the oil wealth of the province, which is siphoned off to Jakarta, while the well-documented abuses of the military have continued to fan the flames of separatism. In Mindanao, Muslim Moro landlessness has been the result of the influx of Catholic settlers, big plantation owners and surrendered communist rebels given land in the south by the Philippine government. Landless, poor, unemployed and subjected to discrimination by the Catholic majority, it is of little wonder that Muslim Moros have taken to rebellion. Both the Moro Islamic Liberation Front and the Abu Sayyaf Group have, over the years, developed well-documented links with Al Qaeda, representing the merger of old and new terrorism.

In Patani, the low economic, social and political status of Muslims prior to 1977, when the official policy of the Thai government was assimilation, translated into Muslim rebellion. In contrast to Aceh and Mindanao however, the Thai government has brought the situation under much better control through its broad political strategy, emphasizing development, and a much more sensitive approach to religion and culture.[11]

Dealing with the new terrorism thus requires a broad, multidimensional approach which must include military and defensive measures, as well as attention to winning hearts and minds, for which development and the addressing of fundamental political, economic and social grievances which lie at the root cause of rebellion and terrorism, are essential. The salience of development cannot be dismissed readily despite the presence of educated middle-class militant activists which make up the core of the new terrorism. History is replete with examples of revolts led by the conscience-stricken middle-class aghast at the sea of alienation, injustice, poverty and dislocation they see. Nor is such a broad political strategy necessarily directed only at the alienated societies in the Middle East that are feeding the new terrorism. In Western Europe, for instance, socio-economic disparities and the discrimination faced by migrant communities, have also contributed to the spread of radical Islam.

Intelligence

Clearly, a broad political strategy is required. While this is a long-term measure, in the short term, what is absolutely essential at the tactical level is to obtain and share timely intelligence to contain the activities of militant groups, and to prevent terrorist attacks. Indeed, information-sharing at the inter-agency level, among governments, and internationally, is absolutely essential in confronting the new terrorism, given its global reach and transnational mode of operation. However, the problem of failing to share information between intelligence and national security agencies, which are unwilling to break down bureaucratic barriers and are predisposed to guard sensitive bureaucratic turf, afflicts every modern state, not just the United States.

In Southeast Asia, Singapore has been at the forefront of measures to better coordinate responses and to share intelligence. Domestically, it has set up a National Security Secretariat to coordinate counter-terrorism at the strategic level, a Joint Counter-Terrorism Centre which shares intelligence on terrorism and a Homefront Security Centre to oversee security operations and joint counter-terrorist exercises. Regionally, Singapore has called for all ASEAN states to each create a single body similar to its Joint Terrorism Centre, which would make it easier to track terrorist threats and speed up intelligence-sharing on a regional basis.[12]

However, merely sharing intelligence is not sufficient. The type and quality of intelligence is also important. Massive Western investment in technical surveillance has been helpful but what is lacking has been quality human intelligence and the capability to assess the collected data and information. Enhanced human intelligence working close to or within targeted terrorist groups would clearly be valuable assets.[13] In addition, there is a need for better cooperation with the private sector, particularly with business people and journalists, who possess a reservoir of local knowledge and perspectives.

Yet, whilst collection efforts have been at the highest ever, the capacity to assess the collected intelligence may well be lacking. As Richard Betts puts it succinctly in the aftermath of September 11:

> If the U.S. is going to have markedly better intelligence in parts of the world where few Americans have lived, studied or understood local

mores and aspirations, it is going to have to overcome a cultural disease: thinking that American primacy makes it unnecessary for American education to foster broad and deep expertise on foreign, especially non-Western societies ... the disease has even affected the academic world, which should know better. American political science, for example, has driven area studies out of fashion. Some "good" departments have not a single Middle East specialist on their rosters, and hardly any at all have a specialist on South Asia, a region of more than a billion people, two nuclear-armed countries and swarms of terrorists.[14]

Clearly, academia needs to address such glaring deficiencies, which have contributed to the dearth of specialists who can make sense of the collected data and intelligence, and provide the in-depth, quality analyses that are required.

There is clearly a need to develop specialists who can build up the necessary expertise on specific terrorist or militant groups, and to share their expertise and information with other agencies and countries. In particular, it is vital to build a shared profile of radical terrorist groups. Monitoring of such organizations requires an accurate typology of radical groups which will enable deeper analysis of their organizational capability, political intent, links to other organizations and political forces, willingness to act, the motivation for their actions, and the domestic context in which they operate. This close, on-going monitoring of radical groups, in terms of where they are going and when they might cross the line into violent terrorist activity, is essential for early warning and preventive actions.[15] However, this can only be done by properly-trained analysts/specialists conversant with the language, culture and history of the groups in question.

There is another compelling reason why specialists are required. Given the increasing reluctance of states to support radical and terrorist groups, these groups have increasingly turned to establishing links with organized crime groups or developing structures to engage in organized crimes such as human smuggling and narcotics. They have also established legitimate businesses, charities and NGOs to help generate funds, making it difficult for governmental detection. Militant groups have also succeeded in penetrating migrant communities worldwide, including the West, where their support networks are deeply enmeshed.

Given the complex organization and sophisticated nature of the new terrorism, new specialized counter-terrorist capabilities are therefore needed. There is, thus, a need to develop specialists on specific terrorist groups such as Al Qaeda and other militant groups. Improved knowledge of how these groups evolve, think and function, will assist greatly in fighting the war against terrorism.[16]

Yet, specialization by itself is not sufficient. There is also a need to develop critical thinking to accompany it. Only by constantly challenging assumptions, exchanging ideas and experimentation can specialized analysts and academics provide the policy-relevant inputs that will help governments and free societies keep ahead of the new terrorism.[17] An environment conducive to the free exchange of ideas and information among analysts and specialists is, therefore, essential.

The threat is clearly very real. September 11 has dramatically heralded the emergence of the new terrorism. Yet, despite military action in Afghanistan and the efforts of governments all over the world, Al Qaeda has not been vanquished. Despite disarray, the overwhelming majority of its top leadership remains at large. But the problem goes beyond Al Qaeda and the current war against terrorism. In the new age of post-Cold War globalization, globalized fanaticism will be a growing challenge to open and free societies. Militant and apocalyptic groups, whether Muslim or Christian, or others (such as the Japanese Aum), will emerge in the evolving globalized world, posing a global threat to national and human security.[18] With increasing networking of computers, communications and economic relationships that are integral to globalization, these groups could potentially cause catastrophic damage to critical infrastructure and achieve significant political, psychological and economic impacts through "new" terrorist activities. For this reason, it is time for a change in mindsets, and to make the necessary effort to learn about the new terrorism and devise new methods to deal with it.

Postscript

The dramatic bomb attack at the popular Kuta Beach in Bali, Indonesia, on 12 October 2002 which killed nearly 200 people (the majority Australians), is the most serious terrorist attack since 11 September 2001. While previous bombing attacks have taken place elsewhere, these have mostly been smaller in scale. Foreign and Indonesian officials have linked Al Qaeda, through operatives in the local radical group, the JI, to the attack, given the size and sophistication of this act of terrorism. Symbolically, the attack on 12 October also coincided with the anniversary of the USS Cole attack in 2000. As the first major terrorist attack since 11 September 2001, it demonstrates that terrorism remains a major security threat; its success will motivate radical terrorists to further atrocities. What is also clear is that the war against terrorism has been brought home to Southeast Asia, and that the threat emanating from it remains serious and needs to be taken seriously. The Indonesian government under Megawati has responded by passing a presidential decree on internal security and arrested the alleged head of the JI, Abu Bakar Bashir. But its resolve remains to be seen given the domestic political sensitivities. It seems the war against terrorism will be long drawn out.

Notes

1   *The Straits Times* (Singapore), 12 September 2001, p. 1.
2   Hoffman, "The Confluence of International and Domestic Trends in Terrorism," *Terrorism and Political Violence*, Vol. 9, No. 2 (Summer 1997), p. 2.
3   Bruce Hoffman, "The Confluence of International and Domestic Trends in Terrorism," p. 2.
4   Hoffman, "The Confluence of International and Domestic Trends in Terrorism," pp. 8–9.
5   "Terrorists Relying Less on State Sponsors," *The Straits Times* (Singapore), 3 May 2000, p. 7.
6   A point made by Jusuf Wanandi.
7   "ASEAN Plan to Fight Terror," *The Straits Times* (Singapore), 18 May 2002, p. A14.
8   See Andrew Tan, *Intra-ASEAN Tensions* (London: Royal Institute of International Affairs, 2000).
9   *The Straits Times* (Singapore), 22 May 2002.
10   A point made by Kumar Ramakrishna.
11   See Andrew Tan, *Armed Rebellion in the ASEAN States: Persistence and Implications* (Canberra: Strategic and Defence Studies Centre, Australian National University, 2000).
12   "ASEAN nations set to work closer on terrorism," *The Sunday Times* (Singapore), 19 May 2002, p. 18.
13   A point made by Rohan Gunaratna.
14   Richard Betts, "Intelligence Test: The Limits of Prevention," in James F. Hoge, Jr. and Gideon Rose (eds.), *How Did This Happen: Terrorism and the New War* (New York: Public Affairs/Council on Foreign Relations, 2001), p. 161.
15   A point made by Donald Porter.
16   A point made by Rohan Gunaratna.
17   A point made by Bruce Hoffman.
18   A point made by Bruce Hoffman.

INDEX